PENGUIN BOOKS

EXHUMATIONS

Christopher Isherwood was born in Cheshire in 1904 and educated at Repton School and Corpus Christi College, Cambridge. He was a private tutor in London for a time and then studied medicine at King's College, London, from 1928 to 1929. He published his first novel, *All the Conspirators*, in 1928 and *The Memorial* (1932) appeared while he was in Berlin, where he had gone to teach English in 1930. The outcome of this Berlin experience was *Mr Norris Changes Trains* (1935) and *Goodbye to Berlin* (1939) (both Penguin Modern Classics). He returned to London in 1934 and in the following year appeared the first of his three plays written in collaboration with W. H. Auden: *The Dog Beneath the Skin* (1935), *The Ascent of F.6.* (1937) and *On the Frontier* (1938). He also collaborated with W. H. Auden in *Journey to a War* (1939), which told the story of their travels in China in 1938, the year in which *Lions and Shadows*, his autobiography, was published. He worked for a while with Gaumont-British and with Metro-Goldwyn-Mayer, and *Prater Violet* (also a Penguin Modern Classic) appeared in 1945. Christopher Isherwood became a citizen of the United States in 1946.

In 1947–8 he travelled in South America, and as a result wrote *The Condor and the Cows* (1949). Since then his novels have been *The World in the Evening* (1954), *Down There on a Visit* (1962), *A Single Man* (1964; in Penguins) and *A Meeting by the River* (1967). *Exhumations* was published in 1966. He is also the author of *Ramakrishna and his Disciples* (1965), and the translator of Baudelaire's *Intimate Journals* (1947) and, with Swami Prabhavananda, of *The Bhagavad-Gita* (1944), *Shankara's Crest-Jewel of Discrimination* (1947), and *How to Know God: The Yogi Aphorisms of Patanjali* (1953).

Christopher Isherwood has held appointments at universities in Los Angeles and California. He is a member of the U.S. National Institute of Arts and Letters, and now lives at Santa Monica, California.

CHRISTOPHER ISHERWOOD

Exhumations

STORIES · ARTICLES · VERSES

PENGUIN BOOKS

Penguin Books Ltd, Harmondsworth, Middlesex, England
Penguin Books Australia Ltd, Ringwood, Victoria, Australia

—

First published by Methuen 1966
Published in Penguin Books 1969
This collection copyright © Christopher Isherwood, 1966
The stories 'I am Waiting' (1939) and
'Take It or Leave It' (1942)
copyrighted © in the respective years shown
by The New Yorker Magazine, Inc.

—

Made and printed in Great Britain
by Hazell Watson & Viney Ltd
Aylesbury, Bucks
Set in Monotype Baskerville

This book is compiled chiefly for those who already feel some interest, never mind how slight, in my writings and, hence, in me. I cannot pretend that it is a self-sufficient, self-explanatory artwork. It is just a lot of bits and pieces, fragments of an autobiography which tells itself indirectly, by means of exhibits – exhibit A, exhibit B, and so forth; dug up for display in a museum (if you wish to study the past) or a court-room (if you hope to convict the author of hitherto unpunished crimes).

If I am in a museum, I am beyond excuses; the past does not have to excuse itself. If I am in a courtroom, it is the business of someone else to defend me. So I will try hard to avoid self-excuse, as distinct from critical comment, in my notes on this material.

Exhibits should not be tampered with. I have made very few cuts, all of which are acknowledged, and done absolutely no rewriting.

C.I. *1965*

Contents

CONTENTS

Acknowledgements

THE author wishes to thank the editors and publishers concerned for permission to include material which originally appeared in the following sources:
'Mapperley Plains', *Public School Verse 1921–22*, Volume III, William Heinemann Ltd, 1923; 'The Common Cormorant', *The Poet's Tongue*, G. Bell & Sons Ltd, 1938; 'Some Notes on Auden's Early Poetry', *New Verse*, London, 1937; the review of *T. E. Lawrence by His Friends*, *The Listener*, 1937; the review of *The Grapes of Wrath*, *Kenyon Review*, 1939; the preface to *Baudelaire's Intimate Journals*, Marcel Rodd, 1947, and Methuen & Co. Ltd, 1949; the essays on *Parade's End*, *H. G. Wells*, *R. L. Stevenson*, *World Within World*, *Katherine Mansfield* and *Dominations and Powers* all appeared in *Tomorrow* during 1950 and 1951; the preface to *Prison Etiquette*, Retort Press, 1950; the prologue to *Mr Norris and I*, Allan Wingate, 1956; the foreword to *All the Conspirators*, Jonathan Cape Ltd, 1957; 'Hypothesis and Belief', 'The Gita and War', 'Vivekananda and Sarah Bernhardt', 'The Wishing Tree' and 'The Problem of the Religious Novel' all appeared originally in *Vedanta and the West*, a magazine published in California (the first four were later included in *Vedanta for the Western World*, Allen & Unwin, 1948, the fifth in *Vedanta for Modern Man*, Allen & Unwin, 1952); 'The Head of a Leader', *Encounter*, 1953; 'Virginia Woolf', *Decision*, May 1941, USA; 'Klaus Mann', *Klaus Mann – zum Gedächtnis*, Querido Verlag, Holland, 1950; 'Escales', an article written with W. H. Auden, *Harper's Bazaar*, 1938; 'Coming to London', *Coming to London*, Phoenix House, 1957; 'Los Angeles', *Horizon*, 1947; 'The Shore', originally entitled 'California Story', *Harper's Bazaar*, 1952; 'An Evening at the Bay', *New Country*, Hogarth Press, 1933; 'The Turn Round the World', *The Listener*, 1935; 'A Day in Paradise', *The Ploughshare*, 1935; 'I am Waiting', *The New Yorker*, 1939; 'Take It or Leave It', *The New Yorker*, 1942.

VERSES

M Y first exhibit, *Mapperly Plains*, is included only because it was my first publication, outside of school magazines. It appeared in 1923, in the third volume of *Public School Verse*, an anthology edited by Martin Gilkes, Richard Hughes and P. H. B. Lyon. Among the contributors were Graham Greene and Peter Quennell, both representing Berkhamsted School. Quennell had already published a book of his own, *Masques and Poems*, the previous year, as a schoolboy of seventeen.

I was listed in the table of contents as C. W. B. Isherwood – the name of a least-likely-to-be-read author, if ever I heard one. My friend Patrick Monkhouse pointed this out to me and suggested that in future I should publish as Christopher. I am lastingly grateful to him for this good advice; and to Katherine Tynan, who mentioned the poem favourably in *The Bookman*, thus becoming my first reviewer.

One summer at Repton, while I was at school there, the authorities had the charming idea of holding a toy balloon race. It was a sort of aerial sweepstake. You paid a small entrance fee, for which you received a balloon with a stamped and addressed postcard tied to it. On the card was a message to whoever might find it, asking him to please mail it back to us after filling in the name of the place where he had picked it up. Each card was numbered for identification, and the one which was found farthest away from Repton would bring its owner the prize. To this day, I can remember the solemn beauty of the great cluster of balloons, as they were released and rose high above the cricket field, drifting slowly apart in their many colours against the blue sky.

One of the postcards (not the winning one) was returned from Mapperley Plains. The name thrilled me the instant I heard it, and I repeated it to myself again and again. My poem was an attempt to describe what it made me feel. Why do some names have this extraordinary power? Certainly, it has very little to do with the places they represent. Surabaya, Far Rockaway, Miraflores, Tristan da Cunha – I have visited the first three with disappointment and seen thoroughly depressing photographs of the fourth; yet the magic is still there for me. In 1961 I unexpectedly found myself driving through Mapperley Plains for the first time in my life. The experience was both moving and ridiculous. 'The weird plains seize the hearts of men. ...' It is a residential suburb of Nottingham.

My recollection is that I wrote this poem late one afternoon in my study at school, after getting back from an Officers' Training Corps field-day. (This may explain the reference to marching!) I had been making it up in my head for hours and now sat down in a feverish hurry, dirty and sweaty in my uniform, to put the precious words on paper before I forgot them.

In 1925 I became friends with an Anglo-French family named Mangeot. (I call them 'Cheuret' in my autobiography, *Lions and Shadows*.) Sylvain Mangeot, the younger son, was then eleven years old. He had a talent for painting; and, one day, he began making illustrations for a book which he called *People One Ought to Know*. The 'People' were all animals; but some of them were shown dressed and behaving like humans – a ferret fishing, a horse playing football, a hare dancing ballet. As soon as Sylvain finished a picture, I wrote verses for it. There were about thirty of them altogether.

We had intended the book to be just a family entertainment, but in due course it got passed around among friends. One of these was W. H. Auden. In 1938 he put *The Common Cormorant* into his anthology, *The Poet's Tongue*, listing its author as Anonymous. Since then, it has appeared anonymously in several other anthologies, both British and American. Auden must have copied the verses from memory, for he made a couple of small mistakes. Here is the correct version. I have taken it from a facsimile of the original book, with tracings of Sylvain's illustrations, which my mother made years ago with her usual beautiful skill and care. I believe the Mangeots still have the original.

While Auden was up at Oxford, he worked as part-editor of two volumes of *Oxford Poetry*, 1926 (with Charles Plumb) and 1927 (with Cecil Day Lewis). In the 1927 volume there is a poem by me, called *Souvenir des Vacances*. It is a feeble attempt to parody the current *avant-garde* poetic manner; not worth exhuming. This, too, had to appear anonymously, because I wasn't an Oxonian.

I haven't published anything in verse since then, except translation: the poems from Brecht's *Dreigroschenroman* and certain passages from the *Bhagavad-Gita*. Yet, because I collaborated with Auden on three plays which are largely in verse – working only on the plotting and part of the prose – I am still referred to now and then as a poet. A few people have even assured me, with apparently firm conviction, that my poetry meant a great deal to them when they were young!

For a long while now I haven't felt the urge to versify. *On His Queerness* is one of my last efforts. It came uninvited into my head one day in 1943, while I was trying hard to concentrate on a religious ceremony.

For those who need an explanation: the poem refers to two characteristic tourist attractions at an English seaside resort – a municipal aquarium and the remains of an ancient Roman fort, sometimes locally called a camp.

Mapperley Plains

By the swift ways of shade and sun
We trod the morning. Spring was white
And hushed in lovely pools of light –
But we were eager to have won
Mapperley Plains, so strange and fair;
Nor guessed what should await us there.

And strong noon bridged half Heaven in flame
And day swung down from blue to blue . . .
We marched untired, for we knew
Daylight could never be the same,
Or Glory half so glad, as when
The weird plains seize the hearts of men.

Their beauty is the sword that cleaves
Youth, royally lived in pride and laughter,
From blank, prosaic Age. Hereafter
A bright day's ending . . . fallen leaves –
Mapperley Plains are years behind,
Their music dies within the mind.

The Common Cormorant

The common cormorant (or shag)
Lays eggs inside a paper bag,
You follow the idea, no doubt?
It's to keep the lightning out.

But what these unobservant birds
Have never thought of, is that herds
Of wandering bears might come with buns
And steal the bags to hold the crumbs.

On His Queerness

When I was young and wanted to see the sights,
They told me: 'Cast an eye over the Roman Camp
If you care to,
But plan to spend most of your day at the Aquarium –
Because, after all, the Aquarium –
Well, I mean to say, the Aquarium –
Till you've seen the Aquarium you ain't seen nothing.'

So I cast an eye over
The Roman Camp –
And that old Roman Camp,
That old, old Roman Camp
Got me
Interested.

So that now, near closing-time,
I find that I still know nothing –
And am not even sorry that I know nothing –
About fish.

BOOKS

I WROTE *Some Notes on Auden's Early Poetry* for the November 1937 'Auden Double Number' of *New Verse*. At that time, only seven years after the publication of his first book of poems, Auden was probably the most famous literary figure of his generation. His departure for Spain, at the beginning of 1937, to offer his services to the Spanish Government in the Civil War, inspired a number of young Englishmen to do likewise. If Auden had been killed in Spain, or had even died there of 'flu, he would doubtless have become a hero-poet like Byron or Rupert Brooke.

The years of our literary collaboration were 1935 to 1939. *The Dog Beneath the Skin* was first performed in January 1936; *The Ascent of F.6* in February 1937. By the time Auden returned from Spain, *F.6* had already started its run. So he had not been present at the rehearsals, in the course of which Rupert Doone, our director, had made several changes with my full approval. The night I went with Auden to see the play he turned to me, a few minutes after the curtain had gone up, and said in a loud reproachful whisper, '*my dear*, what have you *done* to it?' The theatre was tiny and most of the audience heard this, with vast amusement.

When Auden and I left for China in January 1938 our departure inspired no one. The emotional climate had changed. The Spanish Civil War had become over-crowded with celebrities. The Chinese War, as viewed from England, seemed very far away, politically confused and quite lacking in glamour. If we had died, as I suppose we easily might have – the danger being from bugs far more than bullets, in that toxic land – it would have been just another occupational accident to two amateur war correspondents.

We returned to England that July and went to work on

our Chinese travel-book, *Journey to a War*. We also finished our third and last play, *On the Frontier*. It was produced in October. In January 1939 we left for the United States.

During that part of my life, I still saw Auden, to some degree, as the small boy, three years my junior, whom I had known at my first boarding-school. I still saw him as the brilliant teenager who had sent me his poems for my criticism, after our reunion in 1925. (See *Lions and Shadows*, in which Auden is called 'Hugh Weston'.) I was still his despotic, possessive, slightly envious mentor and elder brother. I wanted the world to know that I had first claim upon him. I claimed the right to interpret him to the world. At the same time, my own admiration for him rather embarrassed me. This explains the somewhat aggressive, patronizing tone in which these *Notes* are written. I think I already knew then that Auden was a great poet. But it was several years before I realized that he is also a great man.

The first two of Auden's poems quoted in my *Notes* and three of the four quoted in *Lions and Shadows* had not been previously published. (*Rain* first appeared in Spender's privately printed volume.) All six poems were in the first batch Auden sent me in 1925.

In the *Notes* I write that we revised the best parts of our earlier, unpublished play, *The Enemies of a Bishop*, and used them again in *The Dog Beneath the Skin*. This statement is oddly misleading. *The Dog Beneath the Skin* was based almost entirely on a later play, *The Chase*, which Auden wrote independently in 1934. He sent it to me, I made some suggestions, and thus found myself collaborating with him on its revision and expansion.

During 1935, 1936 and 1937, I wrote about thirty-five book reviews for *The Listener*, nearly all of them unsigned. As a reviewer, I dare say I was no more or less dogmatic, spiteful, irresponsible and smart alecky than my colleagues or the run of people who do the job today. But I have come to feel that it is a job to be avoided, unless you are badly in need of money or want to recommend some book you greatly admire.

In the present state of our literary journalism, most short reviews are merely advertisement or anti-advertisement. You tell the reader why he should or shouldn't read this particular book; and that is all. He isn't supposed to be interested in general critical considerations, and you have no space for them, anyway. Each book is presented as a unique event, unrelated to the career and development of its author.

Within a year or two, this kind of writing becomes almost unreadable. The favourable notices are even duller than the unfavourable; a tedious synopsis of a plot, decorated with tarnished superlatives. That is why I am including only one of my *Listener* reviews, and only one of the reviews I published during my first years in the States. I have also excluded some much later reviews – of Ray Bradbury's *The Martian Chronicles*, 1950, of Calder Willingham's *End as a Man*, 1952, and of Edward Upward's *In the Thirties*, 1962. This does not mean that my admiration for these writers has lessened. I will reaffirm it here and say that I think that *The Martian Chronicles* is a masterpiece; that Calder Willingham is a writer of genius, still grossly neglected despite his *Geraldine Bradshaw* and *Eternal Fire;* and that Edward Upward's trilogy – to judge from this first volume – may well be one of the greatest novels of our time.

I include my review of *T. E. Lawrence by His Friends* (*The Listener*, 1937), because it suggests something of my own attitude to Lawrence of Arabia, and why my friends and I found him so fascinating. He was the myth-hero of the thirties. Auden and I consciously tried to recreate him in our character of Michael Ransom in *F.6.*

I include my review of *The Grapes of Wrath* (*Kenyon Review*, autumn 1939) because it contains some perhaps interesting observations about art and propaganda. However, I have cut out five paragraphs which merely retell the story and a sixth which seems superfluous.

In connexion with *The Grapes of Wrath*, I remember how, during the summer of 1941, some of us used to collect bundles of clothes from the American Friends Service Committee centre in Los Angeles and deliver them to the work-camps for the Okies which had been set up in the farmlands of the San Joaquin Valley. These camps were certainly an improvement on the 'Hoovervilles' described by John Steinbeck, but they were miserable enough; long, narrow, corrugated iron huts which must have become uninhabitable ovens in the midday heat. My friends and I were as socially selfconscious about these expeditions as debutantes before a ball. What should we wear? We didn't want to look offensively prosperous or appear to be dressed for slumming. As a matter of fact, we seldom got to speak to the Okies themselves and saw them mostly in the middle distance. A Quaker volunteer worker would receive our bundles, and back we would go. On one occasion, one of the Quakers said to me: 'Can you get us a tuxedo – we need it for theatricals?' So I gave mine to them, feeling that this was somehow a symbolic act of purgation. I have never owned a dinner jacket since.

In 1929 (I believe) Auden got a tutoring job at a wealthy home in London. The mother of his pupil wished to start a small press and publish limited editions. With admirable taste, she had decided on an English version of Baudelaire's *Journaux Intimes*, so she asked Auden if he knew of a good translator. Auden, who believed in keeping everything in the family, answered that he knew one of the best living writers of English prose, who had also a perfect command of French – me!! So I got the job. With my youthful assurance, I didn't worry for a moment about being able to handle it. I had lots of French friends to help me, and could surely bluff my way through somehow.

But, alas, some truly ghastly mistakes got into the text, due to my ignorance of the language and of classical mythology. For example, I translated *fille* as 'young girl', and *Et que, comme Ixion, j'embrassasse une nue* as 'And that, like Ixion, I embraced a naked woman'! The few critics who reviewed the book were rightly merciless; but my beginner's luck saved me. On the title-page my name had been printed as Ch. Isherwood, and this was naturally taken to be Charles. So Charles Isherwood the translator took my place on the scaffold, like a Sydney Carton, and vanished from the literary world for ever. All that survives this fiasco is the masterly introduction by T. S. Eliot, which is reprinted in his *Selected Essays*.

In 1947 my translation was republished by Marcel Rodd, after Professor Myron Barker of the University of California, Los Angeles, had helped me revise it. This time, Auden wrote the introduction. My own preface is to this later edition only. In his *New Year Letter* Auden speaks of 'trim dualistic Baudelaire' as being the

> Poet of cities, harbours, whores,
> Acedia, gaslight and remorse.

In my preface, I say something about Baudelaire under each of these six headings. I have cut out the last four paragraphs here, because they consist only of technical details.

In 1950 the American magazine *Tomorrow* asked me to do a series of what they called essay-reviews. This was a chance to try my hand at criticism rather than advertising. Between October 1950 and July 1951 I wrote seven pieces for them. Six I include here; the seventh, on Ray Bradbury, I omit for the reasons mentioned above.

The review of the Robert Louis Stevenson omnibus was written without benefit of the more reliable books about him, notably *Voyage to Windward* by J. C. Furnas. It seems that Kate Drummond never existed; and that it is very doubtful if Stevenson ever even began a novel about a streetwalker. Henry James wrote *The Author of Beltraffio* with reference to J. A. Symonds and his wife, not the Stevensons; and Fanny must have realized this, for she is known to have liked the story very much. Stevenson did destroy the first draft of *Dr Jekyll and Mr Hyde* after Fanny had criticized it unfavourably. But Fanny's objections had nothing to do with the presence of a Kate-character; she thought *Dr Jekyll* should be an allegory rather than just a horror-story. Stevenson protested at first; then agreed with her and rewrote it.

In other words, my facts at this point are all wrong; but I don't feel that this invalidates the psychological conclusions I draw from them. So it seems simpler to admit to my mistakes here and leave the text of the review unaltered.

Prison Etiquette is one of the most fascinating books to be produced as a result of the Second World War. What it has to say is just as relevant to our present so-called peacetime. It should be republished without delay.

The original edition, published in 1950, was hand-set, hand-bound and printed on a footpedal press by its editors, Holley Cantine and Dachine Rainer, at Bearsville, New York. They called themselves the Retort Press. The book was illustrated by Lowell Naeve, himself an imprisoned objector, a distinguished artist and the author of another extraordinary book about pacifists in prison, *A Field of Broken Stones*.

I wrote this preface at the invitation of the editors. Aldous Huxley also wrote a favourable comment which was printed on the cover.

If you don't know who 'Mr Norris' is, my prologue to Gerald Hamilton's *Mr Norris and I* (1956) will not be of much interest to you. But you don't have to have read my novel in order to enjoy Hamilton's autobiography. *Mr Norris and I* contains episodes of real-life farce such as I would never have dared to invent; the story, for example, of how he modelled for the statue of Winston Churchill.

In 1956 the firm of Dell in New York commissioned me to edit a paperback anthology of English stories in a series of 'Great Short Stories' of different nations. I wrote an introduction to each of the stories I chose. When I applied to the Trustee of the Conan Doyle Estate for permission to include *The Speckled Band* from *Adventures of Sherlock Holmes*, it was strongly hinted to me that I must first revise my introduction; my remarks about Holmes as a comic character had caused offence.

I refused to agree to this condition, partly because I thought it an unallowable form of censorship, partly because I couldn't honestly convict myself of the least disrespect to Conan Doyle, whose memory I honour and whose work I dearly love. *Great English Short Stories* was therefore published (1957) without *The Speckled Band* or my introduction to it, which here appears for the first time.

All the Conspirators is my first novel; published in England in 1928 by Jonathan Cape. In 1957 they reissued it. In 1958 it was published for the first time in the United States by New Directions. I wrote forewords to both these later editions. The American foreword differs greatly from the British and is better, I think; so it is reprinted here.

Some Notes on Auden's Early Poetry

IF I were told to introduce a reader to the poetry of W. H. Auden, I should begin by asking him to remember three things:

First, that Auden is essentially a scientist: perhaps I should add 'a schoolboy scientist'. He has, that is to say, the scientific training and the scientific interest of a very intelligent schoolboy. He has covered the groundwork, but doesn't propose to go any further: he has no intention of specializing. Nevertheless, he has acquired the scientific outlook and technique or approach; and this is really all he needs for his writing.

Second, that Auden is a musician and a ritualist. As a child, he enjoyed a high Anglican upbringing, coupled with a sound musical education. The Anglicanism has evaporated, leaving only the height: he is still much preoccupied with ritual, in all its forms. When we collaborate, I have to keep a sharp eye on him – or down flop the characters on their knees (see *F.6* passim): another constant danger is that of choral interruptions by angel-voices. If Auden had his way, he would turn every play into a cross between grand opera and high mass.

Third, that Auden is a Scandinavian. The Auden family came originally from Iceland. Auden himself was brought up on the sagas, and their influence upon his work has been profound.

Auden began writing poetry comparatively late; when he had already been several terms at his public school. At our prep-school, he showed no literary interests whatever; his ambition was to become a mining-engineer. His first poems, unlike Stephen Spender's, were competent but entirely imitative: Hardy, Thomas and Frost were his models.

The Carter's Funeral

Sixty-odd years of poaching and drink
And rain-sodden waggons with scarcely a friend,
Chained to this life; rust fractures a link,
   So the end.

Sexton at last has pressed down the loam,
He blows on his fingers and prays for the sun,
Parson unvests and turns to his home,
   Duty done.

Little enough stays musing upon
The passing of one of the masters of things,
Only a bird looks peak-faced on,
    Looks and sings.

Allendale

The smelting-mill stack is crumbling, no smoke is alive there,
Down in the valley the furnace no lead ore of worth burns;
Now tombs of decaying industries, not to strive there
    Many more earth-turns.

The chimney still stands at the top of the hill like a finger
Skywardly pointing as if it were asking: 'What lies there?'
And thither we stray to dream of those things as we linger,
    Nature denies here.

Dark looming around the fell-folds stretch desolate, crag-
        scarred,
Seeming to murmur: 'Why beat you the bars of your prison?'
What matter? To us the world-face is glowing and flag-starred,
    Lit by a vision.

So under it stand we, all swept by the rain and the wind there,
Muttering, 'What look you for, creatures that die in a season?'
We care not, but turn to our dreams and the comfort we find
        there,
    Asking no reason.

The saga-world is a schoolboy world, with its feuds, its
practical jokes, its dark threats conveyed in puns and
riddles and understatements: 'I think this day will end
unluckily for some; but chiefly for those who least expect
harm.' I once remarked to Auden that the atmosphere of
Gisli the Outlaw very much reminded me of our school-
days. He was pleased with the idea: and, soon after this,
he produced his first play, *Paid on Both Sides,* in which
the two worlds are so inextricably confused that it is
impossible to say whether the characters are really epic
heroes or only members of a school O.T.C.

Auden is, and always has been, a most prolific writer.
Problems of form and technique seem to bother him very

little. You could say to him: 'Please write me a double ballade on the virtues of a certain brand of toothpaste, which also contains at least ten anagrams on the names of well-known politicians, and of which the refrain is as follows ...' Within twenty-four hours your ballade would be ready – and it would be good.

When Auden was younger, he was very lazy. He hated polishing and making corrections. If I didn't like a poem, he threw it away and wrote another. If I liked one line, he would keep it and work it into a new poem. In this way, whole poems were constructed which were simply anthologies of my favourite lines, entirely regardless of grammar or sense. This is the simple explanation of much of Auden's celebrated obscurity.

While Auden was up at Oxford he read T. S. Eliot. The discovery of *The Waste Land* marked a turning-point in his work – for the better, certainly; though the earliest symptoms of Eliot-influence were most alarming. Like a patient who has received an over-powerful inoculation, Auden developed a severe attack of allusions, jargonitis and private jokes. He began to write lines like: '*Inexorable Rembrandt rays that stab* ...' or '*Love mutual has reached its first eutectic* ...' Nearly all the poems of that early Eliot period are now scrapped.

In 1928 Spender, who had a private press, printed a little orange paper volume of Auden's poems. (This booklet, limited to 'about 45 copies', is now a bibliophile's prize: the mis-prints alone are worth ten shillings each.) Most of the poems were reprinted two years later, when Messrs Faber and Faber published the first edition of their Auden volume: here is one of the few which were not:

> Consider if you will how lovers stand
> In brief adherence, straining to preserve
> Too long the suction of good-bye; others,
> Less clinically-minded, will admire
> An evening like a coloured photograph,
> A music stultified across the water.

The desert opens here, and if, though we
Having ligatured the ends of a farewell,
Sporadic heartburn show in evidence
Of love uneconomically slain,
It is for the last time, the last look back,
The heel upon the finishing blade of grass,
To dazzling cities of the plain where lust
Threatened a sinister rod, and we shall turn
To our study of stones, to split Eve's apple,
Absorbed, content if we can say 'because';
Unanswerable like any other pedant,
Like Solomon and Sheba, wrong for years.

I think this poem illustrates very clearly Auden's state
of mind at that period: in this respect, its weakness is its
virtue. Auden was very busy trying to regard things 'clini-
cally', as he called it. Poetry, he said, must concern itself
with shapes and volumes. Colours and smells were condemned as romantic: form alone was significant. Auden
loathed (and still rather dislikes) the sea – for the sea,
besides being deplorably wet and sloppy, is formless.
(Note 'ligatured' – a typical specimen of the 'clinical'
vocabulary.)

Another, and even more powerful, influence upon
Auden's early work was non-literary in its origin – in
1929, during a visit to Berlin, he came into contact with
the doctrines of the American psychologist, Homer Lane.
(Cf. Auden's own account of this, in his *Letter to Lord
Byron*, part four.) Auden was particularly interested in
Lane's theories of the psychological causes of disease – if
you refuse to make use of your creative powers, you grow
a cancer instead, etc. References to these theories can be
found in many of the early poems, and, more generally,
in *The Orators*. Lane's teachings provide a key to most of
the obscurities in the *Journal of an Airman* (Mr John
Layard, one of Lane's most brilliant followers, has pointed
out the psychological relationship between epilepsy and
the idea of flight).

The first collaboration between Auden and myself was

in a play called *The Enemies of a Bishop*. The Bishop is the hero of the play: he represents sanity, and is an idealized portrait of Lane himself. His enemies are the pseudo-healers, the wilfully ill and the mad. The final curtain goes down on his complete victory. The play was no more than a charade, very loosely put together and full of private jokes. We revised the best parts of it and used them again, five years later, in *The Dog Beneath the Skin*.

It is typical of Auden's astonishing adaptability that, after two or three months in Berlin, he began to write poems in German. Their style can be best imagined by supposing that a German writer should attempt a sonnet-sequence in a mixture of Cockney and Tennysonian English, without being able to command either idiom. A German critic of great sensibility to whom I afterwards showed these sonnets was much intrigued. He assured me that their writer was a poet of the first rank, despite his absurd grammatical howlers. The critic himself had never heard of Auden and was certainly quite unaware of his English reputation.

The scenery of Auden's early poetry is, almost invariably, mountainous. As a boy, he visited Westmorland, the Peak District of Derbyshire, and Wales. For urban scenery he preferred the industrial Midlands; particularly in districts where an industry is decaying. His romantic travel-wish was always towards the North. He could never understand how anybody could long for the sun, the blue sky, the palm-trees of the South. His favourite weather was autumnal; high wind and driving rain. He loved industrial ruins, a disused factory or an abandoned mill; a ruined abbey would leave him quite cold. He has always had a special feeling for caves and mines. At school, one of his favourite books was Jules Verne's *Journey to the Centre of the Earth*.

A final word about Influences – or perhaps I should say, crazes. For Auden is deeply rooted in the English tradition, and his debt to most of the great writers of the past is too obvious to need comment here. The crazes were all short-lived: they left plenty of temporary damage but few lasting traces. The earliest I remember was for Edwin Arlington Robinson. It found expression in about half a dozen poems (all scrapped) and notably in some lines about 'a Shape' in an Irish mackintosh which malice urges but friendship forbids me to quote. Then came Emily Dickinson. You will find her footprints here and there among the earlier poems: for example,

> Nor sorrow take
> His endless look.

Then Bridges published *The Testament of Beauty*, and Auden wrote the poem beginning: 'Which of you waking early and watching daybreak ...', which appeared in the first Faber edition, but was removed from later impressions. Finally, there was Hopkins: but, by this time, Auden's literary digestive powers were stronger: he made a virtue of imitation, and produced the brilliant parody-ode to a rugger fifteen which appears at the end of *The Orators*.

T. E. Lawrence by His Friends,
edited by A. W. Lawrence

EIGHTY-ONE writers – scientists, soldiers, professional men of letters, politicians, professors, as well as relatives and humbler friends – have contributed to this anthology of Lawrence reminiscences; and the result is surprisingly satisfactory. Surprisingly because composite biographies too often resemble the pompously inscribed and slightly faded heap of flowers on a tomb: everything in perfect taste and so very, very tactful. T. E. Lawrence himself was anything but tactful (except when engaged in wangling on behalf of his friends) and his memory, perhaps for this reason, has inspired a collection of tributes which are all that any man could wish to earn: affectionate, candid, unadorned, sincere. Also, the various contributions do not, essentially, contradict each other; each one adds something to the general effect, and the portrait thus collectively painted is clear in outline, vivid and brilliantly penetrating. It is difficult to imagine that a better study of Lawrence's character could be produced by any single man.

Physically, one's first impression was of his smallness. (It must be remembered that a highly trained body – that of a ballet-dancer, for example – will always appear smaller than it actually is, because its disciplined and economical movements occupy so little space in comparison with those of an ordinary clumsy person. Several observers remark that Lawrence could 'vanish' from a room; meaning that he didn't, like most of us, trip over the mat, fumble with the door-knob, kick the door with the side of his shoe.) Then his eyes, of an immensely burning blue; and his bright gold, sun-bleached hair. Bernard Shaw, Forster and Kennington were all struck by his apparent boyishness; even after the horrors of the desert campaign he looked ten years younger than his age. He had a giggling laugh, played practical jokes, and interspersed his conversation with schoolboy slang. His enthusiasm for mechanical dodges and gadgets, too, had an adolescent quality. 'Powerful and capable as his mind was,' writes Shaw, 'I am not sure that it ever reached full maturity.'

It was easiest to approach him by way of technicalities; archaeological, mechanical or literary. Leonard Woolley, E. M. Forster and his many Tank Corps and Air Force friends understood this. Others, who did not, found themselves blankly ignored, impishly snubbed, or face to face with the terrifying little despot who had once ordered two thousand prisoners to be executed to avenge the death of a mutilated Arab woman. Lawrence loved to talk shop; but woe unto those who did not know their subject or strayed into unfamiliar territories of knowledge. He exposed their ignorance in a second; quietly, brutally. All his life he remained something of an Oxford don.

Like most very unhappy people, he was at ease with children and with people of a humbler class or race. With his social equals his behaviour was unpredictable; moods of gaiety, chatter and hospitality would alternate with shyness and a strange, distant humility which could hardly be distinguished from the extremes of arrogance. He was at his most neurotic when dealing with journalists and publicity in general. L. B. Namier writes:

He was retiring and yet craved to be seen, he was sincerely shy and naïvely exhibitionist. He had to rise above others and then humble himself, and in his self-inflicted humiliation demonstrate his superiority. A deep cleavage in his own life lay at the root of it.

What did Lawrence really want of life? Forster thinks that his highest ambition was literary, and Lawrence's own letters to Cape and Edward Garnett bear this out. He had hoped that the *Seven Pillars* would stand beside *Karamazov*, *Zarathustra* and *Moby Dick*, 'to make an English fourth'. When the work was finished he despaired. He had written some of the best descriptive prose in our language, but this was not enough. *Seven Pillars* had failed in its purpose – to be the great psychological masterpiece of war: it had failed because it was not absolutely frank. Lawrence had been unable to bring himself to record the full history of the 'deep cleavage' in his own nature. Beside this failure, the triumphs and trophies of his military success, the praises of Churchill and Lord Allenby, the admiration of two continents, seemed nothing; the Arabian campaign shrank to a mere irrelevant episode – he was no use, he said, with an almost satanic pride; he was done for, finished. So he went back, lonely, to his motor-boats and his solitary, hated companion – the tough faithful body which, already, he had punished so cruelly for its obstinate will to remain alive.

There are those who have tried to dismiss his story with a flourish of the Union Jack, a psycho-analytical catchword or a sneer; it should move our deepest admiration and pity. Like Shelley and like Baudelaire, it may be said of him that he suffered, in his own person, the neurotic ills of an entire generation. There is much here to ponder over; much to instruct and warn.

The Grapes of Wrath by John Steinbeck

O UT in the Dust Bowl of Oklahoma, the earth is dying of sheer exhaustion. Three generations back, white men took this land from the Indians. Their children grew poor on it, lost it, and became sharecroppers. Now, when the sharecroppers' landlords can no longer pay the interest on their debts, the banks step in to claim what is legally theirs. They will plough up the small holdings with their tractors, and farm them for cotton, until that crop, too, is exhausted. The land will pass to other owners. The cycle of futile, uneconomic possession will continue.

Meanwhile, the sharecroppers have to leave the Dust Bowl. They enter another great American historical cycle – the cycle of migration towards the West. They become actors in the classic tragedy of California. For Eldorado is tragic, like Palestine, like every other promised land. After the Land Rush, the Gold Rush, the Movie Rush, comes the Fruit Rush. The poor farmers are only too ready to believe the handbills which assure them that there will be work for everybody in the orchards and orange-groves of the Pacific Coast. They swarm over the mountains and across the deserts in their broken-down automobiles, they suffer epic and incredible hardships – only to find that they have exchanged a bad life for a worse. The fruit-picking is overcrowded, the season is short, wages have been forced down to starvation level. The 'Okies' themselves are naturally unwelcome to a resident population which sees with dismay and resentment this fresh influx of competition into the labourmarket. The native Californians arm themselves to protect their own hard-won economic security. Camping miserably like nomads, on the fringes of the towns, the starving strangers are persecuted by the police. Most of them are dazed into submission. Some wander away elsewhere, or return to their ruined homesteads. A few grow angry. These form the nucleus of a future revolt. Violence will give birth to violence, as always. *The Grapes of Wrath* are ready for the vintage.

Such, very briefly, is the background of Mr Steinbeck's latest novel. We follow the wanderings of the Joads, a typical sharecropper family, from the moment of their eviction from an Oklahoma farm. We accompany them on their tragic and exciting journey, across Texas, New Mexico, Arizona, dogged by accident and disaster. We are present at the final scene of their disintegration, less than a year later, in the heavy rains of a Californian winter.

Readers of the earlier novels and stories do not need to be reminded that Mr Steinbeck is a master of realistic writing – a master among masters, for America is extraordinarily rich in his peculiar kind of talent. In the presence of such powers, such observation, such compassion, such humour, it seems almost ungrateful to make reservations – to ask that what is so good should be even better. But a writer of Mr Steinbeck's calibre can only be insulted by mere praise; for his defects are as interesting as his merits. What are these defects? Why isn't *The Grapes of Wrath* entirely satisfying as a work of art?

It is a mark of the greatest poets, novelists and dramatists that they all demand a high degree of cooperation from their audience. The form may be simple, and the language plain as daylight, but the inner meaning, the latent content of a masterpiece, will not be perceived without a certain imaginative and emotional effort. In this sense, the great artist makes every one of his readers into a philosopher and poet, to a greater or lesser degree, according to that reader's powers. The novelist of genius, by presenting the particular instance, indicates the general truth. He indicates, but he does not attempt to state it – for to state the general truth is to circumscribe it, to make it somewhat less than itself. The final verdict, the ultimate synthesis, must be left to the reader; and each reader will modify it in accordance with his needs. The aggregate of all these individual syntheses is the measure of the impact of a work of art upon the world. It is, in fact, a part of that work. In this way, masterpieces, throughout the ages, actually undergo a sort of organic growth.

At this point arises the problem of the so-called propaganda-novel, and the often repeated question: 'Can propaganda produce good art?' 'All art is propaganda,' the propagandists retort – and, of course, in a sense, they are right. Novels inevitably reflect contemporary conditions. But here the distinction appears. In a successful work of art, the 'propaganda' (which means, ultimately, the appeal to the tribunal of humanity) has been completely digested, it forms part of the latent content; its conclusions are left to the conscience and judgement of the reader himself. In an imperfect work of art, however, the 'propaganda' is overt. It is stated, and therefore limited. The novelist becomes a schoolmaster.

Mr Steinbeck, in his eagerness for the cause of the sharecroppers and his indignation against the wrongs they suffer, has been guilty, throughout this book, of such personal, schoolmasterish intrusions upon the reader. Too often we feel him at our elbow, explaining, interpreting, interfering with our own independent impressions. And there are moments at which Ma Joad and Casy – otherwise such substantial figures – seem to fade into mere mouthpieces, as the author's voice comes through, like another station on the radio. All this is a pity. It seriously impairs the total effect of the novel; brilliant, vivid, and deeply moving as it is. The reader has not been allowed to cooperate, and he comes away vaguely frustrated.

Overt political propaganda, however just in its conclusions, must always defeat its own artistic ends, for this very reason: the politico-sociological case is general, the artistic instance is particular. If you claim that your characters' misfortunes are due to the existing system, the reader may retort that they are actually brought about by the author himself. Legally speaking, it was Mr Steinbeck who murdered Casy and killed Grampa and Granma Joad. In other words, fiction is fiction. Its truths are parallel to, but not identical with, the truths of the real world.

The *Intimate Journals* of Charles Baudelaire

WHAT kind of a man wrote this book?

A deeply religious man, whose blasphemies horrified the orthodox. An ex-dandy, who dressed like a condemned convict. A philosopher of love, who was ill at ease with women. A revolutionary, who despised the masses. An aristocrat, who loathed the ruling class. A minority of one. A great lyric poet.

By nature Baudelaire was a city-dweller. He was born (1821) and died (1867) in Paris. He loved luxury and fashionable splendour, the endless cavalcade of the boulevards, the midnight brilliance of talk in the artists' cafés. Paris taught him his vices, absinthe and opium, and the extravagant dandyism of his early manhood which involved him in debt for the rest of his life. Even in extreme poverty, he preferred the bohemian freedom of the Latin Quarter to the sheltered respectability of his family home. The atmosphere of Paris was the native element of his inspiration. He speaks of the 'religious intoxication of the great cities'. 'The pleasure of being in crowds is a mysterious expression of sensual joy in the multiplication of Number.'

Brussels, in the eighteen-sixties, was not a great city. It was a provincial town. Baudelaire hated it. Expressing his contempt for a man, he calls him 'a Belgian spirit'. But no doubt this attitude was also due to the state of his affairs and his health. Baudelaire did not come to Brussels until 1864, when he was already ruined, financially and physically. He was miserably poor. His work had failed to obtain proper recognition. Six of the poems in *Les Fleurs du Mal* had been judged obscene and suppressed by court order. His publisher had gone bankrupt. He was slowly dying of syphilis. Violent nervous crises made him dread insanity. 'Now I suffer continually from vertigo, and today, 23rd of January, 1862, I have received a singular warning. I have felt the wind of the wing of madness pass over me.'

Baudelaire was one of the first writers of 'the poetry of departure'. His longing for escape – from the nineteenth century and himself – fastened nostalgically upon ships. 'When', he imagines them asking, 'shall we set sail for happiness?'

When Baudelaire was a boy of twenty his parents became alarmed by the wildness of the life he was leading. They persuaded him to take a long ocean voyage, hoping that it would change his tastes and ideas. The ship was bound for Calcutta. Baudelaire insisted on leaving it at the island of Réunion and being sent back to France. He detested the sea and his fellow-passengers, but he never forgot this glimpse of the tropics. It is characteristic of him, and of the romantic attitude in general, that he later pretended to have been in India, told fantastic lies about his adventures, and always regretted the opportunity he had missed.

Shy men of extreme sensibility are the born victims of the prostitute. Baudelaire's mulatto mistress, Jeanne Duval, was a beautiful, indolent animal. She squandered his money and slept with his friends. The biographers usually condemn her: most unjustly. Few of us would really enjoy a love-affair with a genius. Jeanne had to endure Baudelaire's moods and listen to his poems; she understood neither. But, in some mysterious manner, these two human beings needed each other. They stayed together, on and off, for twenty years. Baudelaire always loved and pitied her, and tried to help her. Hideous and diseased, she limps out of his history on crutches and disappears.

Like many lesser writers before and after him, Baudelaire suffered constantly from Acedia, 'the malady of monks', that deadly weakness of the will which is the root of all evil. He fought against it with fury and horror. 'If, when a man has fallen into habits of idleness, of daydreaming and of sloth, putting off his most important duties continually till the morrow, another man were to wake him up one morning with heavy blows of a whip and were to whip him unmercifully, until he who was unable to work for pleasure worked now for fear – would not that man, the chastiser, be his benefactor and truest friend?' The *Intimate Journals* are full of such exclamations, coupled with resolves to work – 'to work from six o'clock in the morning, fasting at midday. To work blindly, without aim, like a madman. ... I believe that I stake my destiny upon hours of uninterrupted work.' It is terribly moving to read these passages, knowing that the time is close at hand when Baudelaire will be lying dazed and half-paralysed; when he will no longer be able to remember his name and have to copy it, with tedious care, from the cover of one of his books; when he will not recognize his own face in the mirror, and will bow to it gravely, as if to a stranger.

In his lifetime Baudelaire witnessed the dawn of the Steam Age – a false, gaslit dawn, loud with engines and advertisement, faithless, superstitious and blandly corrupt. Baudelaire foresees the future with dismay and denounces it in the magnificent outburst which opens with the words: 'The world is about to end. ...' Elsewhere he writes: 'Theory of the true civilization. It is not to be found in gas, or steam, or table-turning. It consists in the diminution of the traces of original sin.' After two world-wars and the atomic bomb, we of today should understand him better than his contemporaries.

Baudelaire's nervous, unstable temperament, his contempt for bourgeois ethics and his impatience of mediocrity led him into a series of quarrels – with his family, his friends and his business associates. For his mother – the only important woman in his life except Jeanne Duval – he experienced mingled feelings of love, exasperation, pity, rebellion and hatred. He sincerely admired his distinguished stepfather, General Aupick; but the two men were worlds apart, they spoke different languages and could never understand each other. He could appreciate the honesty and good faith of Ancelle, his legal guardian; but the elderly lawyer's primness and caution drove him frantic. Even in middle age Baudelaire often seems touchingly immature, like a defiant schoolboy surrounded by disapproving grown-ups.

His passionate outbursts and bitter words hurt nobody so much as himself. His rage was immediately followed by remorse. His last years were darkened with regrets – regrets for deeds done and undone, for health and vigour lost, for time irretrievably wasted. Yet Baudelaire never gave way finally to despair. He struggled with himself to the very end, striving and praying to do better. His life is not the dreary tale of a talented weakling, it is the heroic tragedy of a strong man beset by great failings. Even its horrible closing scenes should not disgust or depress us. They represent a kind of victory. Baudelaire died undefeated – a warning and an inspiration to us all.

The *Intimate Journals* consist of papers which were not collected and published until after Baudelaire's death. The section called *Squibs* was probably written before 1837; *My Heart Laid Bare* belongs, more or less, to the Brussels period. This latter title is taken from the writings of Edgar Allan Poe, who says that if any man dared to write such a book, with complete frankness, it would necessarily be a masterpiece. Baudelaire certainly dared, but he did not live to carry out his project. What we have here is an assortment of wonderful fragments, cryptic memoranda, literary notes, quotations, rough drafts of prose poems, explosions of political anger and personal spleen.

After some thought, I have decided not to attempt annotation. I have neither the time nor the scholarship for such a task and, anyway, what does it matter to the average reader who Moun was, or Castagnary, or Rabbe? Read this book as you might read an old diary found in the drawer of a desk in a deserted house. Substitute – if you like names from your own world – names of friends and enemies, of bandwagon journalists and phoney politicians. Much of the obscurity is unimportant or on the surface. The more you study these *Intimate Journals* the better you will understand them.

Parade's End by Ford Madox Ford

ONE must begin by congratulating Mr Knopf. *Parade's End* (Knopf) is much more than an ordinary 'omnibus'; it is virtually a new book. In a conventional novel-with-sequels, the author proceeds logically and chronologically, step by step, so that you are always 'with' him at any given point in the story. Such is not Ford's method. Like Proust he is retrospective and discursive; he jumps back and forth across unilluminated chasms of time, and delights in bewildering the reader. You cannot, therefore, judge any part of this work properly until you have read all of it. The four separate books do not stand alone, and Ford always intended them to be published in one volume. That he did not live to see its appearance is especially tragic because, at the time of his death in 1939, it may well have seemed to him that they were doomed to remain disunited and forgotten. Thanks to Mr Knopf this danger has now been removed and *Parade's End* (the overall title was chosen by Ford himself) may be enjoyed as an integrated whole. I believe it will insure its author's belated recognition as one of our most important modern writers.

Some Do Not ..., the first and longest of the novels, introduces us to nearly all the principal characters. They are: Christopher Tietjens, a large heavily-built mathematical genius who works in the imperial Department of Statistics and is a member of a Dutch-descended Yorkshire family whose 'seat' is at Groby; Sylvia his wife, a beauty, a bad Catholic and an hysterical bitch; Mark, his brother, an enormously wealthy mineowner who keeps a French mistress; Macmaster, Christopher's humbly born, ambitious Scotch protégé and Civil Service colleague who is later to become a distinguished but bogus littérateur with a knighthood; General Lord Edward Campion, V.C., an elderly, well-preserved professional soldier, who takes a fatherly interest in Christopher and a sentimental interest in Sylvia; Valentine Wannop, an athletic girl who is a suffragette, one of the best Latin scholars in England, and the daughter of a great Victorian woman novelist.

When the story opens – shortly before the outbreak of World War I – Christopher's marriage is already on the rocks. Having run away with another man and grown bored with him, Sylvia has asked Christopher, in an insolently casual manner, to take her back. Christopher agrees to do this, because 'no one but a blackguard would ever submit a woman to the ordeal of divorce' and for the sake of his small son – if, indeed, the boy *is* his son; even this is not certain.

Christopher and Macmaster take a trip to the country. Macmaster likes golf; Christopher hates it, but is interested in the mathematics of trajectories. Macmaster also wants to meet a clergyman named Duchemin, because Duchemin was a friend of Dante Gabriel Rossetti, and Macmaster is writing a monograph on Rossetti which will start him, he hopes, on his literary career. Duchemin turns out to be a sexual psychopath. There is a luridly funny scene at a breakfast-party, which ends with the clergyman being dragged off, after an outburst of word-fetishism, by an ex-prizefighter disguised as a curate, and with the birth of romance between Macmaster and Edith Ethel, Duchemin's long-suffering arty-snobbish wife. The golf, also, is scandalously interrupted – by Valentine Wannop and a suffragette friend, who heckle one of the players, a Cabinet minister. The friend nearly gets arrested. Christopher has to save her by tripping up a policeman. After this, Valentine and Christopher start to fall in love.

The second part of the novel takes place some time later, during the early part of the war. Christopher has already been in France and has returned home with his phenomenal brain partly incapacitated by amnesia. He is fighting to keep his sanity and Sylvia is doing everything in her power to make him lose it. Tortured by her love-hatred of Christopher and baffled by her failure to break his self-control, she slanders him grotesquely to his friends, involves him in humiliating money troubles, bombards him with accusations of unfaithfulness. Already, she had turned Macmaster and Edith Ethel (now Macmaster's wife) against him; General Campion is wavering and even Mark is distressed by her lies. She is particularly successful with the people to whom Christopher has lent money because most of them want an excuse for not paying it back. Christopher can do little more than endure all these blows with passive stoicism, for he is bound hand and foot by his own principles and by the pride which Sylvia hates. However, just before he returns to France, he finally asks Valentine to go to bed with him. She gladly agrees; but they are prevented by the arrival of Valentine's brother, a conscientious objector, drunk. Next day, Christopher leaves, and Valentine does not hear another word from him until the war is over.

No More Parades and *A Man Could Stand Up* continue the story of Christopher's struggle for sanity amidst the nightmare of military madness, 'the worries of all these wet millions in mud-brown'. First at a replacement camp (magnificently described) where Sylvia suddenly appears during an air raid and creates one of her most complicated and extraordinary scandals, thus compelling General Campion to order Christopher, for his own good, back to the front. Then in the front line trenches, where Christopher gets buried by a shell. He narrowly survives all these ordeals and returns to England and Valentine. On Armistice Night the lovers come together at last.

Last Post is a postwar epilogue. We find Mark, Marie-Léonie (his French mistress, now become his wife), Valentine and Christopher living together in a country cottage. Mark is paralysed and stricken dumb by a stroke. Marie-Léonie nurses him and runs the household with ruthless Gallic efficiency. Valentine, still unmarried, is pregnant. Christopher has a small business selling antique furniture to Americans. On the single day which *Last Post* describes, he is away from home and does not return until the last page but one. But a consciousness of his presence dominates the situation.

The cottage is visited by a party of unwelcome guests, including Sylvia, her son, General Campion, Mrs de Bray Pape (perhaps the most improbable American woman in all British fiction) and Fittleworth, the landlord, whom Sylvia has brought along in an effort to convince him that he should expel his tenants for their immoral way of life. At first Sylvia seems as fiendish as ever, but actually she is slipping. She has already had to give up the pretence that she is dying of cancer, and Fittleworth is beginning to be suspicious of her lies about Christopher and Mark. She has persuaded Mrs de Bray Pape to cut down the historic Great Tree at Groby (which the American has rented); but even this cruel wound to the Tietjens' family sentiment somehow misses its effect. The day is Sylvia's Waterloo. By the end of it she has agreed to divorce Christopher, and has decided to marry poor old Campion (to his great consternation) because, after all, he is going to be Governor-General of India, which might not be

too utterly boring. They go away at length. And then
Christopher returns and Mark dies. Christopher and
Valentine are now free to marry, and they will no longer
be poor – so the story has a moderately happy ending.
This summary of it is as unfair and misleading as all such
summaries must be. But I must pass on to a more important question: what is *Parade's End* really about?

Mr Robie Macauley, in his always interesting and sometimes brilliant introduction, suggests that Ford wanted to
show the Age of Reason, in the person of Christopher
Tietjens, giving way to our modern era of chaos, madness
and squalor, in which 'there will be no more Hope, no
more Glory. Not for the World, I dare say. *There will be
no more parades.*' Tietjens, the Truly Reasonable Man
born out of his time, stands surrounded by (I quote Mr
Macauley) 'fragmentary people, uncertain, confused,
without values. They sense that Tietjens belongs to a
moral frame of reference that both makes the world intelligible and wards off its shocks. To their jumbled and
neurotic lives he stands as a reproach, and they must
destroy him if possible.'

Such, no doubt, was Ford's conscious design when he
started to write this book. We are told that the character
of Tietjens was modelled after an actual friend, Arthur
Marwood, a Yorkshireman and a statistical mathematician
of genius, of whom Ford said, 'he possessed the clear
eighteenth-century English mind which has disappeared
from the earth ... He was, beneath the surface, extraordinarily passionate – with the abiding passion for the
sort of truth that makes for intellectual accuracy.' One
does not question the genuineness of Ford's admiration
for his friend, but Christopher Tietjens is obviously something other than a simple image of Marwood. He has
taken on characteristics of his own. The relation between
an author and his characters is exceedingly complex; and
Ford's attitude towards Christopher seems to have gone
through many changes. It ends by appearing, to say the
least, ambiguous. Christopher is constantly being pre-

sented to us as charitable, gentle, generous, just, loyal and courageous, a near-saint; and yet one has the impression that Ford does not really like him – that he agrees, in fact, with Sylvia, in finding Christopher a maddeningly inhuman, arrogant, prig, who, beneath his mask of Job-like patience, can be obstinately and coldly cruel. 'If you had once in your life said to me: "You whore, you bitch ... May you rot in hell ..." you might have done something to bring us together.'

Ford's secret sympathy with Sylvia has resulted in one of the most compassionate portraits of a neurotically unhappy woman ever drawn in fiction. The more we see of her the better we understand her, until it becomes possible even to love her. But how are we to love or admire a man of whom his creator writes: 'If he had to go into partnership and be thrown into close contact with anyone at all he did not much care who it was as long as it was not either a bounder or a man of his own class and race. To be in close mental communion with either an English bounder or an Englishman of good family would, he was aware, be intolerable to him. ... In electing to be peculiarly English in habits and in as much of his temperament as he could control ... Tietjens had quite advisedly and of set purpose adopted a habit of behaviour that he considered to be the best in the world for the normal life'?

I suggest, therefore, that Ford's conscious design underwent a radical – but possibly subconscious – change during the process of its execution. What he has actually shown us is not the sane Past confronting the insane Present, but a contrast between two kinds of insanity. The cold madness of self-righteous Reason opposes the hot madness of uncontrolled Instinct; and the result of their collision is War.

According to this view of the book, its real heroine is Valentine Wannop. Valentine is able to survive unharmed amidst our modern chaos because she is a whole, sane individual. She has resolved the Christopher-Sylvia conflict within her own life. She is a suffragette who can fall in love with a man, a Latinist who does not shrink from earning her living by scrubbing floors. One hopes that, in time, she will be able to cure Christopher; but this seems doubtful. His madness is much more deeply seated than Sylvia's because it always disguises itself as common sense. And Sylvia, the Catholic, has the advantage of having known a real saint, an Irish priest named Consett. Father Consett becomes innocently involved in the Casement affair, and is hanged by the British; but his influence continues to work upon Sylvia during her more lucid moments, and there are signs, towards the end of the story, that it is growing stronger. (It is at least partly responsible for her decision to give Christopher his freedom.) Christopher, the unimpeachable, will perhaps get the justice he deserves. Sylvia, the inexcusable, can be sure of mercy.

If *Parade's End* is really such a remarkable achievement, why has it been neglected for so long? Partly – as I have already suggested – because you cannot see it properly until you see it as a whole. The four novels appeared over a period of five years, and there can have been few readers who first collected them all and then sat down and read them consecutively. Taken separately, any one of the novels would seem exasperatingly inconclusive. *Last Post* would be almost unintelligible. And this brings me to the other reason for Ford's neglect: his narrative technique.

It is not that Ford is difficult to read – in the sense that James is sometimes difficult, or Meredith. But you have to follow him in a mood of alert relaxation; you must not mind being mystified, detained, dragged backward, pulled forward, cheated, hoaxed. You must suspend curiosity and wait patiently until he is ready to explain. You must be content simply to enjoy what is going on (or what seems to be going on) at any particular moment. Ford's approach to his audience is extraordinarily disingenuous, playful and sly. He would have made an ideal Ancient Mariner – accosting you with the air of one who asks only

a minute of your time, just enough for the merest anecdote; and then enweaving and enwinding you in his great,
dazzlingly complicated web.

Parade's End is the most subjective of novels. Every
page of it is pure Ford. And Ford's voice, speaking through
the minds of the characters in turn, is often so loud that
it seems they must shout against it to be heard. The
immense vitality of this book is the vitality of Ford's own
enjoyment. He is having such a wonderful time. Even
when he is obviously trying to take the situation seriously,
his writing has strange, mocking overtones. And at times,
his glee is positively fiendish. How he delights in Duchemin's crazy breakfast party; and the air raid on the camp,
when Private O Nine Morgan gets half his face blown off
and Christopher keeps Lt McKechnie from hysterics by
betting he cannot translate an improvised sonnet into
Latin; and the Walpurgis of Armistice Night, when
McKechnie finally goes mad, and the Colonel dies in a
cab, and Sylvia throws herself downstairs! I suppose this
glee might occasionally be described as bad taste; but it
has its own antiseptic quality which saves the book from
mawkishness, even in the weakest passages. Mark's death,
for instance, is potentially a nauseatingly sticky scene;
but Ford has managed to make it sound like a peculiarly
spiteful parody of Galsworthy.

Christopher and Sylvia, Mark and Valentine, Campion
and the Macmasters are not complete, detached, objective
portraits in the manner of the classic novel. They are, at
all times, projections of Ford's consciousness. But what
they may lack in substance they make up for in liveliness.
Hearing Ford tell about them is like listening to a very
amusing and perceptive friend describe a group of people
he has met. You know he is exaggerating and distorting.
You know that no one could possibly be quite like that.
And you do not care in the least. For caricature has its
own, equally valid, kind of truth. And you would much
rather listen to Ford.

H. G. Wells

To write a biography of Wells is a peculiarly difficult undertaking, as Antonina Vallentin would be the first to admit. 'He was so infinitely sensitive to the changes taking place around us,' she says, in the foreword to her book (*H. G. Wells, Prophet of Our Day*, by Antonina Vallentin (John Day)), 'so far ahead of our time and yet so closely, so intensely present in it, that he sums up its whole content. He *is* the history of our day.' That is precisely the problem – how to determine the relation of a social and political thinker to an epoch which we cannot yet properly survey, because we ourselves are still in the middle of it. For this reason alone, it would seem doubtful that a really adequate biography of Wells is possible at present. However, Madame Vallentin has certainly made a courageous try. Her book is always informative, occasionally profound and never dull. It is a valuable guide to the enigmas, the fascinating but self-contradictory fragments of Wells' own autobiographical work. Daphne Woodward's translation from Madame Vallentin's French original is commendably free from Gallicisms.

Towards the end of his life Wells wrote: 'I came up from the poor in a state of flaming rebellion, most blasphemous and unsaintly.' The phrase jars on one a little; its swagger seems affected. Wells, to be sure, knew bitter poverty in his youth, semi-starvation and serious illness. But he doesn't quite fill this suggested role of a proletarian revolutionary, marching to the barricades with broken chains dangling from his wrists. He was, in fact, the son of a housemaid and a gardener 'who had gone into a precarious business as small shopkeepers, not through any urge for independence but because they had lost the employment in which they had been perfectly happy. His mother looked upon "service", dependency, as

53

heaven, a haven of security; it represented all she had known of kindness and beauty, the romantic element in her life, the light that still shone through her poverty-stricken days.' What Wells 'came up from' was, therefore, not the unashamed poverty of the proletariat but the apologetic poverty of the lower middle class, the nine-teenth-century heirs of feudal serfdom, with their pitiful yearnings towards 'respectability', their clean lace curtains hung to hide bare rooms from prying neighbours. And it was against this concept of respectability, of preordained subservience, of 'knowing your place', that he primarily rebelled. He grew up hating, above all things, the feudal philosophy of the Big House, with its smugly defined scale of virtues and values, its fatty conscience and its false God. When Bernard Shaw, on the occasion of Wells' death, remarked that Wells had never been a gentleman, he made a cruel but extremely pertinent observation. For throughout his life, despite wealth and worldwide fame, Wells remained painfully and most aggressively conscious of his origins. He loathed the pretensions of birth and rank and felt himself fully entitled to fight them with any weapons that came to hand. An inverted snob, he seemed sometimes to glory in caddishness. He confronted established authority with that kind of comically cocky, underdog defiance which has been classically represented by Charlie Chaplin. And yet – like the rest of us – he was perversely attracted to what he loathed. Many of the heroines of the novels, and many of the real women he loved, display the aristocratic arrogance, the easy con-tempt for convention which is so characteristic of a privi-leged ruling caste.

Wells had no false modesty, but he held some curious and humble views about himself and his talents. He in-sisted upon his ordinariness. Once, happening to meet Madame Vallentin on the railway station at Nice: 'It's funny you recognize me,' he said with his crooked smile, 'I'm so exactly like all the middle-class, middle-aged Englishmen who come in swarms to the Riviera.' Discuss-

ing his mental capacities, he declared that 'if brains could
be put on show, like cats and dogs, he did not believe his
own would win even a third prize'. This is obviously
untrue; but perhaps Wells meant that he lacked a certain
quick-witted, superficial cleverness which he greatly
admired in others. He had, indeed, that measure of
stupidity – or obstinate, plodding slowness – which is an
aid, not a hindrance, to clear and careful thinking. The
merely clever man brings forth a phrase and mistakes it
for an idea. The 'stupid' thinker, lacking this agility, never
trusts a phrase until he has taken it to pieces; he goes
deeper.

Incredible as it sounds, Wells also believed that he
lacked vitality. Yet his vitality was the very essence of his
genius. His vital appetite for experience and knowledge
was prodigious, and he preserved it into his late seventies.
He always wrote straight out of his immediate interests
and enthusiasms, bubbling over with excitement. He
could hardly wait to tell the world what was happening
to him, what he was thinking – and, indeed, he had to
hurry, or he would be thinking something else. To an
altogether extraordinary degree, he had a sense of the
present moment, with all its urgency, menace, opportunity and challenge. He was aware of the stars in their
courses, the earth turning, time passing, Gandhi spinning,
Lenin dying by inches at his desk, Proust (whom he didn't
like) writing, the bus-driver's wife cooking supper, China
starving, America drunk on bathtub gin, the scientists
trying to split the atom, the men of goodwill trying to
unite Europe, and the peoples of the world already shivering in the shadow of another war. Not only was he aware
of all this – as any ordinary journalist might be – but he
reacted to his awareness with passion. He didn't just sit
back and watch. He accepted his share of responsibility, of
guilt, of duty. What could he do, before it was too late?
How could he help? He was prepared to do anything. He
bustled hither and thither, with his ready pen and his
squeaky voice, joining this movement, resigning from

that, minding other people's business, offering suggestions wanted or unwanted, contradicting himself, attacking, accusing. He travelled in many countries, always telling his hosts exactly what he thought of them; he bearded statesmen in their studies, he confronted dictators and generals. He was utterly fearless and reckless, and so clearly above the common motives of ambition and greed that he ended by achieving a privileged position. Like Shaw, he was allowed to write things which no newspaper would dare to publish over any other signature. Unlike Shaw, he made effective use of this privilege. By the time of his death, many of his fellow human beings had dismissed him from their consciences as a nagging and erratic nuisance. It would have been too uncomfortable to listen to him, so they laughed at him and called him absurd. No doubt he often *was* absurd; but this very absurdity put their cowardly apathy to shame.

Wells thought of himself as an historian, an educator, a sociologist, a political pamphleteer, rather than as a literary artist. He was inclined to be impatient with those who believe that style is an end in itself, well worth the practice and effort of a lifetime. 'I write, like I walk,' he said, 'because I want to get somewhere.' He was impatient, also, with Henry James who (while praising him warmly) complained that the heroines of his novels were mere projections of their author's personality: 'the ground of the drama is somehow most of all in the adventure for *you* — not to say *of you*, the moral, temperamental, personal, of your setting it forth'. Wells felt that the novel in its traditional form was out of date. 'It was a fixed frame, apparently established for ever, where individual destinies were played out in an independence that seemed unnatural to the social being of today.' He added that the novel 'was unlikely to be very important in the intellectual life of future generations. It was quite likely to die out and be replaced by more sincere and revealing biographies and autobiographies.' Nevertheless, Wells was capable of fine writing, when he wasn't in too much of a hurry; and, throughout his career, he continued to produce novels.

As a matter of fact, Wells had all the gifts which go to make a 'traditional' novelist. He could create solid characters, write lively, naturalistic dialogue, and evoke the atmosphere of houses and places. His humour was Dickensian, lapsing sometimes into facetiousness but bold and warm at its best. These qualities are most apparent in *Kipps*, *Tono-Bungay* and *Mr Polly*, three books which drew largely upon the experience of Wells' own childhood and adolescence. Wells was always at his most vivid when he returned to that period; no doubt because he could look at it from a distance, objectively. He never gave himself time to do this in dealing with his later life. Everything had to be reported at once, as it happened — like the scribbling of a war correspondent in the midst of a still-smoking battlefield. There was no time to worry about form, or the technical problems of presentation; there was no question of excluding any portions of the given material because they didn't happen to 'fit'. Every bit of it had to go in.

The majority of Wells' realistic novels (I shall speak of his scientific fantasies later) deal with the impact upon their author of a person, or an idea, or a situation. The person is usually a woman, one of the many in Wells' life, very thinly disguised. The idea or the situation is presented subjectively, just as it struck Wells himself. This initial impact (the impact, for example, of World War I upon Wells in *Mr Britling Sees It Through*) is the author's point of departure into speculations and theorizing. 'What does it mean?' he asks himself aloud, 'what do I think about this?' (Wells isn't sure, because he is thinking even as he writes, thrashing the problem out before our eyes.) Along the lines of these speculations, which are like spacious corridors leading off in all directions, wander the minor characters. These are often brilliantly drawn, and their personal circumstances and doings engage our interest, even when they are somewhat irrelevant to the main theme. And then, beyond the open-ended, incomplete structure of the novel, we are aware of the surrounding contemporary world, with all the diversity of its business and its anxieties, ever present on the horizon of the author's consciousness.

It is a measure of Wells' genius that he was able to make these big untidy talkative books so alive and readable. From an artistic standpoint, most of them can only be described as failures; they simply don't 'compose'. But Wells achieved a larger kind of success; he showed how the tight classic form of the novel might be expanded to include a much wider area of reference. That he himself didn't know when to stop, that he expanded the novel until it burst, is not so important. You can't make experiments without explosions. He remains a great pioneer. The novel-of-ideas is out of fashion at the moment, but it will come back – and when it does, Wells will be reread with admiration and excitement. (Incidentally, Madame Vallentin doesn't say whether he knew *The Magic Mountain*. And one wonders what he would have made of *Dr Faustus*.)

Several of Wells' realistic novels were hugely popular, at the time of their publication, because of their topicality and the shock value of the problems they discussed. To-day, his reputation is based chiefly upon the *Outline of History* and half a dozen of his scientific fantasies. Wells would not regret the survival of the *Outline*; it is a masterpiece. But he might well resent our preference for *The Time Machine, The Island of Dr Moreau, The Invisible Man, The War of the Worlds, The First Men in the Moon* and *The War in the Air*. No author cares to have his early works (these were all written before 1909) preferred to his later ones; Wells continued to write scientific fantasies throughout his life, but these, like the realistic novels, became increasingly discursive and were never very successful. Besides, he would probably complain that we have failed to understand the inner meaning of the stories themselves. We regard them as enjoyable thrillers – just as we regard *Gulliver's Travels* as a quaint book for children.

We are quite ready to honour Wells as a prophet – but only in a limited and rather ludicrous sense of the word. We marvel that he foretold the invention of television, motion pictures, dishwashing machines, prefabricated houses, helicopters and tanks. But very few of us (as Madame Vallentin points out) appreciate the real significance and drama of Wells' lifelong struggle with the mystery of the future.

When he looked into the future, Wells alternated between extremes of optimism and pessimism. The early scientific fantasies are deeply pessimistic; a fact which we usually overlook. There is the unutterable sadness of the Time Traveller's last glimpse of the dying world; the reversion of Moreau's fabricated humans into beasts; the wretched fate of the Invisible Man. Life and individual genius end in frustration and defeat. Nearly fifty years later, in his book *Mind at the End of its Tether*, Wells repeated this message: 'The end of everything we call life is close at hand and cannot be evaded.' Yet his own character was essentially optimistic. A natural Utopian, he continued, despite many disappointments, to cling to his vision of a World State; he was still fighting for it in his old age, in the midst of World War II. He believed in world socialism as the only force which could abolish frontiers and rival national sovereignties. 'We do not deplore the Russian Revolution as a revolution,' he said. 'We complain that it was not a good enough revolution and we want a better one.'

'In a crowded English or French or German railway carriage of the later nineteenth century, it would have aroused far less hostility to have jeered at God than to have jeered at one of those strange beings, England or France or Germany. ... (Yet in the background of the consciousness of the world, waiting as silence and moonlight wait above the flares and shouts, the hurdy-gurdys and quarrels of a village fair, is the knowledge that all mankind is one brotherhood, that God is the universal and impartial Father of mankind, and that only in that universal service can mankind find peace, or peace be found for the troubles of the individual soul.)'

Wells' exclusion of this striking passage from the later editions of his *Outline of History* is significant; it marks the end of his 'theological excursion', his uneasy phase of public relations with the concept of God. In his youth, Wells hated God and violently denied His existence; for 'God', in those days, was the God of the Big House, the feudal Overlord. But *Mr Britling*, shaken by the horror of the First World War, found that some Ultimate Reality was, after all, necessary to his peace of mind: so Wells rediscovered Him as 'the Captain of Mankind', a sort of supernatural President of the future World State. This God appears in two further novels, *The Soul of a Bishop* and *The Undying Fire*; but it is doubtful if Wells found Him either comforting or convincing. Indeed, He appears to be little more than a metaphor. His chief quality is negative; He is fundamentally opposed to His Church and to all organized Religion. He makes a last bow, in the guise of a weary and cynical old man, in *Joan and Peter*, telling the young hero that, if he doesn't like the world, he must change it himself.

Wells' 'theological excursion' was doomed to failure because he could never quite escape from the dualistic religious concepts of his upbringing: God high in Heaven and we, His servants, hopelessly far beneath. Such dualism is nauseating to any man of Wells' temperament because it immediately confronts him with his old enemy, established authority. Wells might try to persuade himself that 'his' God was different, but he couldn't. The truth was that he didn't really want a Captain of Mankind any more than he had wanted a feudal Overlord. He wasn't a follower. Indeed, he had a horror of 'Great men'.

Nevertheless – and this is Wells' tragedy – he was always dimly but poignantly aware that something was lacking, some vital spark that would bring his New Utopia to life.

Under the influence of Plato's *Republic,* which he had read as a schoolboy, he imagined an Order of Samurai – a group of dedicated and sternly disciplined young people who would give their lives to the work of building the society of the future. His writings on this subject actually inspired the formation of enthusiastic groups which looked to him for leadership. Wells, to his great mortification, was unable to offer them any; he couldn't devise a practical programme. 'Toward the end of his life he remarked on the fact that just about the time he made this unsuccessful attempt at practical construction, Lenin, "under the pressure of a more urgent reality", was quietly and steadily drawing up an "extraordinarily similar plan" – the Communist party organization.' But, even if a revolutionary situation had existed in England at that period, and even if Wells had been a born revolutionary leader, he and his Samurai would have found themselves, sooner or later, in trouble. For a dedicated group demands a faith; without one, it cannot continue to function. Lacking genuinely spiritual inspiration, it will turn to some substitute idolatry, such as nationalism or the cult of a leader; and so the movement defeats itself and the World State can never be founded, much less sustained.

Wells was always proclaiming his faith in the capacities of Man. Yet he refused to take account of Man's highest capacity – that of knowing and drawing strength from what is eternal within himself. Some inhibition or deeply-seated fear, it would seem, made Wells unable to accept the validity of the mystical experience, or to recognize its central importance in the scheme of human evolution. Why he couldn't bring himself to do this, despite all his urgent self-questionings, I don't know. Madame Vallentin doesn't tell us. There is no mention of the subject anywhere in her book.

R.L.S.

RANDOM HOUSE has added to its Modern Library Giants the *Selected Writings of Robert Louis Stevenson*, edited, with an informative and fair-minded introduction, by Saxe Commins. This is an astonishingly roomy omnibus, and its contents are as representative as one could wish – *Treasure Island, The Master of Ballantrae* and *Weir of Hermiston, Dr Jekyll and Mr Hyde, The Suicide Club, The Beach of Falesa*, and seven shorter stories; eight essays and the *Open Letter* about Father Damien; *Travels with a Donkey* and *The Silverado Squatters*; *A Child's Garden of Verses*, five ballads and nine poems. I can hardly blame Mr Commins for leaving out one of my favourite stories, 'The Destroying Angel', since this must be read as part of *The Dynamiter*, an uneven book not worth reprinting in its entirety. I think, however, that he might have included two or three of Stevenson's prayers. Also, since these Modern Library books are designed to be kept, I feel moved to make a general protest against their recently added endpapers. In my opinion, they are messy and undistinguished – quite unworthy to enclose Stevenson, not to mention Augustine and Austen.

Two great legendary figures dominated the literary background of my generation in its youth; the Dying Wanderer and the Martyred Dandy, Stevenson and Oscar Wilde. I don't mean that we necessarily admired either of them very much as writers. But you couldn't deny their personal fascination. Wilde's legend has persisted, almost undiminished, to the present day – despite every attempted debunking; including Mr Edmund Wilson's most damaging suggestion that Wilde wasn't a genuine homosexual at all. Stevenson's legend – as distinct from the popularity of his work – seems quite extinguished. Why should this be so?

It is no sufficient explanation to say that Stevenson was

a poseur. All legendary figures have been poseurs of one sort or another. But Stevenson's poses now seem fatally lacking in style and conviction. He was half-hearted about them; and he changed them too often. The general effect is confused. As the wanderer, he doesn't achieve the glamour of Byron or George Borrow. As the bohemian, he couldn't survive a single evening with Rimbaud. As the bogus feudal patriarch at Vailima, he pales beside the grand old ham of Yasnaya Polyana. As the moralist, he is never crazy or unreasonable enough to be really impressive. (Tolstoy beats him there, too; Stevenson couldn't conceivably have made a remark like 'all prostitutes and madmen smoke'.) As the invalid, he is far too noble; and we turn with relief to the cosy shamelessness of Proust. Even his antics and caprices seem laboured, unfunny and unkind. While at Davos, for example, he sent urgently for the local Anglican clergyman in the middle of the night, allowing him to suppose that he was being called to a deathbed. When the poor man rushed into the room, half-dressed and breathlessly concerned, Stevenson gasped out: 'For God's sake, have you a Horace?' Wilde would never have behaved like that.

In order to become a lastingly legendary character, you have to be, or seem to be, all of a piece. You have to have that immediate, total effectiveness of impact which is common to the great figures of literature or the theatre. We say 'Ah yes – Byron!' in the same tone as we say 'Ah yes – Mr Micawber!' Forty years ago Stevenson still appeared to be one of these splendid simple human masterpieces – the beloved R.L.S., the world's storyteller who had gladly sacrificed his life to his art and now lay romantically buried on a Samoan mountain-top, the sailor home from sea. Today, in the clearer perspective of distance, he is seen to be a highly complex creature; courageous but irresponsible, outspoken but disingenuous, strict-principled but self-indulgent; a man of moods rather than of passions, of wilfulness rather than of will. And so, in our disappointment, we desert his shrine and are now in danger of forgetting that, if less godlike, he is much more interesting than we had supposed.

It is always hard to guess how much or how little J. M. Barrie meant by anything he wrote; for Barrie is one of the most enigmatic of modern writers. But he was certainly in a position to know Stevenson well. (It was in a letter to Barrie that Stevenson said of his masterful wife: 'Hellish energy; can make anything from a house to a row, all fine and large of their kind. ... A violent friend; a brimstone enemy. ... Is either loathed or adored; indifference impossible.') And in *Peter Pan* Barrie seems to have created, consciously or subconsciously, a kind of Freudian nightmare about *Treasure Island* and Stevenson himself. Peter Pan-Stevenson is the gallant little boy who plays father to another man's children (Lloyd Osbourne and his sister) while his own development remains mysteriously arrested; he has 'decided' not to grow up. Instead, he chooses to inhabit an adventure-book world peopled by Indians and pirates. Wendy, the mother-wife, has her counterpart in Fanny Stevenson, who used to look on indulgently while her young husband sat utterly absorbed in playing soldiers with her son on the floor. Captain Hook is not only a reincarnation of Long John Silver but a dream-version of the swashbuckling, crippled Henley – first extravagantly admired, then angrily renounced – whose 'hand of friendship' has been replaced by a deadly weapon. And then there is the crocodile, symbol of sentimental hypocrisy, with its swallowed alarm clock which seems to be saying, 'It's later than you think.' ... One wonders how Stevenson would have enjoyed his friend's play, if he had lived to see it performed.

Personally, I never cared much for *Treasure Island* – John Masefield's sea stories appeal to me far more – but it is impossible not to admit that it is a kind of masterpiece. Why is it so successful? Because, I think, it belongs to that very special class of what one may call, without any suggestion of disparagement, superpotboilers. The superpotboiler is the perfect work of synthesis. It is about our day-dreams about something. It sums up the totality of our fantasies relating to a certain milieu. It presents to our recognition our own nostalgia, so that we almost feel that we have created it ourselves – as indeed, in a sense, we have. *Treasure Island* isn't simply the account of a particular treasure hunt; it is a definitive statement of the treasure-hunt day-dream, and, as such, doubly non-realistic. Other examples of this class are *The Pickwick Papers* (the old-fashioned Christmas), *Carmen* (Spain-as-you-like-it), and *South Pacific* (phallic sailors plus tropical sex). Stevenson tried to produce another superpotboiler, *A Child's Garden of Verses*, about the way grown-ups would like children to feel. As far as I am concerned, he failed – and to fail in this medium is to fail disastrously.

Almost all of Stevenson's stories are set in the past, the eighteenth century or earlier. There is nothing to complain of in this. The greatest novel so far written is an historical novel. But when we describe *Kidnapped*, *Catriona*, *The Master of Ballantrae*, etc., as 'romances' we are certainly implying a criticism. For all their carefully accurate documentation, we feel that they have been subtly glamourized and emotionally falsified. Stevenson's trouble was that he was too fond of the Past for its own sake. He loved it and sentimentalized it, just because it wasn't the present. It was his place of refuge from the dull, smug commercialism of nineteenth-century Britain, which he hated with all his heart. No doubt this hatred was also associated with his revolt from his own father, the admirable but narrowly orthodox engineer. Stevenson refused to find romance in the machine (despite a dutiful poem about his father's lighthouses); otherwise, he might have forestalled Kipling. Though a disciple of Balzac – from whom he acquired his fine flair for melodrama – he did not share his master's enthusiasm for the tremendous melodrama of money. Instead, he wished himself back in the age of 'velvet and iron'.

In view of what has happened and is happening to the modern world, Stevenson's longing to have been a soldier and his cry, 'Shall we never shed blood?' seem merely morbid; and we excuse him by reminding ourselves that he was a very sick man throughout most of his life. Yet Tennyson, who was in perfect health when he wrote, 'Why do they prate of the blessings of peace? We have made them a curse ...', would have understood better what he meant. The 'peace' of the Victorian Age was a sort of fat after-dinner nap on top of many shelved problems and ignored injustices, and it was natural for an impatient man to want to disturb it, no matter how. Where so many healthier and wiser men failed to estimate the cost of violence, we mustn't be too hard on Stevenson. In his innocence, he was thinking in terms of swords and horses, not jet-planes and tanks. He would certainly have found modern war as horrible and sordidly utilitarian as the rest of us do.

Stevenson's only long stories about contemporary London are *The New Arabian Nights* series and *Dr Jekyll and Mr Hyde*. *The New Arabian Nights* are charming in their lively artificiality, and one wishes that he had written more of them. He really did manage to create a magic, never-never London, where extraordinary scenes are being enacted behind every curtained window and any cab is ready to whisk you away into an adventure. Stevenson's London has been largely buried, as it were, beneath the more recent and even more magical Londons of Sherlock Holmes and Chesterton's Father Brown; nevertheless, it forms their foundations.

The origins of *Dr Jekyll and Mr Hyde* are obscure and fascinating. It is worth discussing them here because they are so closely related to Stevenson's whole predicament as a human being and as an artist. As a very young man, a law student at Edinburgh University, Stevenson had an affair with a girl named Kate Drummond, an innocent, simple person who had drifted into the city from a country home in the Highlands and become involved in its slum-nightlife. The affair was a happy one, at any rate from Stevenson's point of view, and he wrote poems to

Kate in which he called her 'Claire'; poems that were for many years suppressed. Stevenson never forgot Kate. More than ten years later, married and living in the South of France, he decided to write a novel about her. Fanny Stevenson made a terrible scene, declaring that this would ruin his reputation as a clean, wholesome family author, the author of *Treasure Island*. So Stevenson abandoned the novel which would probably have been his best and most adult work, and thereby, it is said, gave Henry James the idea for his *The Author of Beltraffio*. Shortly after this, back in England, Stevenson had a nightmare which inspired him to write *Dr Jekyll and Mr Hyde*. Again, Fanny violently objected – because, it has been suggested, the figure of Kate appeared prominently as Jekyll's temptation and Hyde's victim. Be that as it may, Stevenson destroyed his original draft and produced the now published version, from which Kate is entirely absent. (Hollywood, disagreeing with Fanny, has put Kate right back where she belongs, to the considerable improvement of the story.)

Kate or no Kate, we find here the symptoms of a tension which was dominant in Stevenson's character; the struggle between his inherited Puritanism and his natural inclinations. Dr Jekyll is the average sensual man whose sensuality is inhibited by his sense of duty and his regard for the proprieties. 'I had learned', he says, 'to dwell with pleasure, as a beloved day-dream, on the thought of the separation of these elements. If each, I told myself, could be housed in separate identities, life would be relieved of all that was unbearable. ...' And so he sets himself to discover the drug which will separate him from Mr Hyde.

Unfortunately, Stevenson's Puritanism obscured his psychological insight and caused him to mis-state the Jekyll-Hyde problem completely. What he has given us, with Fanny's assistance, is a ridiculous and thumpingly effective melodramatic tract. We all love Mr Hyde – he is the world's favourite horror sweetheart – and we roar with joy as he goes skipping off towards the redlight district, trampling on a little girl to show how wicked he is. But he doesn't fool us for an instant. He may be an ugly customer, greedy and brutal and dangerous when roused, but he is no more essentially evil than a big savage dog. The real tragedy of Jekyll – as Stevenson would have seen if he had permitted himself to face it – is that he disowns Hyde, his libido, and calls him evil; just as Stevenson himself was being forced to disown the young man who made love to Kate in the Edinburgh slums. Hyde, driven forth into the streets, becomes a fierce outcast with his hand against every man, but Jekyll, the cruel proud hypocrite wearing a mask of benevolence, is ten thousand times wickeder than he. Perhaps this doesn't matter very much today, when we can enjoy the story as simply entertainment, but the book did a great deal of harm in its time, providing material for fashionable preachers who hailed it in their sermons as a new and edifying proof that Sin is not respectable. If there is a Purgatory for literary characters, Jekyll will have to stay in it until he has hugged Hyde to his bosom and they have gone out on the town together, arm in arm, with all the neighbours watching.

Of the two travel books included in this volume, I much prefer *The Silverado Squatters*, which gives you a vivid glimpse of the Californian back-country and its inhabitants in the eighteen-eighties. Left all alone with Stevenson and his donkey in the Cevennes, I find myself frequently bored. As a travelling companion he is inclined to be sententious. Imagine being with a man who turns to you in a Trappist Monastery and solemnly declares, 'And yet, apart from any view of mortification, I can see a certain policy, not only in the exclusion of women, but in this vow of silence'! One can't help wishing that D. H. Lawrence, and not Stevenson, had made this trip. Just think what he would have made of Modestine!

We have a certain prejudice, nowadays, against the middleweight essay; the kind that Stevenson wrote. The middleweight essayist seems to us to be neither serious nor silly enough, and we neglect him for Aldous Huxley or James Thurber. Unjust though this attitude may be, it cannot be denied that Stevenson often gives one the impression of a man playing solitaire, neatly dealing out his opinions with what Chesterton calls 'a dainty equity', a little on that side, a little on this. He is too fond of words like 'withal' and locutions like 'a-tiptoe on the highest point of being'. At his worst, he adopts a tone of humourless sprightliness which is tiresome and embarrassing.

Stevenson's greatest defect as a writer is his vanity, and this becomes most evident when he really has something important to say. Throughout the whole of his magnificent and rousing attack on the Reverend Dr Hyde of Honolulu – the missionary who libelled Father Damien – we are never for a moment allowed to forget Stevenson himself, arising in his righteous anger to defend a poor, dead, saintly priest. 'If I have at all learned the trade of using words to convey truth and to arouse emotion, you have at last furnished me with a subject,' he tells Dr Hyde – and one is reminded of some famous and conceited defence counsel warming to his work. It isn't that Stevenson is insincere, but he is a little too pleased with his own sincerity.

The final period of his life – the six years he spent in the South Pacific – gives us some idea of the lines along which his personality and his powers would have developed, if the cerebral haemorrhage hadn't killed him. Towards the end of it, we see him solidly established as an international celebrity and local potentate, the ceremonious Master of Vailima. After all his wanderings, he has found, in Samoa, a sort of tropical-baroque version of the respectability he fled from in his own country. He makes speeches at lavish feasts, composes family prayers, and has his mother sitting as a guest at his table.

What is more, he has at length gratified his ambition to intervene in the sphere of action, though unsuccessfully and on a tiny scale. He has supported one native chieftain against another in a fight for control of the Samoan kingdom. His candidate Mataafa has been defeated and banished, and he has had to accept a truce with the victorious rival; but he has made a public stand as champion of the oppressed and has been treated as a person of political consequence – or at least as a serious nuisance – by the German and British authorities.

Nevertheless, he is melancholy, restless and terribly homesick for Scotland. (Had he lived, he would probably have returned there sooner or later – his health, his pride, and Fanny permitting. It is possible, also, that he would have gone into politics.) His mind dwells chiefly on Scottish themes. He writes *Catriona* and begins *Weir of Hermiston*.

The extraordinary quality of the *Hermiston* fragment doesn't necessarily prove that this would have been Stevenson's masterpiece. Mr Commins points out how often his longer books begin strongly and end weakly, in the carelessness of fatigue. But *Hermiston* does show that Stevenson died with his genius unimpaired and growing. Adam Weir, unfinished, is still finer than the wonderful completed portrait of James Durie, in *Ballantrae*. Stevenson could never have created Weir if he hadn't entirely forgiven his own father; the character is too deeply understood to have been conceived in hatred. How his rapidly maturing mind would have come to feel about the Kate Drummond episode, and how he would have resolved these problems in his art, are questions which remain unanswered. But they suggest that we may have lost a much greater writer than the Stevenson we know.

World Within World by Stephen Spender

WHEN one of your best and oldest friends tells you that he is writing his autobiography, you naturally feel excited. You know that you will appear in it, and you are curious to see what you'll look like. You know that it will reclaim large areas of your own past life. You look forward to revisiting them, and perhaps finding there some clues to your present problems. No matter how little the book succeeds as a piece of literature it is sure to fascinate *you*, if only for these reasons.

However, if Stephen Spender's *World Within World* (Harcourt, Brace) had merely gratified my private nostalgia or tickled my vanity, I most certainly shouldn't be reviewing it. I am doing so because I sincerely believe that this is a very important book; an outstandingly clear and courageous statement of certain personal and social problems which concern all of us – Americans just as much as Europeans – today. Because this statement is made in the form of an extremely lively, moving and amusing autobiography, I feel sure that it will appeal to many readers in this country, even if they know very little about the individuals, places and events to which it refers.

World Within World is a true autobiography, not a volume of memoirs. That is to say, it presents a central character to whom all other characters and all events are directly related, and by whose mind all experiences are subjectively judged. Memoirs, on the other hand, should ideally be written by an insignificant, almost invisible observer, with the utmost possible objectivity. Authors who waver between these two approaches to their material usually produce shapeless, incoherent books.

Good autobiography is only achieved when its live original has qualities which would make him a suitable hero for a novel. Many men and women of great ability do not have such qualities; and so, when they write about their lives in this style, we get bored with them and wish they would step back from the middle of the stage. One never gets bored with Spender. He can stand on his own feet as a fictional creation. And the fact that he happens to be one of our best living poets has no bearing on one's enjoyment of his story.

What makes Spender a suitable hero for a novel? There are, I think, two aspects of his personal predicament which have universal dramatic value. He is the liberal individualist hesitating before the false options of our totalitarian world. ('There's only two sides, nowadays. Come on, you've got to choose one or the other.') He is also the victim of 'puritan decadence' (his own phrase, which I shall explain later), torn between indoctrinated sex-guilt and the lure of neo-Freudian licence. ('*Do what thou wilt* shall be the whole of the Law.') In both these roles, he has teetered back and forth, and even now his balance is uncertain. 'I have learned largely from mistakes,' he writes, 'so that this book seems to me, among other things, a catalogue of errors. ... I do not want my behaviour to appear attractive or fashionable. Nor do I offer any consoling picture of myself living now in detached philosophic calm, having survived my life like a grave illness.'

Lest this should sound formidably serious, I must immediately add that Spender is, and knows himself to be, an essentially comic character. 'The wonderful thing about Stephen,' a mutual friend said to me recently, 'is that he's the right kind of idiot' – meaning that he is one of those rare people who aren't afraid of making fools of themselves, and who actually help and inspire others by allowing themselves to be laughed at. Thinking of him, one conjures up a sort of parody-Parsifal; or a mock-Goethe hero with sorrows as funny as the Sorrows of Werther. He has something of the conscious *naïveté* of Novalis ('This morning I wept much; and again after dinner'); something of the sly madness of Hölderlin (whose poems he has translated with extraordinary insight). Even as I picture him now, I find myself starting to grin.

It seems natural to compare Spender to these German poets because he himself has a partly German ancestry. His mother's side of the family was German, Danish and Jewish. Both his parents were writers; but he would seem to have inherited most of his artistic sensibility from his mother. 'At school, where there were many Hampstead

Jews, I began to realize that I had more in common with the sensitive, rather soft, inquisitive, interior Jewish boys, than with the aloof, hard, external English.' From Harold Spender, his father, who was temperamentally more of a journalist and a politician than a novelist, he got his liberal idealism, his ambition, and his chronically acute anxiety about world affairs. 'I grew up in an atmosphere of belief in progress curiously mingled with apprehension.' Both parents had died by the time Spender was eighteen, leaving him to make the best of the talents and weaknesses they had bequeathed to him.

For his father, during the last years, he felt a sort of fascinated hatred, so intense that it has continued to influence his own life and work, down to the present day. With the passing of time, such an emotion becomes gradually indistinguishable from love; and, indeed, there is much love in his beautiful poem called *The Ambitious Son*, in which the son freely admits that he shares his father's besetting sin. 'When I realized that the desire to be Prime Minister was in itself only a thirst for notoriety, I shifted my ambition. ... I turned back to poetry. But although I wanted a truer fame, I cannot deny that I have never been free from a thirst for publicity very like that of my father. Even today it often disgusts me to read a newspaper in which there is no mention of my name.' Nevertheless, Harold Spender could not possibly have written the passage I have just quoted; that is where father and son are unlike. Harold's political exhibitionism disgusted the adolescent Stephen just because it was unconscious and humourless, as well as being ineffectual. When Harold stood for Parliament, he was defeated. When he lectured, half the audience was secretly laughing at his pomposity. And thus it came about that when Stephen – after a period of agonizing shyness at Oxford – began to emerge as a successful public figure, he began also, by a self-protective instinct, to accentuate those clownish, self-mocking elements in his own personality which would prevent him from ever becoming 'the wrong kind of idiot', from turning into a pitiful bore like poor Harold. His father, if he were alive, would understand Stephen now as little as he understood him then. No doubt he would be proud to read the headline in a French newspaper which recently announced 'Stephen Spender tells us how we can save civilization'. But he wouldn't see the joke.

In his political books, articles, poems and speeches, Spender speaks always as an individual who reserves the right to doubt, to criticize, to change his mind and to shift his position. 'To believe that my individual freedom could gain strength from my seeking to identify myself with the "progressive" forces was different from believing that my life must become an instrument of means decided on by political leaders. I came to see that within the struggle for a juster world there was a further struggle between the individual who cares for long-term values and those who are willing to use any and every means to gain immediate political ends – even good ends. Within even a good social cause, there is a duty to fight for the pre-eminence of individual conscience.' Such an attitude becomes increasingly daring and valuable in the world of today, where every effort is being made to separate mankind into two snarling, terrified packs. Its danger is only that the protagonist of the individual conscience may easily – if he escapes murder or imprisonment – turn into a coldly self-righteous prig, acting always on principle and from the highest motives but in fact quite inhumanly. This sort of prig is tolerated because he is impotent. He is impotent because he has lost touch with the way ordinary people feel.

When one considers the fate of the individualist prig one begins to recognize in Spender's behaviour – his indiscretions, rash decisions and public humiliations – an instinctive flair, amounting to genius, for revealing truth through farce. Spender's principles often get mixed and his motives are sometimes far from lofty, yet he always seems to preserve an ultimate integrity simply by virtue of laying himself so ridiculously open to criticism. And, in the end, it is the critics who betray themselves; for in the presence of naked absurdity we are all embarrassingly unmasked.

This book recounts the tragi-comic saga of Spender's involvement in the Spanish Civil War. During the winter of 1936, he impulsively joined the British Communist Party on the invitation of its Secretary, Harry Pollitt, believing, as many of us then did, in the sincerity of its cooperation with the united front against fascism, and being willing on this account to agree to differ about the justice of the Moscow trials. Mr Pollitt, no doubt, simply wanted to gain another prominent convert for propaganda purposes, and lost interest in him as soon as the party card was signed. At all events, he allowed the *Daily Worker* to send Spender off to Spain immediately, on a fruitless hunt for information about the interned crew of the Russian steamer *Comsomol*, which could probably have been obtained in ten minutes by phoning the Italian Consulate. (Spender's adventures as an amateur intelligence agent, snooping around Gibraltar and Tangiers, would make a great satirical novel, and I often beg him to write it.) But those who try to exploit people like Spender always live to regret it. His article in the *Daily Worker*, setting forth with annihilating innocence the reservations with which he had joined the Party, offended many of its influential members. And worse was to follow. For Spender, now back in Spain, began making attempts to help a friend who had deserted from the International Brigade. These attempts were entirely honourable and legitimate, but they caused some scandalous gossip which was extremely embarrassing to his fellow Communists. He was never again asked to work for the Party in any capacity, and his membership lapsed. The last phase of his Spanish experiences, as a delegate to the International Writers' Congress in Madrid, is hilarious and should be studied carefully by all who wish to understand the literary life of the thirties. Much that has been written about the Civil War is noble and passionate, much is wise and profound.

Yet I know of no one who gives you a more vivid sense of its atmosphere, from a foreigner's point of view, than Spender does here. His blazing indignation, his guilt and pity, his love for the landscape and the language, his keen sense of the ridiculous and his own personal anxieties all combined to sharpen his awareness of the situation as a whole. And I believe that, in spite of all he suffered there, he was happier in Spain than he had ever been before.

Speaking of happiness, and thus implying its opposite, takes one back again to Spender's boyhood; for he assures us that this was worse than anything he has experienced since. Miseries of homesickness at his first school were followed by torments of guilt at the oncoming of adolescence. 'My brothers and sister and I were brought up in an atmosphere which I would describe as "puritan decadence". Puritanism names the behaviour which is condemned; puritan decadence regards the name itself as indecent, and pretends that the object behind the name does not exist until it is named. ... To the son of the puritan decadent, his body is a nameless horror of nameless desires which isolate him within a world of his own. He is divided between a longing to become like the others who walk about in their clothes without desires and as though they had no bodies, and a sense that nevertheless for him his guilt gives him back his body.' In this state of acute tension Spender grew up and went to Oxford, where he met W. H. Auden. Auden was then a disciple of the American psychologist Homer Lane, one of the early pioneers of what we now loosely call psychosomatic medicine. Lane's teaching was, very briefly, as follows: 'Don't fear and hate your desires. Make friends with them. If you are sick, this merely means that your desires are urging you, through sickness, to do what you really want, not what you think you *ought* to do. Follow their guidance, no matter how wicked or crazy it may seem, and you will get well and be good and natural and happy.'

This was thrilling news to Spender. And when, a little

later, Auden introduced me to him, he decided that I was the healer who was going to lead him out of his puritan captivity into the promised libido-land. When we are young, we love to cast our friends in these great symbolic roles; and I can't deny that I threw myself into the character with enormous enthusiasm, for I too was a Lane disciple. I was living mostly in Berlin at the time, which seemed especially romantic to Spender; for Germany was then pre-eminently the country of the wander-vogel movement, of nudism, hiking-trips, leather shorts, accordions and free love. So Spender came to Germany, and wrote in his diary: 'Now I shall begin to live.'

What he actually did there was to write some of his best early poems; and to expose the utter absurdity of the sex-freedom myth by living up to it with his usual ruthless *naïveté*. He also, quite unconsciously, exposed me as a bogus healer. I didn't like this, and we had a short quarrel which ended by our dropping the symbolic relationship and becoming permanent friends.

The German period was undoubtedly good for Spender, nevertheless. It cured him of a lot of his fear. The pendulum of his life had swung over as far as possible, so to speak, in the forbidden direction; but it hadn't flown right off, as he had perhaps half-expected, and plunged him into destruction. It began to swing back again; and, in future, its arc would be shorter and its limits known. The guilt-nightmares and the freedom-daydreams faded. His world became populated with real people, instead of heroes, healers and tyrants. He found himself capable of serious love-affairs and lasting friendships.

To become a genuine adult is, among other things, to learn not to be afraid of words; to refuse to allow them to dominate one's life and confine it to a dictated pattern. 'I leave it to the reader to apply the psychiatric labels to the various relationships which I have to describe. Yet I come to wonder whether many contemporaries do not also condemn themselves to a kind of doom of being that which they consider themselves in the psychological textbook. ... What I am concerned with here is adjusting my acceptance of my own nature to the generally held concept of the normal. ... For the artist to feel cut off from this warm flow of the normal general life ... is a grave disadvantage.' This is wisely said. But those who find themselves under the 'grave disadvantage' of being in prison on a moral charge might well protest that it is not they, but our lawgivers and our police, who have done the labelling.

At forty-two, famous, actively creative, happily married and the father of two children, Spender is still admirably open to doubt and experience, still rash and spontaneous in his reactions, still inquiring and growing. He is eagerly concerned with the problems of the younger generation. He sees the young British writer of today in search of a status, a position of individual responsibility within yet independent of the collectivized state. He sees his own country reduced to a position of second-rate importance and helplessly involved in the great struggle between Russia and the United States. 'I am for neither west nor east, but for myself considered as a self – one of the millions who inhabit the earth. ... If it seems absurd that an individual should set up as a judge between these vast powers ... I can reply that the very immensity of the means to destroy proves that judging and being judged does not lie in these forces. For supposing that they achieved their utmost and destroyed our civilization, whoever survived would judge them by a few statements ... a few words of those men who saw outside and beyond the means which were used and all the arguments which were marshalled in the service of those means.'

In his preface, Spender acknowledges the help of Frances Cornford: 'Whatever improvement there may be in this over my other prose I owe to her.' I admit the improvement, but must confess to a partiality for Spender's prose style even at its oddest and least grammatical; it so vividly suggests his personality. I can find here only one example of the Spender *nonsequitur* – 'despite her titantic strength, she was not particularly clean' – and only a few specimens of his verbal impressionism, such as 'the river-winding countryside'. But there is plenty of characteristic Spender humour, which consists of grandiosely exaggerated comparisons and the sudden introduction of absurdly irrelevant details. 'Edmund Blunden exclaimed: "Whatever you do, don't review books as I did", as Paolo and Francesca relate that it was reading a book which led to their downfall.' 'J. B. Priestley ... went on to explain how, as a consequence of his early poetic discipline, trains were at that moment being loaded with copies of *The Good Companions*.' Spender describes how he made a fool of himself on a transatlantic broadcast during the war. 'Fortunately the broadcast was not "live", and what I said was cut out with a needle made of some precious stone.'

World Within World is full of scenes and portraits. Most memorable of the scenes are Spender's first school, Oxford in the late twenties, the romantic Hamburg of 1929 merging into the terrible bomb-ruins of 1945, civilwartime Madrid, and the Christmas party at the Fire Service sub-station of which he was a member, in 1942. Many well-known people appear: T. S. Eliot, Virginia Woolf, Edith Sitwell, W. H. Auden, Yeats, Cyril Connolly, Ezra Pound – and always something is told which brings each one of them to life. But the best and most finished portraits are of 'private' individuals: the ex-guardsman friend whom Spender calls 'Jimmy Younger'; Inez, Spender's first wife; 'Tristan', the fellow-undergraduate who became a fanatical Communist; Spender's brother Michael, the scientist and apostle of efficiency, who claimed to have reduced the margin of error in his activities to a minimum and said that 'he could not remember ever having held a subjective opinion'. Most wonderful of all is the strikingly Proustian character of Hilda Schuster, Spender's maternal grandmother, who is a year older than Bernard Shaw, and still alive at the time of writing. Mrs Schuster's warmth and innocence, her agonized sympathy for the oppressed, her eagerness to understand the minds of the young ('Dear Stephen, say something quickly to shock me'), and her Spartan insistence on fantastically trivial economies, are beautifully conveyed. 'Arrived in her unheated room, she surprised me by inquiring whether I would like a cup of tea. "Oh, I'm so glad," she said to my eager assent. "I was afraid it would be wasted. You see it was brought to me early this morning and I couldn't drink it." She reached to a cupboard in which a cup of almost frozen tea was waiting, and asked me whether I would also care for a bun. Cautious now, I replied that I was not hungry.'

World Within World closes aptly with the dying words of Spender's mother: 'Tell them I have had a very happy life.' I say 'aptly' because this is an essentially joyful book, full of profound delight in human experience; a book which gives you fresh courage to live your own life and new eyes with which to examine its meaning.

Katherine Mansfield

MISS SYLVIA BERKMAN's *Katherine Mansfield: A Critical Study* (Yale University Press) is a concise, well-documented book which contains much interesting biographical material and some penetrating judgements. Miss Berkman's style is somewhat lacking in warmth and humour; but I think that, under the circumstances, these are faults on the right side. For her approach to her subject is deliberately academic, as befits an Assistant Professor of English at Wellesley College, and she is admirably determined to weigh and measure accurately what others have overpraised or undervalued. Where so many have lavishly emoted, Miss Berkman tidies up the mess with grave common sense. If she doesn't communicate the kind of enthusiasm which would send new readers to Katherine Mansfield, she should at least make every confirmed admirer pause and re-read and ponder. And the resulting reassessment will certainly be to both the author's and her admirers' advantage.

There are some writers you revere; others you fall in love with. The loved ones are seldom the greatest; indeed, their very faults are a part of their charm. For several years I was violently in love with 'Kathy', as my friends and I (who never knew her personally) used to call her. Then the love-affair turned sour and ended in unfair belittlement. I am truly grateful to Miss Berkman for bringing us together again. From now on, I am sure my affection will be more constant, more intelligent and much less sentimental.

I realize that I loved Mansfield ('Kathy' sounds mawkish now, and 'Miss Mansfield' absurdly formal) for her life rather than for her work. I identified myself romantically with her sufferings and her struggle. And today I still find it impossible to think of Mansfield simply as the author of her stories, without relating her to the Journal and the Letters. For she is among the most personal and subjective of all modern writers; and, in her case, fiction and autobiography form a single, indivisible opus.

Katherine Mansfield's life is so fascinating because – despite its surface tangle of moods, impetuous reactions and rash decisions – it presents a very simple symbolic pattern. This is a variant of the Garden of Eden theme. A childhood paradise is lost. An apple of knowledge is eaten, with bitter consequences. And then, under the curse and blessing of that knowledge, comes the attempt to regain the paradise. It is a deeply moving story but not really a tragic one, for it ends in sight of success.

In 1906, after some years of schooling in England, Mansfield returned at the age of eighteen to her native New Zealand. There, amidst the comforts and social activities of her wealthy family home, she at once began to feel restless and miserable. The people she met in Wellington seemed unendurably stuffy and provincial. As a disciple of Oscar Wilde, she longed to demolish 'the firm fat framework of their brains' and drown them, for their own good, in 'a mad wave of pre-Raphaelitism'. She saw herself as the Artist in Exile, alienated by her own finer sensibilities from the vulgar herd. 'Here in my room I feel as though I was in London – in London. To write the word makes me feel that I could burst into tears. Isn't it terrible to love anything so much? I do not care at all for men, but *London* – it is Life.' Substitute 'Moscow' for 'London' and this is the cry of Irina in *Three Sisters*. No doubt much of the affinity which Mansfield later felt with Chekhov (whom, of course, she had never met) was based on memories of this period, when she herself had been, most unwillingly, a Chekhov character.

Katherine's father was a generous-minded man who continued to love his daughter even when her conduct puzzled and pained him. Eighteen months after her return home he agreed to let her go back to England in unconditional freedom and with a small living-allowance. She never saw New Zealand again.

But Mansfield's 'London' proved to be a mirage; and the first three years of her life in the real city were squalid and disenchanting. Hiding her desperate loneliness behind a mask of intellectual arrogance, she inhabited the trivial bohemia of St John's Wood and surrounded herself with pitiful, trashy little pretensions of 'sophistication'. She had a skull decorated with flowers and candles, and a room containing nothing but a Buddha and two black-draped couches. She got involved in messy love-affairs and a brief, incompatible marriage. She gave birth to a stillborn illegitimate child. Such behaviour is characteristic of a very innocent nature which takes this world's shams at their surface value and learns everything the hard way. Those who have Mansfield's kind of innocence often appear, from the outside, to be more artificial, more cynical, more depraved than the rest of us. Actually, they are purging themselves through excess.

In 1911 Katherine Mansfield met John Middleton

Murry, who was later to become her second husband. Their relationship was beset with many difficulties, both financial and temperamental, but it survived them all and remained, until the end, a central, steadying emotional factor in Katherine's life.

For Mansfield the writer, however, the really decisive event was still to come. This was the death of her brother Leslie on the Western Front, in October 1915. Before going over to France with his regiment, Leslie had spent a week's leave at the Murrys' house in London, where the brother and sister had long talks, nostalgically recalling the days of their New Zealand childhood. In retrospect, every detail of it seemed magically beautiful, flawlessly happy. Katherine seems to have forgotten or discounted her more recent boredom and wretchedness in Wellington. She planned eagerly to return with Leslie to New Zealand as soon as the war was over.

When Leslie was killed, that plan was automatically abandoned; but the childhood memories he had aroused seemed to Katherine more precious, more sacred than ever. While still under the immediate and terrible shock of his loss, she wrote in her Journal: 'The people ... whom I wished to bring into my stories don't interest me any more. The plots of my stories leave me perfectly cold. ... Now – now I want to write recollections of my own country.' And again, addressing her dead brother: 'Now, as I write these words and talk of getting down to the New Zealand atmosphere, I see you opposite to me. ... Ah, my darling, how have I kept away from this tremendous joy? Each time I take up my pen *you* are with me.' It was in this mood of spiritual collaboration with Leslie that Mansfield began to write the New Zealand stories which contain so much of her finest work: *Prelude, At the Bay, The Doll's House, The Garden Party, The Stranger.*

In order to re-enter her childhood paradise, Mansfield wanted to turn herself back into a child. And, of course, she couldn't. Whether she liked it or not, she was a beautiful, highly complex woman in her late twenties, with much worldly experience behind her; a woman possessed of (to quote Katherine Anne Porter) 'a grim, quiet ruthlessness of judgement, an unsparing and sometimes cruel eye, a natural malicious wit, an intelligent humour'. To her undoing, Mansfield began increasingly to hate her own adult personality, dwelling harshly on its defects and rejecting its virtues. Above all, she hated her 'cleverness'. 'I look at the mountains, I try to pray and I think of something *clever*'; her journal is full of such disgusted self-accusations. Mansfield did well to condemn the cheapness and artificiality of which she had sometimes been guilty; but in going to this extreme she was really trying to annihilate herself as a writer and as a human being.

This acute internal conflict could only end in disaster. I myself believe that it was at least partly responsible for the tuberculosis which Mansfield developed in 1918, and which killed her five years later. In the present state of our medical opinion, such conjectures are still usually dismissed as fanciful and ridiculous. But it is worth recalling how Homer Lane, one of the earliest and most daring pioneers of psychosomatic medicine, used to maintain that pulmonary tuberculosis is the characteristic disease of those who desire to escape into their childhood, since the lungs are the first organs used by the new-born baby.

We can never return to the childhood paradise in a state of primitive simplicity. For we have eaten the apple of experience and we cannot unlearn the knowledge it has brought us. What we can do, however, is to reconcile experience with innocence, intellect with instinct; thus we become integrated and able to accept life in its wholeness. This acceptance is another kind of simplicity. The simplicity of the integrated adult is not the simplicity of the child.

This is what Mansfield slowly started to learn during the last bitter years of her life. She travelled feverishly back and forth between England, Switzerland and the South of France; she suffered the wretched loneliness of the invalid; she had brief hopes of recovery followed by heartbreaking relapses; she consulted many doctors and submitted to drastic treatments. At the end of it all she was no better; and, during the summer of 1922, she came to a revolutionary decision. She would stop going to doctors altogether. She would stop trying to heal her body simply *as* a body. 'It seems to me childish and ridiculous to suppose that one can be cured like a cow *if one is not a cow.*' Instead she would put herself in the hands of someone who could heal her divided psyche. Once the spirit had been made whole, she felt the body would imitate its wholeness and grow well.

The healer chosen by Mansfield was Gurdjieff, who at that time was the head of a community near Fontainebleau, outside Paris. In this community a number of men and women practised a strict routine of manual labour, rhythmic exercises and psychical instruction which was designed to develop a harmonious balance of the intellectual, emotional and spiritual functions. Much has been said against Gurdjieff, and there is no doubt that he was something of a charlatan. But his basic ideas were perfectly sound, and he certainly helped many of his pupils toward self-integration. Indeed, he was already helping Mansfield. Her last letters are full of faith and exaltation; and the fact that she had begun to question his claims to be an omniscient prophet is a very healthy sign. Had she lived, she would naturally have outgrown Gurdjieff and gone on alone, with increasing self-reliance; but it was he who put her feet upon the path. It was not his fault that she came to him too late, a mortally sick woman. In January 1923, having spent less than three months in the community, she was seized by a violent haemorrhage and died.

In the second part of her book, which deals with Katherine Mansfield's art, Miss Berkman spends a considerable time discussing the resemblances and differences between Mansfield's technique and that of Chekhov and of James Joyce in his pre-*Ulysses* period. Miss Berkman's examples are well chosen; she certainly proves her point. But I can't say that I find this kind of criticism very rewarding; it is really just an amusing game. When all has been said, the fact remains that the literary personalities of Chekhov and Joyce are quite unlike the literary personality of Mansfield. Purely technical comparisons are, at best, extremely superficial.

What is Katherine Mansfield's literary personality? What is the total impression that she makes upon the reader? Such distinguished critics as Eliot, Maurois, Miss Porter and H. E. Bates have described her as 'feminine'. Both Miss Berkman and I quarrel with that adjective, though for slightly different reasons. In my view, a 'feminine' writer is one who writes exclusively out of her experience as a woman; she tells us things that a man could not feel or know. She doesn't necessarily have to write about childbirth or motherhood or the woman's side of marriage, but her perception of the world will be conditioned by the fact that she is biologically female. Anais Nin is such a writer. So is Naomi Mitchison. So is Colette. I don't find this quality to any great degree in Katherine Mansfield. Indeed, as I have already suggested, she rather shrank from the recognition of herself as a woman – at any rate, an adult woman. Her view of the sexual relation is distasteful and pessimistic; and one feels that, much as she loves children, she would rather they belonged to someone else.

The word 'feminine' is also used in a derogatory sense to describe the kind of writing which is (to quote Mr Bates) 'fluttering, gossipy, breathless'. (Stephen Spender once said to me, criticizing a book he didn't like, 'it gives me a feeling of earrings'.) Mansfield was certainly apt to flutter. She often affects a breathless epistolary style, in which she appears to think she can make words take on deeper meanings by simply writing them in italics. And her coyness at its worst can make you hot with shame. But it must be objected at once that these are not exclusively feminine defects. There is plenty of breathless male gossiping in Henry Miller, and plenty of male coyness in Hemingway.

Miss Berkman seems to me to be much nearer the mark when she calls attention to Mansfield's preoccupation with littleness. In the stories, 'tiny' is used over and over again as a synonym for 'beautiful' or 'exquisite'. 'This fascination by the very small,' Miss Berkman continues, 'is a quality found more often in women than in men, but it distinguishes most generally the curious and observant child. ... The enlargement of perception one receives from Miss Mansfield's finest work is of the kind one gains from association with an imaginative and gifted child, who sees, freshly and sharply, imponderables of meaning within the compass of the small. But she was also a woman who had suffered in the world, and it is not often that the untouched apprehension of the child fuses perfectly with the view acquired through the circumstances of her life.'

I would go farther than Miss Berkman. I do not think that the childlike apprehension and the adult view of life were *ever* perfectly fused in any of Katherine Mansfield's stories. In other words her split psyche produced a split writer – or, as one might put it for the sake of clarity, two separate writers. Mansfield's best work was achieved, it is true, by a collaboration between the writers; but it was an uneasy collaboration, likely to end, at any moment, in a fight and resulting confusion. When one writer pushed the other clear away from the desk and tried to work alone, the product was inferior.

Writer A is the childlike, intuitive Mansfield, the poetess. She is capable of those clairvoyant flashes of perception which one associates particularly with the New Zealand stories. Some creature or object – a flower, a painted teapot, a flying bird – is seen, for an instant, in its own right as a marvel, a microcosm of all creation, and the reader gasps with wonder. These flashes of perception have the quality of genius; but they are, by their very nature, spasmodic. Writer A is a medium, with a medium's lapses. A rather dishonest medium, it must be added; for, when nothing is 'coming through', she begins faking, and when she fakes, her tone is false and embarrassingly sentimental. Sometimes, these alternations of poetic truth and sentimental falsehood occur with bewildering frequency; as, for example, in the description of the sunrise which is the opening of *At the Bay*.

Writer B is the critical, witty adult Mansfield, the satirist. She can curb Writer A's sentimentality ruthlessly, whenever Writer A will let her. Writer B can dash off startlingly funny thumbnail portraits, like that of Nurse Andrews in *The Daughters of the Late Colonel*. She can expose the vanity and shallowness of a woman like Isabel in *Marriage à la Mode* with a terrible and beautiful justice. Her only trouble is that she is sometimes too brilliant for her own good. She constructs speciously clever plots for stories, and lures Writer A into helping her with them. We read these stories and are, at first, quite dazzled; then, slowly, the doubts begin. For instance, there is poor old Ma Parker, the charlady, who longs to have one good cry over the sadness of her life. At the climax, she realizes that she can't even enjoy this small relief, because there is no place where she won't be disturbed. Again and again Ma Parker's plight has moved me almost to tears; but afterwards, thinking it over – I'm sorry, I just don't believe it. Or take the case of *Poison*, a study in sexual jealousy which is another near-masterpiece. Here a woman, already tired of her lover, is waiting for a letter which will probably call her away to join another man. In order to prepare her lover for this blow, she begins to talk figuratively about the way in which one partner in a relationship will slowly poison the other, with tiny daily doses of suspicion. The metaphor is admirable and intensely dramatic. But then, right at the end, the lover sips his apéritif and says to himself: 'Good God! Was it fancy? No, it wasn't fancy. The drink tasted chill, bitter, *queer*.' The metaphor is taken literally, so that the lover seems, after all, to be merely play-acting, and the whole

88

situation drops with a bump to the level of a sophisticated parlour-game. I am disgusted. Writer B, with her fatal cleverness, has intervened and spoilt everything.

That Katherine Mansfield was well aware of this split in her literary personality is proved by many passages in the journal and the letters. Had she lived to achieve her own psychological integration she would naturally have merged the two writers into one. A would have submitted to B's critical intelligence; B would have learned when not to interfere with A's intuition. Then the sentimentality and the cleverness would have been gradually refined away. That process had already begun when Mansfield died, and one can only end on a note of deep gratitude for what she has actually left us: the best of her stories – fifteen, at the very least – which still, after thirty years, seem as magically vivid as ever. Yes, and not only the stories. Mansfield left us also – in her journal, her letters and her recorded biography – the human example of one who dedicated her whole being and existence to the perfection of her work. Only the greatest men and women have the courage to do this; and the degree of their success is of secondary importance. What matters, what inspires the rest of us, is the intensity of the attempt. And, by that standard, Mansfield need fear no comparisons.

Dominations and Powers by George Santayana

GEORGE SANTAYANA has been called 'the Mona Lisa of Philosophy'. Such descriptions-by-comparison are usually no more than meaningless journalese (their absurdity has been brilliantly parodied in the famous 'Wagner is the Puccini of Music') but this one is strikingly apt. For, like the Mona Lisa, Santayana presents to the world a personality that is ambiguous and enigmatic; and, like her, he dominates his public with a smile. This smile appears, overtly or subtly, in most of his photographs, and you can almost hear it in the melodious, half-playful tones of prose. His own ideal Philosopher is often pictured as smiling.

Chesterton said of Matthew Arnold that he 'kept a smile of heartbroken forbearance, as of the teacher in an idiot school, that was enormously insulting'. Santayana's smile certainly isn't heartbroken, and it is not exactly insulting; it is superior, however, and somewhat intimidating. It is the smile of a man who invites argument and challenges criticism because he loves to demonstrate the futility of all opinions. It is a smile at once coquettish and foxy.

If I were Max Beerbohm or David Low, it wouldn't be necessary for me to review this book (*Dominations and Powers*, Charles Scribner's Sons); instead, I should draw a cartoon. My proposed cartoon shows Santayana, in an elegant dressing-gown, seated before a chess-table; he is leaning back in his chair and waiting 'not without some merriment' (as he would put it) for his opponent's next move. Opposite to him sits a big muscular college boy whose honest face expresses dismayed bewilderment and whose sweater is decorated with the letters 'U S A'. At a second chess-table sits an aristocratic-looking Oxford undergraduate, similarly frustrated. And at a third chess-table a Russian student, in his uniform blouse and boots, thumbs desperately through a primer of openings compiled by Karl Marx. The Russian is muttering indignantly, 'It isn't dialectical', the Englishman, 'It isn't cricket', and the American, 'It isn't democratic'. The caption under the cartoon reads: 'Mr Santayana simultaneously checkmates the three Dominations.'

But, alas, I am no cartoonist. I am compelled to be more specific, and must try to say what this large, elusive book is all about. Its subtitle is 'Reflections on Liberty, Society and Government', and I think one can safely begin by describing it as a discourse on Politics in the widest sense of the word. (Having said even this much, I am a little uneasy; for I am acutely conscious of Santayana, waiting smilingly to catch me out.) The treatment of the subject is necessarily discursive, since this is a collection of more than a hundred individual though interrelated essays, written over a period of thirty years. Santayana admits that these essays, which are now brought together, revised, in his eighty-eighth year, had no consecutive development. He wrote them from time to time, whenever an idea occurred to him, and filed them away for future arrangement. 'However,' he adds, 'a more vivid apprehension of the actual impact of Dominations and Powers in the political world was forced upon me by the war of 1939–45; for I lived through it in Rome in monastic retirement, with the visible and audible rush of bombing aeroplanes over my head, and of invading armies before my eyes. Most pertinent and instructive, also, has been the experience of the after-effects of that war. The country where I was living was traversed by two foreign armies nominally friendly to it; one came to defend and the other to liberate it; and both united in pillaging it and leaving it in misery and ruins.'

The above quotation is extremely suggestive. It gives one, by means of a concrete illustration, an insight into the nature of this book and of Santayana's psychological approach to his material. Here we have the drama of the present age, in which all of us are forced, however unwillingly, to play a part. The characters of the drama are the individual man-in-the-street, the 'two foreign armies nominally friendly', and the philosophic I, the witness. But these roles can be doubled. For the man-in-the-street may be the philosopher, or he may be a member of one of the armies (which are, nevertheless, entities other than the individual). The philosopher may choose to live in monastic retirement, that is his own affair; but the bombs are just as likely to hit him in his monastery as anywhere else, and his relation to the armies can by no means be denied or ignored. Also, the armies themselves may exchange roles, sometimes playing the hero and sometimes the heavy. It is this complicated interrelationship which Santayana now proceeds to examine. His examination is based upon the meanings which he attaches, quite arbitrarily, to the words 'Dominations' and 'Powers'.

Here I must pause to register a protest against the extraordinary and, as it seems at times, almost malicious vagueness of Santayana's style. He has a trick of writing all around his ideas, without ever simply stating the idea itself. He wriggles out of definite pronouncements by turning them into poetical phrases and uses double negatives to break your hold, like an expert in judo. He has an air of half-disclaiming, half-accepting an opinion; as when, for example, he speaks of 'a principle which we may call defensible, since it is often defended'. It may appear absurd to anyone who has never read him that I should have to hesitate, even for a moment, before producing a plain definition of two terms which are used over and over again, and in a very special sense, throughout this book. But I do hesitate, and I blame Santayana for my hesitation. If, in the effort to interpret, I oversimplify – well, it is all his fault.

By a 'Power', Santayana means – or seems to me to mean – a natural force, or an action which is motivated by the natural needs and interests of any particular human being or creature. Powers are forces or actions which promote growth and development through the unfolding of one's nature, with its potential capacities. For example, there is the principal of physical growth within our own bodies. This is a Power, and any action we may perform to assist growth – such as eating, sleeping, or exercising our muscles – is also a Power. And in our growth we are assisted, also, by external Powers, such as the sun and the surrounding atmosphere.

A Domination, on the other hand, is an imposed force. A Domination does not promote free growth and development; it inhibits and impedes them. It is unnatural in that it threatens to overthrow the laws of an individual's nature. It is therefore 'bad' in the same sense in which a

Power is 'good'. 'The distinction between Dominations and Powers,' says Santayana, 'is moral and not physical.'

These definitions should make it immediately evident that the two words can only be used relatively, according to the viewpoint of any given individual. Our lives as Earthmen are harmoniously related to the gravitational pull of the Earth; but visitors from another planet of a different mass would find this same Power an unbearable Domination. Water is a Power from the viewpoint of the fish, a Domination from the viewpoint of the drowning sailor. 'The same government that is a benign and useful power for one class or province may exercise a cruel domination over another province or another class.' Under certain circumstances, a Power may turn into a Domination and later change back again into a Power. Indeed, the individual himself may be responsible for the change. For instance, our individual 'fate' or physical environment is a Power as long as we accept it and use it to promote our mental growth. We may go through a phase of rebellion against this fate; then it has become a Domination and our rebellion itself is a Power, making for growth of another kind. Finally, we may decide to accept, after all; then fate and environment are Powers again. But the acceptance, needless to say, must be voluntary and creative, not involuntary and passive. You cannot turn a Domination into a Power by simply ceasing to struggle against it. The Nazi occupation of France was equally a Domination to those who joined the underground movement against it and to those who merely resented it and did nothing.

Santayana considers this interplay between Powers and Dominations as it functions within three spheres – or, as he calls them, 'Orders'; the Generative, the Militant and the Rational. Before examining each of these Orders in detail, we must remind ourselves that a Power (and, hence, a Domination) can appear in any one of several forms. It may be an external force of nature, or an internal force within the body. It may be a passion, a need, an interest, an action or an idea. It may be represented by another human being, or by a whole group of human beings, such as family, a race, a nation or an organization. And, by the same token, it may affect us in many different ways: physically, psychologically, economically or politically.

'The first powers and dominations to be studied in politics are those on which the individual is most radically dependent, by which his nature is most radically modified. Now in the human race, the initial helplessness of children and their prolonged immaturity makes the ascendance of parents first and of custom later both inevitable and decisive. Yet the ways of parents are often erratic; and customs ... are diverse and arbitrary; so that both parental authority and native ways exhibit Domination in acute forms.' When Powers and Dominations operate in the sphere of growth, custom and tradition, Santayana classifies them as belonging to the Generative Order. Such Powers and Dominations affect the individual as a member of a family or a tribe.

When the individual enters into voluntary associations other than those of the family or the tribe, he becomes subject to a second order of Powers and Dominations, the Militant Order. For example, the individual may enter a military organization, or a political party, or a religious sect, or he may practise one of the parasitical arts.

The adjective 'parasitical', employed in this manner, needs explanation. An art is said to be parasitical when it does not contribute, directly or indirectly, to the maintenance of animal life, i.e. the production of food and shelter from the elements. (One assumes that 'animal life' means primitive life; and that its maintenance is limited to agriculture, hunting and rough carpentry. But it could, I suppose, be argued that the need for food makes necessary the Colony Restaurant and a fleet of merchant ships, while the need for shelter demands mink coats and the Empire State Building. Santayana doesn't make it clear exactly where he draws the line.) As soon as food and shelter have been secured, these other optional arts are sure to arise; for Man is always seeking to embellish the crude simplicity of the animal life and enlarge the area of his enjoyments. When Man begins to practise arts which are not strictly necessary, he functions on a new level. He now has to determine in what proportion the necessary and optional arts shall be allowed to develop. 'The criterion will no longer be merely the contribution made to food ... but will be some ideal of the free use to be made of life.' In the exercise of such social discrimination we become subject to the third order of Powers and Dominations, the Rational Order. The art of reasoning may itself be described as a parasitical or optional art – at any rate in the sense in which Santayana uses the word 'Reason'. 'Rationality,' he says, 'is a secondary habit in the animal psyche, a not indispensable synthesis of functions each capable of asserting itself separately, and apt, in rough weather, to lose all contact with its neighbours.' Rationality is not necessary for the maintenance of animal life; but any coherent social life is unthinkable without it.

As soon as our childhood is over, we find ourselves living under all three Orders at once. The Generative Order conditions, consciously and subconsciously, the basic pattern of our behaviour, because it was the first of the three to be experienced in our early years. As individuals, we continue throughout our lives to feel the influence of the family with its traditions, the homeplace with its customs, and the benevolent or unkind attitudes of our parents. As human beings, we are perpetually alternating between war and alliance with our environment; now cooperating with fine weather to bring in a good harvest, now fighting droughts and floods. Meanwhile, under the Militant Order, we engage in other kinds of loyalties and enmities, not directly concerned with the family or the tribe. And, at the same time, we live as thinking creatures under the Rational Order and employ that faculty of evaluation without which the whole experience of social and economic life would degenerate into senseless madness.

Generative Man knows hunger and thirst and pain, repletion and physical ease. He is jealous of his father, proud because he was born in Texas, ashamed because he broke a promise to his mother not to touch whisky until he was twenty-one. He can never forgive the unfair whipping he got at the age of six, when it was his brother who had really stolen the apples. In middle life, he still defiantly wears gaudy socks because his sister, long since dead, once told him that they were vulgar. He mistakes his creative intuition for a Domination and fears it as something disgusting. The middle-class prejudices which his parents taught him in boyhood he regards as Powers. He often ends up on the couch of a psychoanalyst, who reintroduces him, with the utmost difficulty, to himself.

Militant Man knows patriotism, fanaticism, sectarian passion and crusading zeal. He is an Elk, a Republican, a Baptist, a Mason, a Democrat, a Catholic. He paints abstract oils and makes objects out of wire and wood, devotedly, in an attic. He loathes Picasso, Churchill, Stalin and the Pope. He loves everybody who believes in the Immaculate Conception, socialized medicine, birth control and a bigger Navy. To him, Russia was a Domination in 1939, a Power in 1941, a Domination in 1946. He runs back and forth through the years in a fever of activity, talking into two telephones at once, shooting off machine-guns, conducting filibusters, building gigantic monuments and tearing them down again. He often ends up with ulcers.

Rational Man knows the calm of meditation, the excitement of disinterested logic, the sadness of disillusionment. Incapable of fanaticism or fervour, he is melancholy in his awareness that there are two sides to every question but happy in the clarity with which he sees them. He will take up arms, if need be, in defence of the lesser evil; but without passion. He recognizes with disenchanted eyes the Powers that men neglect and abuse and the Dominations of which they are not even aware. 'What a pity,' he exclaims, 'that they won't stop to think, and use a little common sense!' On the whole, he finds the world a depressing place; and, unless he can face it with Santayana's detached and almost disembodied kind of humour, he often ends up by committing suicide.

Rational Man's ultimate despair arises from a species of stupidity which is inherent in pure Reason; the stupidity of the academic pattern-maker. His beautifully reasonable political blueprints for a just society have one fatal defect: they bear little or no relation to the needs and drives of Generative and Militant Man. The psychoanalyst might help him here, but the psychoanalyst's own outlook on life is all too often circumscribed by his own concept of normality. However hotly he may deny it, he is really trying to produce a Standard Man. He talks a great deal about 'adjustment'; but he means, in most cases, the adjustment of the individual to a predetermined common standard, not the adjustment of the individual to the Powers of his own particular nature. As for Militant Man, his advice to the individual is: 'Forget about yourself and your private problems. Join up with us, and before you know it we'll have you so excited about the Cause that you won't have time to worry about anything else.' This is no more helpful than telling a friend to go out and get drunk. The hangovers of fanaticism are as terrible as the despairs of sober reason.

At this point we find ourselves on the subject of Religion. For Religion claims to make life liveable and supremely significant by translating it into the terms of a timeless, transcending Meaning. Santayana, a self-confessed materialist, finds himself unable to accept this Meaning, even as a hypothesis. But he handles the problem with extreme politeness, as befits his status of house-guest in a convent. 'Suppose now we define a religion to be the recognition of the Powers on which our destiny truly depends, and the art of propitiating those Powers and of living, as far as the power in us avails, in devout harmony with them. We should not be friends of religion if we confined it to proclaiming imaginary powers, and living under the real ones in ignorance or despair. A religion worth having must recognize true Powers, however poetical the form may be which that religion lends them; and it must tend to establish peace and sanity in the mind, not fanatical madness.' Nobody could quarrel with these statements, but they do not take us very far. And, elsewhere, Santayana writes as if Religion were simply a kind of aesthetic performance in rather dubious taste. He seems unaware of the whole history of empirical mysticism, and of the historical significance of the saint. His system of Orders seems to me to be incomplete, since it does not include a fourth, the Order of Spiritual Man.

Santayana expresses the greatest respect for the freedom of the individual; but this does not mean that he is at all enthusiastic about democracy. He doesn't believe that it works. 'Anyone who wishes to maintain literally the claim of the people to govern themselves would need to reduce all legislators and administrators to executants of exact instructions issued by the persons who had elected them. Yet obviously such instruction could never anticipate the terms of all measures that would have to be voted on or executed. A certain initiative must therefore be left to a representative agent to decide particular questions, on the understanding that he will be faithful to the general intentions and sentiments of his supporters.' But '... almost always, at his election, besides the numerous absentees, there will have been a large minority who would have given him contrary instructions. These the conventional sentiment of democracy allows, or even commands, him to oppose or to ignore altogether.' Of liberalism Santayana says: 'The virtue of liberalism is a sort of intellectual kindness or courtesy to all possible wills. Yet what a melancholy kindness is this, to leave the inoffensive liberal helpless before unkindness! Government needs to be based on the principle that men are by nature fundamentally helpless and automatic.'

In other words, Santayana doubts that the individual knows what is good for him, since he so often fails to recognize and accept his own Powers. So he has got to be told what it is that he really wants. The will of the people is the criterion of the people's good; but that will is not conscious, and its real demands can only be formulated by those who function within the Rational Order. The paradox in this kind of argument is obvious, for Santayana's whole thesis has been framed to show that there is, in fact, no such creature as the exclusively rational man. And when he goes on to advocate a form of government by selected rulers and managers, who would display 'the most perfect disinterestedness', and would themselves select new rulers and managers from time to time, as required, one has difficulty in believing that he expects to be taken seriously.

Failing the establishment of his ideal managerial government, Santayana thinks that our best chance of an harmonious future lies in the imposition of some sort of *Pax Romana*; the control of the world by a nation that is all-powerful and yet liberal in its treatment of its subjects. The candidates he considers for this position are the United States, Russia and Britain, and he regretfully rejects them all. Britain would try to turn mankind into synthetic Englishmen. Russia is incapable of toleration. The United States always insist on exporting their constitution and their fundamentalist ethics along with their soft drinks and ice-boxes. So the prospects are far from bright, and we may expect the present state of anarchy to continue indefinitely.

Dominations and Powers ends on a note of blandly pessimistic agnosticism. Santayana disclaims any intention of trying to foretell the future, or of offering a new political creed. He is dubious as to the prospects of a 'final peace between order and liberty'. He feels that the utmost service that the best imaginable government could render would be to display 'the modesty of a physician' and recommend only 'what can enable us to escape or to overcome the assaults that natural accidents can make upon us'. One pictures his Head Manager telling the public, 'I shouldn't do that, if I were you,' then adding, 'and what's more, I won't let you do it.'

It is very easy, on the strength of some of the theories referred to above, to label Santayana as a neo-Fascist corporativist, or as something shorter and even ruder. But no do so would, I think, be to discount the real value of this book. The Zen Buddhists employ, in the training of their monks, a philosophical device known as a *koan*. The *koan* is presented in the form of a seemingly nonsensical question, such as, for example: 'Suppose you have a duck in a bottle; how will you get it out without breaking the bottle or hurting the duck?' The pupil attempts to give a rational answer to this question, finds that he cannot, and is thereby reduced to a state of acute intellectual agony verging on madness, from which, it is claimed, he is sometimes released by a flash of intuitive enlightenment. Suddenly, he understands, in some non-rational manner, that his dilemma is unreal. The duck-bottle relationship is not fundamental. It is only a symbol of an imaginary bondage in which we live and from which we could free ourselves at any moment.

Dominations and Powers seems to me to be a sort of political *koan*. Santayana's ambiguity, his frivolous proposals, his self-contradictions and his maddening style all combine to drive us into the mood of desperation experienced by the Zen pupil and the three young men in my cartoon. Doesn't he, in presenting us with all these irreconcilable opposites, these irresistible Dominations opposed to immovable Powers, slyly endeavour to make us transcend them? Isn't he really trying to show us that the only true solution of our problems is to be found in a refusal of all solutions? How else, in the presence of our contemporary disaster, could he sit there in his study and smile?

Prison Etiquette, edited with an Introduction by Holley Cantine and Dachine Rainer

THE men who have written this book were all members of the extreme pacifist minority which resisted the U.S. conscription system during World War II. *Extreme pacifist* is the best description I can think of, but it is unsatisfactory and vague; for the group contained several sorts of anarchists, individualists, religious and non-religious objectors. Some of them had refused even to register for the draft, holding that registration itself implies acceptance of the military machine; others, having registered, found themselves unable to accept any of the compromises offered to the conscientious objectors by the State – forestry camps, medical projects, or non-combatant service with the armed forces. So they chose prison, and served terms ranging from one to five years in various penitentiaries and road camps up and down the country. Some were even arrested and sentenced twice.

Prison Etiquette may, as its title indicates, be regarded simply as a manual of living-technique for prisoners in general. It is also a statement, written with great power, insight and occasional humour, of the whole anarchist-pacifist position. As such, it will have its own, necessarily limited, appeal. But I want to recommend it, now, to a far wider public.

Maybe you will never go to prison, either willingly or unwillingly. Maybe you disagree completely with the stand which these men took, or feel, at any rate, that they were unreasonably radical and unnecessarily uncooperative. (I myself was a law-abiding and somewhat apologetic objector during the same period.) But that is neither here nor there. For the problems raised by this book extend far beyond the usual categories of 'right' and 'wrong', expediency and inexpediency. They touch all our lives.

We all – much as we may hate to admit it – have a foot in both camps. Each one of us is an individual. Each one of us has a measure of responsibility for the existing machinery of the law-making and law-enforcing state. We may imagine that the relations between our individual and our social selves is stabilized, permanently adjusted. It is not. It cannot be. It ought not to be.

Therefore we all owe an enormous debt of gratitude to those daring and dissatisfied spirits who strike out, no matter why, into the dangerous no-man's-land beyond the laws and the social conventions, to find the inner truth of our human relationships and to restate it in action. By a sort of atomic fission, they generate new and terrific discharges of power from old, worn-out, everyday words like 'brotherhood', 'peace', 'compassion'. Such men have much in common with those few genuinely original artists who, in every age, restate the inner truth of form, sound, colour and meaning. The artist challenges and forces us to re-examine our ingrown habits of perceiving and feeling. The anarchist-objector forces us to re-examine our habits of social thinking and the society which represents them.

All of these men have suffered, physically and psychologically, in a way which most of us can hardly even imagine. Yet it would be as absurd and insulting to offer them our pity as to feel sorry for Baudelaire or Van Gogh. Our tribute to their endurance must be this: that we try with all our might to understand what their action meant to them, what it means to ourselves, and why it was necessary. If we honestly do that, then we can say, not callously, but with grateful humility, that their sufferings were well worth while.

I hope (and I am sure the authors hope) that this book will not be dismissed, or too easily accepted, as just another indictment of the U.S. prison system. It is so very much more than that. And indeed, the wardens and guards who appear, very fairly presented, in these pages, are more often bewildered and half-apologetically re-proachful than positively brutal. ('You fellows do so much objecting that if we opened the gate right now and told you to go home, some of you would get half-way out and then come back and object about that.') One can sympathize with them even at their worst. A lifetime of routine and rule-of-thumb psychology in dealing with ordinary prisoners is unlikely to prepare you for a man like Lowell Naeve. The average type of guard could not possibly be subjected to a more exquisite form of mental torture than passive resistance. No wonder if some of them cracked under the strain and responded with acts of violence.

Certainly, there are prisons in this country which are very bad, and no doubt much could be done to reform them, even within the framework of the existing penal system. It goes without saying that such reforms are desirable: but, in working for them, we must never allow ourselves to forget that the great central problem remains unsolved – the problem of Man's freedom within society. Because this book sets that problem squarely before you, I wish it could be read by everybody in the United States.

Mr Norris and I by Gerald Hamilton

Now and then I am asked if the character of 'Mr Norris' in my novel (called *Mr Norris Changes Trains* in England and *The Last of Mr Norris* in America) is based on my old friend Gerald Hamilton. Sometimes I answer No to this question, sometimes Yes – according to my mood and the suspected motives of the questioner. Neither answer is more than partially true.

What do most of us mean when we say that we know

someone well? We mean that we have constructed a mental image of that person, a sort of robot which functions adequately, except perhaps in revealing moments of crisis, and thereby saves us the fatigue of continually wondering what our friend is 'really like'. We have decided, once and for all, what he is like – arbitrarily accepting certain aspects of his personality and rejecting others – and our robot embodies our decision.

It follows, therefore, that any connexion between a live person and a character in a novel is at a double remove. Between Gerald and Mr Norris stands the robot, Gerald-as-I-choose-to-see-him. It is from such a robot, and never directly from a live person, that a character in a novel must be adapted and developed.

I have stated these obvious truths because they are too frequently forgotten or wilfully ignored. The inquisitive and the malicious are eager to discover in every novel a *roman à clef*. But their miserable little key fits nothing but the broken padlock of their own discretion; it will never open the doors of Life or of Art. How, indeed, *can* a fictional character 'be' a live person? They inhabit two different worlds and breathe two different kinds of atmosphere. Just imagine poor Gerald trying to participate in the impossibly melodramatic plots of Mr Norris and his fellow-conspirators! His prudent and fastidious nature would shrink in horror from such irresponsible antics. Just imagine Mr Norris daring to substitute himself as host at one of Gerald's inimitable lunches! His attempts at conversation would expose him instantly as a puppet who had lost his ventriloquist.

When I came to Germany in 1929 I was twenty-four years old and in many respects very immature for my age. One of my chief motives for wanting to visit Berlin was that an elderly relative had warned me against it, saying that it was the vilest place since Sodom. For months I had been day-dreaming of it as unrealistically as a child dreams of the jungle; he hopes to meet tigers and pythons there, but doesn't expect them to hurt him. A favourite

line of mine at that time – I chose to take it altogether out
of the context of the play – was Iago's

> There's many a beast then, in a populous city,
> And many a civil monster.

I arrived in Berlin on the lookout for civil monsters. And,
since my imagination had very little contact with reality,
I soon persuaded myself that I had found several.

What repels me now about *Mr Norris* is its heartless-
ness. It is a heartless fairy-story about a real city in which
human beings were suffering the miseries of political violence and near-starvation. The 'wickedness' of Berlin's
night-life was of a most pitiful kind; the kisses and em-
braces, as always, had price-tags attached to them, but
here the prices were drastically reduced in the cut-throat
competition of an overcrowded market. (I remember
hearing of a boy who told a psychiatrist quite seriously
that he was 'homosexual – for economic reasons'!) As for
the 'monsters', they were quite ordinary human beings
prosaically engaged in getting their living by illegal
methods. The only genuine monster was the young
foreigner who passed gaily through these scenes of desolation, misinterpreting them to suit his childish fantasy.
This I later began to understand – which is why my
second book about Berlin is at least somewhat better
than my first.

Berlin was only one of the many scenes of my meetings
with Gerald. I can picture him more clearly against other,
more recent backgrounds: straw-hatted on the beach at
Ostend; enlivening a party of friends in the torture cham-
ber at The Hague, where we had taken shelter during a
rain-storm; involved in a grotesque plumbing-disaster at
Sintra, caused by his almost surgical standards of cleanli-
ness; holding forth against the evils of smoking, in his
London flat. How little that well-known face has changed
in the passing of twenty-five years! The cheeks are, if anything, more innocently rosy than ever; bespeaking an
untroubled digestion or conscience, or both. Time has

added few wrinkles, and has taken nothing away – nothing but a mere artificial adjunct; and most of us agree that Gerald looks much more distinguished without it. To be frank, it never fitted perfectly. They so seldom do.

Here, heaven knows, is no monster. But the word 'civil' is certainly applicable – though not in the sense in which Iago uses it. If there *is* anything essentially of Gerald in Mr Norris, it is his marvellous urbanity – and to that I fear I have failed to do justice. Some men raise the morale of their fellows by setting them an example of aggressive courage or of calm self-control. But Gerald has brightened many a dark hour for his friends by simply being his immaculate self. He has the art of creating social occasions by dressing as if they existed, and nobody understands better than he how to make the most unpleasant phases of life tolerable by the observance of the small ceremonies of courtesy. In this respect – as he himself has said – he is a true disciple of Confucius.

The Speckled Band by Arthur Conan Doyle

SINCE I was ten years old, the adventures of Sherlock Holmes have been my favourite escape-reading; again and again I have turned to them in times of sadness, boredom and ill-health and never found myself disappointed. (Next to them, for this purpose, I rate *The Arabian Nights* in the Mardrus-Mathers translation. Unfortunately, they don't come within the scope of this anthology.) Today – seventy years after the first of the Holmes novels was published – the name of Holmes is still a household word, even among those who have never read anything that Conan Doyle wrote about him and have caught only a few distorted glimpses of him in some television serial or newspaper cartoon. Perhaps he will survive to bury Doyle's books and turn into a purely legendary figure whose creator has been forgotten.

In my opinion, Holmes is one of the truly great comic characters in our literature; but it is doubtful if Doyle himself would have agreed with this statement or even if he would have taken it as a compliment. Admittedly, Holmes was not conceived in comedy, like Falstaff and Micawber; he can only be considered comic in retrospect, if at all – like Captain Ahab. His comic quality seems to me to be this: he is the classic caricature of the Amateur Detective, in whose person the whole art of detection is made ridiculous. I don't believe that Doyle consciously intended this ridicule – and yet it is what makes Holmes lovable and immortal.

It is hard to love the Amateur Detective, either in fiction or in real life. That a man should hound his fellowmen for pay is quite bad enough; and we, his paymasters, must all share in his guilt. But that an unpaid dilettante should do the same thing for his own amusement is infinitely worse. No amount of fine phrases about civic responsibility can alter that simple human truth. The more the Amateur Detective tries to justify his hobby, the more contemptible he becomes.

But Holmes is different. He isn't contemptible and he needs no justification. He has the sanction of his own peculiar kind of madness. Like Captain Ahab, he is possessed by the insanity of the chase. Holmes's Moby Dick is Dr Moriarty, the arch-criminal; and Doyle's instinct was sound when he made Moriarty turn to bay and kill Holmes, just as the White Whale killed Ahab. I find Holmes's subsequent resurrection both embarrassing and unnecessary – for Doyle could easily have pre-dated his later stories about Holmes, just as he did pre-date *The Valley of Fear* in order that Moriarty could reappear in it.

To get properly acquainted with Holmes, one should begin at the beginning – with *A Study in Scarlet*. Dr Watson, back from the Afghan War, is looking for someone with whom he can share the expenses of furnished rooms. He consults a colleague, who recommends Sherlock Holmes – though with reservations:

'Holmes is a little too scientific for my tastes – it approaches to cold-bloodedness. . . . He appears to have a passion for definite and exact knowledge.'
'Very right too.'
'Yes, but it may be pushed to excess. When it comes to beating the subjects in the dissecting-rooms with a stick, it is certainly taking rather a bizarre shape.'
'Beating the subjects!'
'Yes, to verify how far bruises may be produced after death. I saw him at it with my own eyes.'
'And yet you say he is not a medical student?'

Watson's innocent question seems to me to touch the very nerve of comedy. But this is only the beginning of a wonderfully sustained sequence, in which he vainly tries to discover what Holmes's profession is and gets repeatedly bewildered by the variety of Holmes's tastes and the extraordinary gaps in his knowledge. Holmes is quite ignorant of literature, philosophy and astronomy; he neither knows nor cares if the earth goes round the sun or vice versa. On the other hand, he is 'well up in belladonna, opium and poisons generally', can play the violin, box, fence, and tell you which part of London you have been walking through by glancing at the mud-splashes on your trousers. . . . Finally the mystery is solved – long, long after every reader has guessed the solution; this being of the essence of the comedy – Holmes is a private detective.

No one Holmes story can do more than add a few details to the composite portrait. For a long time I hesitated fondly between *The Red-headed League* with its absurdly over-ingenious conspiracy and *Silver Blaze* with its famous exchange of dialogue between Holmes and the Inspector:

'Is there any point to which you would wish to draw my attention?'
'To the curious incident of the dog in the night-time.'
'The dog did nothing in the night-time.'
'That was the curious incident,' remarked Sherlock Holmes.

But I have chosen *The Speckled Band*, although it is so

well known, because it displays Holmes in several of his most pleasing aspects. (As the genial host: 'Ha! I am glad to see that Mrs Hudson has had the good sense to light the fire.' As the well-bred muscle-man, straightening the poker which that vulgar show-off, Dr Roylott, has twisted: 'I am not quite so bulky, but if he had remained I might have shown him that my grip was not much more feeble than his own.' As the moralist, while casually capturing a swamp-adder and locking it in a safe: 'Violence does, in truth, recoil under the violent, and the schemer falls into the pit which he digs for another.') Also, this story contains an unusually horrible murder and a really full-blooded villain. Characteristic of Doyle's love of verbal mystification is the use he makes of the band of gipsies and the dying woman's reference to a 'speckled band'.

In his Sherlock Holmes stories, Doyle became one of the great exponents of the romance of London at the turn of the century – city of Night, pea-soup fogs, gaslight, hansom-cabs and opera-hats. Robert Louis Stevenson was before him in this field, with his *New Arabian Nights*. G. K. Chesterton was his successor. Hollywood took over the London they had created, slightly modernized it and put it again and again upon the screen. When, at last, it became outmoded (since, nowadays, most films about London are actually made there) a leading English newspaper lamented the fact, saying: 'We have lost a city that we had learned to know almost as well as our own.'

Foreword to *All The Conspirators*

A cormorant, startling them with its queer cry, broke flapping from unseen rocks below and vanished into the empty gulf of light westward, like an absurd impulse of desperation, towards America.

IT amuses me to regard the above sentence – the last of

the first chapter of this novel – as an unconscious pro-
phecy. Nearly twenty years ago its author, with his queer
cry, flapped his way across the Atlantic. His eldest book
now belatedly follows him and comes to roost for the first
time in America, beside some of its younger brothers on
the friendly perch of New Directions.

I started writing *All The Conspirators* in the spring of
1926, when I was twenty-one years old. Two years later,
after rejections and revisions, it was published in London
by Jonathan Cape. If you should care to read about its
origins I must refer you to my autobiography, *Lions and
Shadows*.

Cyril Connolly, in his brilliant but too generous introduction to Cape's 1939 reissue of this novel in their
Travellers' Library series, writes politely of its author's
'austere and conscientious assumption of a cooperative
and intelligent reader'. If you flatter yourself that you are
cooperative and intelligent, see what you can make of, for
example, the first three and a half pages of the last chapter! I now detect a great deal of repressed aggression in
this kind of obscurity. Young writers are apt to employ
it as a secret language which is intelligible only to members of their group. Outsiders are thereby challenged to
admit that they do not understand it or dared to pretend
that they do – to be unmasked in any case, sooner or later,
as squares.

My instinctive use of this modern epithet – for which
I cannot even think of an earlier equivalent – makes me
ask myself: could the author of this novel conceivably be
described as a prehistoric Angry Young Man? Well – as a
young man, he was certainly angry – God help us if the
time ever comes when young men are not! – but his
anger had a different frame of reference. Today's Angry
Young Man (who will curse me for using that silly but
convenient label once again) is angry with Society and its
official representatives; he calls them hypocrites, he challenges the truth of what they teach. He declares that a
social revolution has taken place of which they are trying

to remain unaware. He accuses them of reactionary dullness, snobbery, complacency, apathy. While they mouth their platitudes, he exclaims, we are all drifting towards nuclear war.

The Angry Young Man of my generation was angry with the Family and its official representatives; he called them hypocrites, he challenged the truth of what they taught. He declared that a Freudian revolution had taken place of which they were trying to remain unaware. He accused them of reactionary dullness, snobbery, complacency, apathy. While they mouthed their platitudes, he exclaimed, we were all drifting towards mental disease, sex crime, alcoholism, suicide.

Nevertheless, there is always an emotional solidarity between rebels. And if the Allen Chalmers of my story could have been taken to see John Osborne's plays he would have been sympathetically thrilled by their anger, just as I am in my middle age today.

All The Conspirators may be regarded as a very very late Victorian novel, for it recalls the days when parents were still heavies. It records a minor engagement in what Shelley calls 'the great war between the old and young'. And what a war that was! Every battle of it was fought to a finish, with no quarter asked or shown. The vanquished became love-starved old maids, taciturn bitter bachelors, chronic invalids, harmless lunatics; or they died, if they were lucky. You may call the motives of these characters trivial, but their struggle is mortal and passionate. And the author is as passionate as any of his characters. He makes not the smallest pretence of impartiality. His battle-cry is 'My Generation – right or wrong!'

Perhaps you will be able to enjoy this book simply as a period piece – smiling at its naïve attempts at a James Joyce thought-stream, its aping of the mannerisms of Stephen Dedalus, its quaint echoes of Virginia Woolf, its jerky flashback narration crudely imitated from E. M. Forster. But even if this were now its only interest, there would still be one thing about it which had not dated,

as far as I was concerned; its dedication. After half a lifetime, Edward Upward is still the friend he has always
been; still the judge before whom all my work must stand
trial and from whose verdict, much as I sometimes hate to
admit it, there is no appeal.

I now extend my dedication to include Edward's wife,
Hilda, their daughter, Kathy, and their son, Christopher.

July 1958

VEDANTA AND THE WEST

D u r i n g the mid-thirties I would have described myself as an atheist, a liberal, a supporter of the Popular Front and an advocate of armed resistance to fascism, in Spain and everywhere else.

However, after our return from China, I began to be troubled by doubts. This was the first time I had actually seen people involved in a war. (I have described my self-questionings elsewhere – in the symposium *What Vedanta Means to Me*, 1960, and in a pamphlet called *An Approach to Vedanta*, 1963.) By the time Auden and I sailed for the United States I had realized that I was, and perhaps had really always been, a pacifist. One of my chief reasons for going on from New York to California in the spring of 1939 was that I wanted to clarify my ideas about pacifism by talking to Gerald Heard and Aldous Huxley. They had settled in the Los Angeles area two years previously.

I found that Heard and Huxley were engaged in the study of Vedanta philosophy and the practice of meditation. They introduced me to their friend Swami Prabhavananda, a Hindu monk of the Ramakrishna Order, who had founded a small Vedanta centre in Hollywood. After I got to know Prabhavananda, I gradually ceased to be an atheist; because I found myself unable to disbelieve in his belief in God. In due course I became his disciple, a devotee of Ramakrishna and a Vedantist. A liberal I have remained to this day.

Vedanta means literally 'end of the Veda' and, hence, that which is taught by the Vedas. The Vedas are the most ancient of the Hindu scriptures. They teach that Man's nature is, in essence, divine, and that the one aim of each man's life should be to become united with his divine nature. (I have tried to explain these teachings in detail in my introduction to *Vedanta for the Western*

World, 1945, and in introductions and commentaries written for the three translations of Hindu religious classics which I have made with Prabhavananda: the *Bhagavad-Gita*, 1944, *Shankara's Crest-Jewel of Discrimination*, 1947, and *Patanjali's Yoga Aphorisms*, 1953.)

In 1941 I went to work with the Quakers at an American Friends Service Committee hostel for refugees from Nazi-occupied Europe, at Haverford, Pennsylvania. While there, I registered with the draft-board as a conscientious objector. However, the draft-age was lowered again, just as I was about to be inducted into a forestry camp and perhaps eventually into the Army Medical Corps. So Prabhavananda invited me to live at the centre and collaborate with him on a translation of the Bhagavad-Gita.

The Swami's English is fluent and he is an excellent Sanskrit scholar. I knew no Sanskrit at all. My job was literary, not linguistic. He told me the meaning of the text, sentence by sentence. We then considered how this meaning could best be conveyed in English. By the time we had finished translating the book, I realized that I had been studying it with an ideal teacher and in the most thorough manner imaginable.

The four articles reprinted here were written some time between 1942 and 1950 and were originally published in *Vedanta and the West*, the magazine put out by our centre.

I think that even the uninitiated reader will find them more or less self-explanatory. To *Vivekananda and Sarah Bernhardt* I need only add the following footnotes:

1. Swami Vivekananda, 1863–1902, was one of the chief disciples of Ramakrishna, 1836–1886, the Hindu religious teacher. Vivekananda founded the Ramakrishna Order after his Master's death, and travelled in America and Europe expounding Ramakrishna's teachings. (I have retold these historical facts in a biography, *Ramakrishna and His Disciples*, 1965.)

2. *Swami* is the title of a Hindu monk, in the same sense that 'Father' is the title of a Catholic priest. *Swamiji* is a more respectable way of addressing a swami. In the Ramakrishna Order, 'Swamiji' is often used as a name for Vivekananda. A *Sannyasin* is a Hindu monk who has taken his final vows.

3. *Samadhi* means in Sanskrit the superconscious state in which man experiences his identity with the ultimate Reality. In Christian literature this is called the Mystic Union.

Hypothesis and Belief

IF a member of the so-called intellectual class joins any religious group or openly subscribes to its teaching, he will have to prepare himself for a good deal of criticism from his unconverted and more sceptical friends. Some of these may be sympathetic and genuinely interested; others will be covertly satirical, suspicious, or quite frankly hostile and dismayed. It will be suggested to the convert, with a greater or lesser degree of politeness, that he has sold out, betrayed the cause of reason, retreated in cowardice from 'the realities of Life', and so forth. Henceforward, his conduct will be narrowly watched for symptoms of pretentiousness, priggishness, prudery and all other forms of puritanism. Certain topics will either be altogether avoided in his presence or they will be presented in the form of a challenge, to see how he will take them.

The convert himself, self-conscious and badly rattled, is almost sure to behave unnaturally. Either he will preach at his old friends and bore them; thus confirming their worst suspicions. Or he will make desperate efforts to reassure them, by his manner and conversation, that he is still 'one of the gang'. He will be the first to blaspheme, the first to touch upon the delicate subject. And his friends, far from feeling relieved, will be sincerely shocked.

One question, especially, he must learn to expect. It will be asked by the most candid, by those who really want to know: 'Yes, of course, I can quite understand why you did it, in a way ... but tell me, do you actually *believe* all that?' This question is particularly distressing to the convert, because, if he is to be honest, he will have to answer: 'No, I don't – yet.'

The 'all that' to which the questioner refers will vary in detail and mode of formulation, according to the religious group the convert happens to have chosen. In essence, however, it can always be covered by what Aldous Huxley has called 'the minimum working hypothesis'. This word 'hypothesis' is extremely significant, but it will probably be overlooked by the outside observer, who prefers to simplify his picture of the world's religions by regarding their teachings as 'creeds' and 'dogmas'. Nevertheless, a statement of religious doctrine can be properly called a creed only by those who know it to be true. It remains a hypothesis as long as you are not quite sure. Spiritual truth is, by definition, directly revealed and experienced; it cannot be known at second hand. What is revealed truth to a Christ is merely hypothetical truth to the vast majority of his followers; but this need not prevent the followers from trusting in Christ's personal integrity and in the authenticity of his revelation, *as far as Christ himself is concerned*. One can feel sure that Einstein is neither a fraud nor a lunatic, and that he has actually discovered the law of relativity, and still fail, in a certain sense, to 'believe' in the conception of Space-Time, just because one has not yet personally understood it.

There is, even nowadays, a good deal of loose and unrealistic talk about 'the conflict between religion and science'. I call this kind of talk unrealistic because it suggests that 'Science', and hence scientists, are one hundred per cent materialistic, and that 'Religion' is based upon the blind, one hundred per cent acceptance of dogmas which are incapable of scientific proof. Modern Science is, of course, very far from being materialistic. In the nineteenth century, it is true, science did pass through a phase of mechanistic materialism. But the scientist himself never has been, and never could be, an absolute materialist. The scientist is a human being. The absolute materialist, if he existed, would have to be some sort of non-human creature, completely lacking the human faculty of intuition, a mere machine for measuring and making calculations. If a human being could become a truly convinced materialist, he would never have the heroism to get up in the morning, shave, and eat his breakfast. His world-picture would be too terrible for even the boldest heart to contemplate; and, within twenty-four hours, he would have committed suicide.

Similarly a religion based upon blind faith could not possibly survive, as all the world-religions have survived, for hundreds and thousands of years. Religion lives, and is revived, from age to age, because of the direct revelation of the few, the saints, who win for themselves a personal knowledge of spiritual reality. Religion survives *in spite* of blind faith, priestly persecution, ecclesiastical politics; in spite of superstition and ignorance amongst the masses of its adherents. Most of us cannot understand this, because our imagination refuses to grasp the gigantic influence and importance of the saint as an historical phenomenon. Whereas the persecution and the ignorance stand out brutally from the pages of history in red and black, plain for all to see. Nine times out of ten, when we use the word 'Religion', we are really referring to the crimes or follies committed in religion's name.

There is no conflict between true Religion and true Science, but there is a great deal of bickering between religious dogmatists and scientific pedants. The dogmatist states his case, or rather, presents his dogmatic ultimatum. The scientifically-trained pedant reminds him, none too patiently, that his assertions cannot be verified by the microscope, the slide-rule, or the laboratory experiment. Therefore, he continues, quite rightly, the dogma is merely another hypothesis. And he will probably add that hypotheses which are incapable of scientific proof do not interest him, anyway. At this point a deadlock is reached, and the two men part in mutual annoyance.

But now let us suppose that, instead of the tiresome, dogmatic convert (who is unconvincing because he has not personally experienced the truth of what he asserts), Christ himself should enter the scientist's laboratory, and make the very same statements which the convert makes. How would the scientist react? If the scientist were a pure, non-human materialist, he would, of course, remain completely unconvinced. But, since he is a creature of emotion and intuition as well as of reason, the chances are that he would be impressed, not rationally but emotion-ally, by the personality of Christ and the tremendous psychological impact of such a meeting. In spite of his scientific training, he would venture to trust his intuition. He would say to himself: 'Although my scientific methods of analysis cannot deal with these statements, my intui-tion tells me that this man has some authority for his words.'

This raises the question of what we may call 'the credi-bility of the witness'. The jury in a court of law does not, or should not, judge a case entirely by scientific (i.e. rational) method: it relies, also, on intuition. It decides to believe a witness or not to believe him – sometimes in defiance of considerable circumstantial evidence. There is, also, the factor of corroboration. If two or more wit-nesses support each other, and make an impression of being truthful, the case is apt to turn in their favour.

When we begin to examine the assertions of the great religious teachers we shall have to behave like jurymen. Reason can help us, no doubt, and it must be brought to bear on the case; but Reason will not take us all the way. It can only deliver a provisional verdict. It can only say: 'This is possible', or 'Perhaps ...' Next, we must ask our-selves: 'What sort of men are telling us this? Are they charlatans? Do they seem sane? Do their lives bear out the truth of what they preach?' And, again: 'Do they, substantially, agree with each other's testimony?' On this second point, however, there can be little argument. The basis of essential agreement between the great religious teachers of the world is very firm, and can easily be demonstrated by documentary evidence. Any student of comparative religion can reconstruct 'the minimum working hypothesis'. Nevertheless, it is quite possible to decide that Buddha, Christ, Shankara, St Francis and Ramakrishna were all mad, or self-deluded, and therefore not to be taken seriously. If that is the verdict, then our inquiry ends.

But if the world's teachers were not mad, then, as all must agree, their teaching has universal application, and implies an obligation to put it into practice, in our own lives. And so we are faced by the next question: 'Am I dissatisfied with my life as it is at present? And, if so, am I sufficiently dissatisfied to want to do anything about it?'

Here the majority and the minority definitely part company. Buddha said that human life is miserable, but he did not say that everybody thinks it is. Not all the socially underprivileged are dissatisfied, as every reformer knows, to his despair. And this is even truer of spiritual poverty than of economic lack. Life contains a number of vivid sense-pleasures, and the gaps of despondency and boredom between them can be filled more or less adequately by hard work, sleep, the movies, drink and day-dreaming. Old age brings lethargy, and morphia will help you at the end. Life is not so bad, if you have plenty of luck, a good physique and not too much imagination. The disciplines proposed by the spiritual teachers are drastic, and the lazy will shrink back from them. They are tedious, also, and this will discourage the impatient. Their immediate results are not showy, and this will deter the ambitious. Their practice is apt to make you appear ridiculous to your neighbours. Vanity, sloth and desire will all intervene to prevent a man from setting his foot upon the path of religious effort.

Disregarding all these obstacles, and they are tremendous, the beginner will have to say to himself: 'Well, I am going to try. I believe that my teacher is sane and honest. I do not believe in his teachings with the whole of my mind, and I will not pretend that I do, but I have enough belief to make a start. My reason is not offended. My approach is strictly experimental. I will put myself into his hands, and trust him at least as far as I would trust my doctor. I will try to live the kind of life which he prescribes. If, at the end of three or four years, I can conscientiously say that I have done what was asked of me and had no results whatsoever, then I will give up the whole attempt as a bad job.'

The Gita and War

IN the course of a year spent studying the Bhagavad-Gita, I have talked about its philosophy to a considerable number of people. Whatever else they had to say, I found them, almost without exception, agreed on one point: that the Gita 'sanctions' War. Some were glad of this. Others were sorry. But all, I think, were puzzled. Educated in the Christian tradition, they were accustomed to a gospel which is uncompromisingly pacifist. However deeply they might be convinced of the justice or necessity of some particular conflict, they did not like what they regarded as a general approval of the use of military force. They themselves, mere human beings struggling in the everyday world, might be driven to fight and kill one another, but they wanted Krishna, like Jesus, to stand for a higher ideal. That was their reaction.

I do not wish to sound superior or conceited when I say that I myself do not put this interpretation upon the teaching of the Gita. I will try to explain why I do not:

not merely for the information of the few people who may be interested, but because I want to straighten out my own ideas. The question is of the greatest importance to me, because I am myself a pacifist, and because I believe the Gita to be one of the major religious documents of the world. If its teachings did not seem to me to agree with those of the other gospels and scriptures, then my own system of values would be thrown into confusion, and I should feel completely bewildered.

Briefly, the circumstances of the Gita dialogue can be described as follows:

Two factions, closely bound to each other by ties of blood and friendship, are about to engage in a civil war. Arjuna, one of the leading generals, has Krishna for his charioteer. Krishna has told Arjuna that he will not fight, but has promised to accompany him throughout the battle. Just before it begins, Arjuna asks Krishna to drive his chariot into the no-man's land between the two armies. Krishna does so. Arjuna looks at the opposing army, and realizes that he is about to kill those whom he loves better than life itself. In his despair, he exclaims: 'I will not fight.'

Krishna's reply to Arjuna occupies the rest of the book. It deals not only with Arjuna's immediate personal problem, but with the whole nature of action, the meaning of life, and the aims for which man must struggle, here on earth. At the end of their conversation Arjuna has changed his mind. He is ready to fight. And the battle begins.

Before trying to analyse Krishna's arguments, I must mention two points which certain commentators have raised with regard to the battle itself. In the first place, it is sometimes said that the battle of Kurukshetra cannot possibly be compared to a battle in modern war. It was, in fact, a kind of tournament governed by all the complex and humane rules of ancient Indian chivalry. A soldier mounted upon an elephant may not attack a foot-soldier. No man may be struck or shot at while running away. No one may be killed who has lost his weapons. And we are told, in the Mahabharata, that the opposing armies stopped fighting every evening, and even visited each other and fraternized during the night. In the second place, it is sometimes said that the whole battle is to be regarded allegorically. Arjuna is the individual man, Krishna is the indwelling of Godhead, the enemies are man's evil tendencies, and so forth.

All this is interesting, of course. But it has nothing to do with our problem. If Krishna is only talking figuratively , or only about War under certain conditions, then the Gita is just a fable, an archaic curiosity: we need not discuss it. Personally, I prefer to forget Kurukshetra and ancient India altogether, and imagine a similar dialogue taking place today, in a plane over the European front or the Japanese positions on a Pacific island. If the Gita has any validity, its reference is equally to this war and this very year.

To understand the Gita, we must first consider what it is and what it is not. We must consider its setting. When Jesus spoke the words which are recorded as the Sermon on the Mount, he was talking to a group of followers in the most peaceful atmosphere imaginable, far from the great city, far from all strife and confusion. He was expressing the highest truth of which man's mind is capable, in general terms, without reference to any immediate crisis or problem. And even in the Garden of Gethsemane, when he told Peter to sheathe his sword, he was addressing a dedicated disciple, a monk, a man who was being trained to preach and live the spiritual life. For Peter, there could be no compromise. He must learn to accept the highest and strictest ideal, the ideal of non-violence.

The Gita is very different. Krishna and Arjuna are on a battlefield. Arjuna is a warrior by birth and profession. He corresponds to the medieval knight of Christendom. His problem is considered in relation to the circumstances of the moment. The Gita fits into the narrative of an epic poem, the Mahabharata, and must be read in the light of previous happenings. It is not simply a sermon, a philosophical treatise.

This, I believe, is the cause of much misunderstanding. We all tend to remember most clearly the part of the book which we read first. The opening chapters of the Gita deal with a particular case: they are concerned with a soldier and the duties of a soldier. Later on, Krishna passes from the particular to the general, and utters those same truths which were afterwards taught by Jesus and the Buddha. But the first impression is apt to remain. The superficial reader closes the book and remembers only Arjuna and the battle. He says to himself: 'Krishna tells us that we must fight.'

Krishna, it must be repeated, is not talking to a monk. We ought to be glad of this, not sorry. The vast majority of mankind are not monks, but householders. What a great teacher has to say to a married man, a soldier, is of immediate interest to the world at large.

We must realize, also, that Krishna, in teaching Arjuna, employs two sets of values, the relative and the absolute. This duality is inherent in the circumstances of the story. For Krishna is both Arjuna's personal friend and his illumined teacher. He is a fellow-mortal and he is God. As God, he expresses the absolute truth, the highest ideal. As a fellow-man, he presents the relative values which apply to Arjuna's particular condition. Considered superficially, this duality of attitude may seem to produce contradictions. Carefully studied, it will be seen to compose into a complete and satisfying philosophical picture. For life itself is double-faced; and any attempt at simplification will only bring us to ultimate confusion.

One circumstance renders Arjuna's compassion suspect: its occasion. Arjuna himself is dimly aware of this. 'Is this real compassion I feel,' he asks Krishna, 'or only a delusion? My mind gropes about in darkness. I cannot see where my duty lies.' Up to this moment Arjuna has not hesitated. He has accepted the necessity of the war. He has assumed responsibility for its leadership. Then, suddenly, he sees the other side of the picture: the blood-shed, the horror. And he recoils.

In the years that followed the 1914–18 war, much paci-fist propaganda was based on gruesome narratives of battle and books of photographs showing mutilated corpses. 'This is what war is like,' said the authors. 'Isn't it horrible? Do you want to go through this again?' And nearly everybody agreed that they did not. But this sort of revulsion is always short-lived, because it appeals, funda-mentally, to our cowardice. When a new war-situation develops, most of us react in the opposite direction, and rightly. Men can never, ultimately, be deterred from any course of action by cowardice alone. Otherwise we should never have evolved from the jellyfish. We have to go forward, and the path is always dangerous, in one way or another. Arjuna has to go forward. Krishna tells him so. Arjuna must accept the sum of his actions up to that moment – and the sum is this battle.

Krishna's reply begins by dealing with Arjuna's feelings of revulsion, on general grounds. Arjuna shrinks from the act itself, the act of killing. Krishna reminds him that, in the absolute sense, there is no such act. The Atman, the indwelling Godhead, is the only reality. This body is simply an appearance: its existence, its destruction, are alike illusory. In the absolute sense, all talk of killing or being killed is meaningless.

> 'Some say this Atman
> Is slain, and others
> Call It the slayer:
> They know nothing.
> How can It slay
> Or who shall slay It?'

Therefore, if Arjuna is objecting to the act of killing, as such, he need have no scruples. For he only seems to kill.

Then, with one of those changes of viewpoint which may bewilder and shock a reader who opens the Gita for the first time and takes only its surface meaning, Krishna begins to talk to Arjuna as man to man:

'Even if you consider this from the standpoint of your own caste-duty, you ought not to hesitate; for, to a warrior, there is nothing nobler than a righteous war. . . .

'But if you refuse to fight this righteous war, you will be turning aside from your duty. You will be a sinner, and disgraced. People will speak ill of you throughout the ages. . . .'

For Arjuna, a member of the warrior caste, the fighting of this battle, in defence of his family and property, is undoubtedly 'righteous'. It is his duty. In the Gita, we find that the caste-system is presented as a kind of natural order. Men are divided into four groups, according to their capacities and characteristics. Each group has its peculiar duties, ethics and responsibilities; and these must be accepted. It is the way of spiritual growth. A man must go forward from where he stands. He cannot jump to the Absolute: he must evolve towards it. He cannot arbitrarily assume the duties which belong to another group. If he does so, his whole system of values will be upset, his conscience can no longer direct him, and he will stray into pride or doubt or mental confusion. 'Prefer to die doing your own duty,' Krishna teaches: 'The duty of another will bring you into great spiritual danger.'

Socially, the caste-system is graded. The merchants are above the servants. The leaders and warriors are above the merchants. The priestly Brahmins are highest of all. But, spiritually, there are no such distinctions. Krishna is very clear on this point. Everyone, he says, can attain the highest sainthood by following the prescribed path of his own caste-duty. In Southern India we are told of seven saints who belonged to the lowest caste of all, the untouchables. And the same principle, of course, holds true if we apply the caste-classification to the social pattern of Europe. Men have grown into spiritual giants while carrying out their duties as merchants, peasants, doctors, popes, scullions or kings.

In the purely physical sphere of action, Arjuna is, indeed, no longer a free agent. The act of war is upon him: it has evolved out of his previous actions. He cannot choose. 'If, in your vanity, you say "I will not fight", your resolve is vain. Your own nature will drive you to the act.' At any given moment in time, we are what we are; and our actions express that condition. We cannot run away from our actions because we carry the condition with us. On the highest mountain, in the darkest cave, we must turn at last and accept the consequences of being ourselves. Only through this acceptance we begin to evolve further. We may select the battleground. We cannot avoid the battle.

Arjuna is bound by the law of Karma, the law of cause and effect which has brought him face to face with this particular situation. Now he is compelled to act, but he is still free to make his choice between two different ways of performing the action. Krishna introduces this great theme – the principal theme of the Gita – in the passage which immediately follows. He proceeds to define the nature of action.

In general, mankind almost always acts with attachment: that is to say, with fear and desire. Desire for a certain result, and fear that this result will not be obtained. Attached action binds us to the world of appearance, to the continual doing of more action. We live in a delirium of doing, and the consequences of our past actions condition the actions we are about to perform. According to the Gita, it is attached action which compels us to revisit this world, to be reborn again and again.

But there is another way of performing action; and this is without fear and without desire. The Christians call it 'holy indifference', and the Hindus 'non-attachment'. Both names are slightly misleading. They suggest coldness and lack of enthusiasm. That is why people often confuse non-attachment with fatalism, when, actually, they are opposites. The fatalist simply does not care. He will get what is coming to him. Why make any effort?

Fatalists are apt to get drunk or spend most of the day in bed. The doer of non-attached action, on the other hand, is the most conscientious of men. He does not run away from life: he accepts it, much more completely than those whose pleasures are tinged with anxiety and whose defeats are embittered by regret. No matter whether he is sweeping out a room, or calculating the position of a star, or taking the chair at a meeting, he does it to the utmost limit of his powers – so carefully, so devotedly, so whole-heartedly, that the dividing line between the chosen activity and the necessary chore disappears altogether. All work becomes equally and vitally important. It is only towards the results of work that he remains indifferent. Perhaps the dog runs across the clean floor with muddy paws. Perhaps his researches are recognized by Harvard University. Perhaps somebody throws a rotten egg at him. It does not matter. He goes right on with his job. We find something of this spirit in the lives of all truly great men and women, including the professed atheists and agnostics. Madame Curie refuses the Legion of Honour with the matter-of-fact words: 'I don't see the utility of it.' Lenin, in 1921, with the White armies converging on Moscow, his régime apparently doomed, his work brought to nothing, calmly sits down and writes the order: 'The peasants in the localities of Gorki and Ziianova are immediately to be supplied with electric light.' This, in its highest development, is the attitude of the saint. When action is done in the spirit, Krishna teaches, it will lead us to true wisdom, to the knowledge of what is behind action, behind all life: the ultimate Reality. And, with the growth of this knowledge, the need for further action will gradually fall away from us. The law of Karma will cease to operate. We shall realize our true nature, which is God.

It follows, therefore, that every action, under certain circumstances and for certain people, may be a stepping-stone to spiritual growth – if it is done in the spirit of non-attachment. All good and all evil is relative to the individual point of growth. For each individual, certain acts are absolutely wrong. Indeed, there may well be acts which are absolutely wrong for every individual alive on earth today. But, in the highest sense, there can be neither good nor evil.

> 'The Lord is everywhere
> And always perfect:
> What does He care for man's sin
> Or the righteousness of man?'

Because Krishna is speaking as God Himself, he can take this attitude, and advise Arjuna to fight. Because Arjuna has reached this particular stage in his development, he can kill his enemies and actually be doing his duty.

There is no question, here, of doing evil that good may come. The Gita does not countenance such opportunism. Arjuna is to do the best he knows, in order to pass beyond that best to better. Later, his fighting at Kurukshetra may seem evil to him, and it *will* be evil – then. Doing the evil you know to be evil will never bring good. It will lead only to more evil, more attachment, more ignorance.

How, in this complex world, are we to know what our own duty is? There is no greater problem. Yet, somehow, we have to find our position and make our stand. For the majority, much self-analysis, much trial and error, would seem to be the only way. But, having found that position, we must accept it in its entirety. The soldier has many responsibilities and duties besides fighting. The pacifist has much else to do besides refusing to fight. These duties and responsibilities extend equally over wartime and peace: they cover our whole life. But, in every case, the final ideal is the same.

The Gita neither sanctions war nor condemns it. Regarding no action as of absolute value, either for good or evil, it cannot possibly do either. Its teaching should warn us not to dare to judge others. How can we prescribe our neighbour's duty when it is so hard for us to know our own? The pacifist must respect Arjuna. Arjuna must respect the pacifist. Both are going towards the same goal. There is an underlying solidarity between them which can be expressed, if each one follows, without compromise, the path upon which he finds himself. For we can only help others to do their duty by doing what we ourselves believe to be right. It is the one supremely social act.

Vivekananda and Sarah Bernhardt

IN Paris, during the late summer of 1900, Swami Vivekananda had a conversation with the most famous woman of the Western world. It was probably, but not certainly, their first meeting. The two-volume *Life of Vivekananda*, by his Eastern and Western disciples, refers somewhat vaguely to an earlier occasion, in the United States, on which Bernhardt 'sought an interview with him' (that hardly sounds like the imperious Sarah, who had made royalty take its hat off in her presence!) 'and expressed her admiration and intense interest in the sublime teaching of the philosophy he so eloquently and truly represented'. The date given for this encounter – 1895 – would seem, in any case, to be wrong. Bernhardt was not in the States that year, though she visited them for a six-month tour in 1896. Moreover, Swamiji himself, writing in 1900 about the people he has met in Paris, particularly mentions that he and Madame Calvé, the singer, were previously acquainted, but speaks of Bernhardt as though they had just been introduced.

His correspondent was Swami Trigunatita, back home in India, and the tone of these travel-letters, which were intended for publication, is instructive, gossipy, explosive, facetious, affectionate and prophetic by turns: they are among the most characteristic things Viveananda ever wrote. 'Madame Bernhardt,' he tells his brother-monk, 'is an aged lady; but when she steps on the stage after dressing, her imitation of the age and sex of the role she plays is perfect! A girl, or a boy – whatever part you want her to play, she is an exact representation of that. And that wonderful voice! People here say her voice has the ring of silver strings!'

In a couple of months the 'aged lady' was going to be fifty-six years old. Even the unkind camera shows us that, 'on the stage after dressing', she did not look a day over thirty. Her photograph in the role of *L'Aiglon*, the Duke of Reichstadt, which she played for the first time in March of that year, presents an astonishingly slender and erect little personage in a riding-coat and high boots with spurs, neither boy nor girl, woman nor man, sexless, ageless, and altogether impossible by daylight, outside the walls of a theatre. Some later references in another of the letters to the story of Napoleon's tragic son suggest that Vivekananda must almost certainly have seen Sarah in this, her greatest dramatic triumph after *La Dame aux Camélias*.

Bernhardt was then on the final peak of her mountainous career. Her acting was probably better than it had ever been before; better, certainly, than in the nineties, when her hit-or-miss noisiness, ranting and hamming had provoked the brilliant scolding of the young theatre-critic Bernard Shaw, and his unfavourable comparisons between her and the more modern restraint of Eleanora Duse. She had disciplined herself, artistically and emotionally. The crazy days of her publicity – of the balloon-trip, the coffin, and the shooting of the St Louis Bay bridge – were far behind her. The shameful tragedy of her marriage with Damala had been ended, long ago, by his death from morphine poisoning. Her extravagance was still immense, but so were her earnings. And the accident in Rio de Janeiro which was to result in her gradual crippling was still five years ahead.

Swamiji seems to have been taken round to visit her in her dressing-room at the theatre after a performance. One wonders who introduced them, what word was used to describe the Swami's occupation to the actress, and whether she had already heard of him. 'Madame Bernhardt,' writes Vivekananda, 'has a special regard for India; she tells me again and again that our country is *très ancien, très civilisé* – very ancient and very civilized.' There must have been a gleam in Swamiji's eye as he politely received this flattering information.

They talked, as was natural, of the only play Sarah had ever produced with an Indian setting. It was *Izéil*, by Morand and Silvestre, an expensive flop. Bernhardt had always obstinately liked this piece, perhaps because it displayed her undoubted talent for theatrical décor. 'She told me that for about a month she had visited every museum and made herself acquainted with the men and women and their dress, the streets and bathing ghats and everything relating to India.'

'Madame Bernhardt,' the letter concludes, 'has a very strong desire to visit India. "*C'est mon rêve* – It is the dream of my life," she says. Again, the Prince of Wales has promised to take her over to a tiger and elephant hunting excursion. But then, she said, she must spend some two lacs of rupees if she went to India! She is, of course, in no want of money. *La divine Sarah* – the divine Sarah – is her name; how can she want money? She who never travels but by special train! That pomp and luxury many a prince of Europe cannot afford to indulge in! One can only secure a seat in her performance by paying double the fees, and that a month in advance! Well, she is not going to suffer want of money! But Sarah Bernhardt is given to spending lavishly. Her travel to India is therefore put off for the present.'

Underneath these few mock-serious, bantering sentences, one senses the warmth of an immediate sympathy and liking. You can picture Swamiji sitting opposite the vivid, Semitic little Frenchwoman, large and jolly, his amused glance taking in the whole luxurious setting, the jewels, the mirrors, the silks, the cosmetics, the marvellous robes. Here, as in all women everywhere, he saluted his own daughter, sister, mother. Here, as always, he bowed to the eternal Godhead, beneath yet another of those queer disguises which bewilder our wanderings towards Self-realization. Here, also, he surely recognized, to an unusual degree, the virtue he prized so highly: courage. Courage was, perhaps, the one quality which these fantastically dissimilar personalities had in common: the courage which had supported Vivekananda in the blackest hours of spiritual torment, of his Master's loss, of all the early struggles and trials of the Order, and which had never deserted him in the jungle or the mountains or the drawing rooms of American millionaires: the courage which had nerved Sarah in her battles to raise her child, in her work during the siege of Paris, in her defence of Dreyfus, in her return to the stage, at the age of seventy-two after the amputation of her right leg. Swamiji must have been aware of this, and loved her for it.

And how did Bernhardt think of him? Perhaps, curiously enough, as a kind of colleague. Had not he, also, appeared triumphantly before the public? Many actors and actresses, including Sarah herself as Joan of Arc, have represented saints – at any rate, to the satisfaction of the audience beyond the footlights. Swamiji, on the other hand, with his superb presence and sonorous voice, might well have been mistaken for a great actor.

In a photograph of this period, we see how the eyes of the young sannyasin, burning almost intolerably with mingled devotion and doubt, have softened and deepened in the face of the mature man. The big lips and the lines spreading from the wide nostrils have a curve of watchful humour, in which there is neither irony, nor bitterness, nor resignation – only a great calm, like the sea, with certainty dawning over it, an absolute, arising sun. 'Are you never serious, Swamiji?' somebody asked him, rather reproachfully, and was answered: 'Oh, yes. When I have the belly-ache.' Even this was an overstatement, for the smiling, joking Vivekananda of 1900 was already a very sick man.

He and Bernhardt never saw each other again. In October the Swami's party left Paris for Austria, the Balkans and Egypt, whence he sailed to India, arriving home at the Belur monastery early in December. Thus ended his last journey to the West. The longer journey, also, was nearly over. One day in July 1902, wishing perhaps to spare his friends the agony of a good-bye, he passed, by stealth, as it were, into *samadhi*, and did not come back.

Sarah survived him by twenty-one years, survived the First World War, lived on into the era of Chaplin and Pickford and the Keystone Cops, appeared in two or three movies herself, and died in action, getting ready to rehearse a new play.

In the half-dozen Bernhardt biographies I have been able to consult, the name of Vivekananda is not even mentioned. In fact, this brief anecdote of their meeting, with its exchange of conventional small-talk and politeness, would seem to have no point whatsoever. That is just what makes it so fascinating and so significant. When poets or politicians foregather, we expect epigrams and aphorisms; for talk is their medium of expression. But talk is not, primarily, the medium of the man of illumination. His way of approach is more direct, more subtle and more penetrating. He makes contact with you below the threshold of everyday awareness. No matter whether he speaks of the Prince of Wales, or of God, or only smiles and says nothing, your whole life will be, to some degree, changed from that moment on.

That is why – despite the biographer's silence, and the lack of high-class philosophical conversation – one dare not say that Swamiji's visit made no great or lasting impression upon Sarah. The spotlight of history, which reveals a tiny area of surface-action so brightly, cannot help us here. All we can venture to say is this: 'One day, the two human mysteries known to the world as Bernhardt and Vivekananda met, exchanged certain signals which we do not understand, and parted, we do not know why. All we *do* know is that their meeting, like every other event in this universe, did not take place by accident.'

The Problem of the Religious Novel

I SUPPOSE that most novelists have considered, at one time or another, the project of writing a religious novel. Every writer of dramatic fiction, irrespective of his individual beliefs or doubts, is eager to find characters who will exhibit the maximum variety of reactions to external events. The saint is pre-eminently such a character. Because his motives are not dictated by fear, vanity or desire – because his every action is a genuine act of free will – you can never predict what he will do next. He accepts life more fully, more creatively, than any of his neighbours. And therefore he is the most interesting person to write about.

The most interesting and the most difficult. For, in attempting to present such a character to his audience of average men and women, the writer cannot rely at all on the factor of familiarity, of self-recognition, which assists him so powerfully when he is describing average people, recognizable social types. He cannot expect his audience to come half-way to meet him, exclaiming, 'Why, that's just like Mr Jones!' The saint, considered as an end product, resembles Mr Jones as little as he resembles a giraffe. And yet Mr Jones and Mr Smith and Mr Brown are all potentially saints. This is what the author has somehow to prove to his audience.

It is a task which demands the utmost persuasiveness, deftness and cunning. At every step prejudices and preconceptions have to be overcome. The public has its preconceived notion of a saint – a figure with a lean face and an air of weary patience, who alternates between moods of forbidding austerity and heart-broken sweetness – a creature set apart from this bad world, a living reproach to our human weakness, in whose presence we feel ill at ease, inferior, and embarrassed. In other words, the dreariest of bores.

If I ever write a religious novel, I shall begin by trying to prove that my saint-to-be really *is* Mr Jones. Somerset Maugham, for example, does this quite successfully in *The Razor's Edge*. Larry, when we first meet him, is an entirely reassuring character, lively, natural, normal, a typical American boy. I think that Maugham's choice of such a character had a great deal to do with the immense popularity of this book.

So far, so good. But now a second and much greater problem arises. How am I going to show, in terms of dramatic fiction, that decisive moment at which my hero becomes aware of his vocation and decides to do something about it? Maugham is rather vague at this point: he merely suggests that Larry's change of heart is caused by his experiences in the First World War. Aldous Huxley's *Time Must Have a Stop* avoids the moment altogether – making a huge jump from Sebastian the precocious, cowardly, uninhibited schoolboy to Sebastian the mature, meditative man, already far advanced in the practice of a spiritual discrimination. One of the classic examples of a conversion scene is, of course, Dostoyevsky's account of the duel, in *The Brothers Karamazov*, which starts the process of turning a stupid young bully of a Russian officer into Father Zossima, the saint. How beautifully Dostoevski handles this moment of transformation – without the least sentimentality, in terms almost of farce, yet with such warmth, insight, and naturalness! We share the young man's exquisite relief when he finds himself suddenly able, by fearlessly asking his opponent's pardon, to break the bonds of a rigid military code which has hitherto conditioned his behaviour, and to perform his first act of pure free will. This is the kind of scene I should like to have in my novel – something slightly comic and entirely natural. In history, we know that many conversions have occurred as the result of a vision. But visions, unless you are writing historical fiction, like *The Song of Bernadette,* seem to me to be undesirable in the early stages of a story, because they excuse the author from explaining what is happening in his hero's mind. Dramatically, they are a form of cheating.

It is all very well to use words like 'conversion' in an article for a religious magazine. They belong to an accepted terminology. I know that my readers will understand what I mean. But this kind of shorthand is never permissible for the novelist, with his mixed and highly sceptical audience. He has to explain, as though they had never been explained before, his hero's motives and objectives; and this, in a religious novel, is particularly difficult. How am I to prove that X is not merely insane when he turns his back on the whole scheme of pleasures, rewards, and satisfactions which are accepted by the Joneses, the Smiths, and the Browns, and goes in search of super-conscious, extra-phenomenal experience? The only way I can see how to do this is with the help of the Joneses themselves. I must show that the average men and women of this world are searching, however unconsciously, for the same fundamental reality of which X has already had a glimpse. Certainly, they look for it in the wrong places. Certainly, their methods are quite unpractical. Mr Jones will find nothing at the bottom of the whisky bottle, except a headache. But the whisky bottle is not to be dismissed with a puritanical sneer; it is the crude symbol of Jones's dissatisfaction with surface consciousness, his need to look more deeply into the meaning of life. The Smiths conform obediently to the standards imposed by the advertisements they read in their newspapers. They drive the prescribed make of car, smoke the recommended brand of cigarettes, spend their leisure time in the ways and at the places which are guaranteed as educational and enjoyable – and yet, at the back of their minds, there is a germ of doubt. Is this really what we were born for? Is this the whole meaning of existence? That doubt may, one day, be their salvation. It is the measure of their kinship with X. For the evolving saint does not differ from his fellow humans in kind, but only in degree. That is why X can only be understood, artistically, when his story is related to that of the Joneses, the Smiths, and the Browns.

The greater part of my novel would deal, of course, with X's struggles towards sainthood, towards complete spiritual realization. I think that most writers have erred in making this phase of their story too sombre and depressing. True, the path of the spiritual aspirant is hard. The mortification of the ego is tedious and painful. But I see no reason for the author to sentimentalize his hero's sufferings, or to allow him to indulge in self-pity. Sports writers find no pathos in the hardships of a boxer's training. The would-be saint is the last person in the world we should feel sorry for. His sufferings are purely voluntary. If his will slackens, they automatically cease. *The Garden of Allah* is not really a tragedy, unless one regards it as a tragedy of weakness. If the runaway monk did not genuinely want to return to the monastery, and was only bowing to public opinion, then it was very weak and silly of him to do so. George Moore, in his two novels, *Evelyn Innes* and *Sister Teresa*, has traced the development of a famous opera singer into a Catholic nun. It is a wonderful and moving story, full of acute psychological observation, amounting almost to clairvoyance. Moore is at his best in describing that moment of spiritual vertigo and despair when Evelyn, listening to the trivial chatter of the other novices, thinks, 'How can I possibly stay here?' and then, remembering the equally trivial chatter at the dinner parties she used to attend, asks herself, 'But how could I possibly go back to the old life?' Nevertheless, I feel that Moore, like many of his inferiors, has made his protagonist's spiritual history too gloomy – perhaps simply because he does not carry it far enough. We say good-bye to Evelyn before she has made any permanent adjustment to her new life, and at a time when she has just lost her marvellous voice. The novel ends on a note of sadness, against which I protest. Surely the mishaps and setbacks which beset the path of spiritual progress can be recounted with some of the humour which invests one's failures in cookery or falls in learning to ski? Maugham, I believe, would agree with me here. There is nothing gloomy about Larry's career. Unfortunately, however, his creator has gone to the other extreme, and one gets the impression that becoming a saint is just no trouble at all.

And so we come to the last phase of the story, the portrait of the perfected saint. Here, I am sure, I should give up in despair. Nothing short of genius could succeed in such a task. For the mystical experience itself can never be described. It can only be written around, hinted at, dimly reflected in word and deed. So far, the novelists have given us nothing but brilliant glimpses – the incident of the Bishop's candlesticks in *Les Misérables*, the few interviews with Father Zossima, Huxley's sketch of Bruno Rontini. These three men are only minor characters in long and crowded stories. Maugham is greatly to be admired for his more ambitious attempt – even if, as I have indicated above, it is not altogether successful. Tolstoy, towards the end of his career, outlined what might have been a masterpiece. We cannot be sure. The life of *Father Sergius* is told in less than fifty pages. Perhaps even Tolstoy felt himself unequal to the undertaking. Perhaps the truly comprehensive religious novel could only be written by a saint – and saints, unfortunately, are not in the habit of writing novels.

PEOPLE

THE 'Leader' in the first of these three pieces is Ernst Toller, the famous German dramatist, poet and revolutionary. Auden translated and adapted the lyrics for the English version of Toller's play, *No More Peace!* Later, he wrote one of his most beautiful poems in Toller's memory.

Toller killed himself in New York in May 1939, about six weeks after the meeting between us which I describe here. That summer I wrote down my memories of him. I avoided mentioning his name and made them sound as much as possible like fiction, lest they should cause offence. But, even as fiction, they seemed to demand a tragic ending, and this I was unwilling to write; which is why the piece stops so abruptly. I finally decided not to publish it for the time being. Years later, I sent it to Stephen Spender, who put it in his first number of *Encounter,* October 1953.

Biographically, my account of these conversations and episodes may be unreliable; I have long since forgotten which details, if any, were invented. But, as subjective impressions, they are genuine.

During March 1941 I was working at Metro-Goldwyn-Mayer studios on the screenplay of a film. One day, one of the movie-columnists, who used to rove around the studios picking up bits of information, dropped into my office and asked if he might use my phone. He wanted to call his own office and find out if any messages had come in for him. I told him to go ahead and turned back to my work, listening with half an ear to him talking to his assistant: 'No – *no*, you dope – the name's Woolf – W-O-O-L-F – sure, I'm sure – sure, I've heard of her, you ignorant bastard – she was a great writer – British –'

That was how I learned of Virginia Woolf's death.

Klaus Mann asked me to write about her for *Decision*, a magazine which he had just started. This piece appeared in the May number of 1941.

I exhume it for the sake of some descriptive passages which do seem to me to evoke Virginia as I knew her. But, of all my exhibits, this is the one I have been most tempted to tamper with. An attempt to speak simultaneously as the public eulogist and the private mourner is almost foredoomed to falseness; all the more so when you feel you are addressing strangers who could never really understand or care. One sentence in particular nauseates me as much as anything I have ever written: 'she was, as the Spaniards say, "very rare" ...' This bit of jargon was undoubtedly inspired by Hemingway's *For Whom the Bell Tolls*, which I had recently read and reviewed enthusiastically (I now admire it less than his other novels). But it would be cowardly to blame Hemingway. To ape the affectations of great writers is never excusable.

I did seriously consider cutting the sentence out of this reprint. Then I remembered that the piece has already appeared in a college textbook which is designed to teach Form and Style in writing modern prose. So let my lapse be recorded here, also, as a warning to the young!

The 'Jeremy' referred to is a pseudonym for Hugh Walpole. Virginia teased him endlessly but was very fond of him, I believe. He took her teasing with good humour, feeling humble and honoured to be in her presence. He seems to have been a generous, warm-natured, thoroughly sympathetic person. I wish I had known him better. In my teens, I used to imitate his way of writing; later, I reacted violently against it. *All the Conspirators* is written in what might be called an anti-Walpole manner. Nevertheless, Walpole was the first well-known writer to praise the book in print.

Klaus Mann died in May 1949. Like Toller and Virginia Woolf, he committed suicide.

This piece was written for a volume called *Klaus Mann*

– *zum Gedächtnis*, which was published by the Querido Verlag of Amsterdam in 1950. Most of the contributors to this memorial volume wrote in German, a few in English, and one in Italian.

Although we saw each other infrequently, Klaus was a close friend of mine for more than fifteen years. I first met him in Germany before the Nazis came into power, and I was with him in California not long before his death. Through Klaus, I got to know Thomas Mann, Frau Mann, Erika and several other members of that brilliant and astonishing family. I felt that I was writing about Klaus for them and for his friends, rather than for the public. So this piece comes nearer to the truthfulness of personal feeling than my two others.

The Head of a Leader

'COMME il est beau!' someone murmured in my ear, at the moment of our first meeting – and I agreed without hesitation. He *was* beautiful, with the immediately striking, undeniable beauty of a peacock, or a great lady of the theatre. But, as he advanced to greet us from the hotel doorway – the smallest central figure of a little group – I could not help noticing that the square vigorous body was a trifle too short for his splendid silver head – the head which a dictator had valued at five thousand dollars.

A girl introduced us, and I found myself looking into those famous, burning dark eyes, which every photograph had failed to reproduce: 'Ah ... Mr Isherwood. This is a great pleasure.' His lips parted, in the most flattering, the most imperious of smiles. Then the glance hardened, became penetrating, commanding. Still grasping my hand, steering me by the elbow, he led me a little aside from the others. They drew back respectfully to let us pass, like the staff officers of a general who wishes to confer with an important messenger. 'Tell me, first – what do you think of Portugal? Ah, we shall have much to talk about!'

But through supper it was he who did most of the talking – and I was glad, like the others, merely to sit and listen; to follow, with amused, willing admiration, his every gesture and word. He was all that I had hoped for – more brilliant, more convincing than his books, more daring than his most epic deeds. It was easy enough to see him on that cinema platform, fifteen years ago, when he told the workers: 'You must occupy the factories. You must resist.' I could picture him at the magnificent moment of defeat, crying out to his judges: 'You can silence me. You can never silence History.' I watched him pace his cell, five years long, in the mountain fortress, aloof and dangerous as the untamed tiger. Yes, he had done all that. And he could do it again – tomorrow, if need be. The years, which had cloaked him with authority, had left the vital spark untouched. The man of forty was as undaunted as the boy of twenty-five.

We spoke of Portugal. 'A great change is coming soon to this country,' he told us. 'The peasants live like the humblest animals. Feudalism is still a reality. But there is much discontentment. The forces of Progress are working underground. The masses are learning to read, and their primer is the Communist Manifesto. It is passed from hand to hand, secretly, like a precious diamond, or a bomb.'

'But, Ernst, how can you possibly *know* that?' one of the boldest members of the party, a beautiful young girl, interrupted. 'Why, you've only been here forty-eight hours. And you don't even speak the language!'

Not the smallest trace of displeasure, or impatience, was visible. With perfect good humour, the lordly, flattering eyes paid tribute to her youth, her charm; pardoned her inexperience: 'My dear Mary,' his voice was very gentle, 'I do not know these things. I feel them. Why should I wish to deceive you? You can trust me.'

We could trust him, as thousands had trusted him,

unreservedly, absolutely. Somebody proposed his health, and we drank it, in the local red wine of Cascaes, which is sour as the blood of the exploited peasants. Slightly blood-drunk, I looked down from a vast height at our party, sitting there in the garden, under the vine-leaves and stars, and saw this evening as a sentence in a great book, a classic, which would one day be written – probably by Ernst himself. Later, he told funny stories, and began to sing, in a fine tenor, the songs of his own ungrateful country. He was in excellent spirits. He made us all laugh. Yet even this moment was somehow solemn, and epic. The general was entertaining his troops; building up their morale on the night before a desperate battle.

It was two years before I saw him again, in London, at a time when the newspapers were full of his activities. Single-handed, he was conducting a propaganda campaign on behalf of his compatriots, the starving refugees who were now scattered over half Europe. His success was sensational. He had contrived, somehow, to reach audiences outside the circles of the Left. He had touched the heart of the huge, apathetic Public. He had caught the ears of the right people, the Powers, and the powers behind the Powers. They invited him to their houses, as an honoured guest. Even the conservative press spoke well of him. He was in the process of becoming a respectable institution.

At last, one evening, I ran into him, in the middle of Regent Street. It was shortly before midnight, and I had just come out of the Café Royal. Hardly to my surprise, he recognized me at once – it was only natural, I felt, that his memory for faces, like everything else about him, should be regal: 'Ah, Isherwood! Good that we meet! And now we shall be together for a few hours, I hope? Tell me, where can we talk?'

I was feeling dreadfully tired; and I had to get up early in the morning to leave London on a long journey. But such was the epic quality of his presence that I felt childishly ashamed to have to admit that I was on my way home to bed. Revolutionaries never sleep. So I muttered something about an important engagement – some kind of meeting, I hinted – and added, with cowardly cunning: 'But Stephen's in there. I've just left him. I'm sure he'd be delighted to see you.' Stephen was a mutual friend.

He accepted my excuses benevolently, with a little pat on the shoulder. He seemed amused and touched by my slight embarrassment. 'Stephen is in there? Good. I shall surprise him.' And turning to a charming girl who, as I now became aware for the first time, had been accompanying him, he commanded, with the most regally natural simplicity: 'Please get me a flower.'

The girl showed no surprise. She must have been accustomed to this sort of thing. She turned back at once, in the direction of Piccadilly Circus, leaving us together on the pavement, dividing the slowly-moving current of the passers-by.

'You have heard about my work?' he asked, immediately.

'Yes, indeed,' I said.

'It is tremendous, Isherwood. Tremendous. I tell you, this has been a revelation to me – of what can be done with these people. In all my experience, I should not have believed it possible. You know my secret? I have discovered how to treat them!'

'And how do you treat them?'

'You see, these men are accustomed to rule an empire. To be obeyed. They are educated to believe in discipline. They do not understand a mere request. They ignore it. They despise it. But they can understand an order!'

'An order?' I laughed. 'That doesn't sound very easy.'

'It *is* easy!' His dark eyes flashed superbly. 'At first, I made many mistakes. I wrote letters, very polite: "Could you please spare me one hundred pounds?" No answer. Then I got impatient, angry. I telegraphed: "Send me one thousand." And I received it immediately. Immediately! By return of post!'

He was as delighted as a child. I nodded encouragingly, being careful not to smile.

'Yes, it is easy ... But when one sees what could be done in this country – what one man with the absolute determination could achieve ... I think to myself: Suppose this power were to be used for evil? For destruction? Seriously, Isherwood, there are moments when I feel frightened!'

But he did not look frightened. Standing there, under the street lamp, he seemed positively drunk with triumph – the fine nostrils were dilated, the lips curved in an imperial smile. His vanity was not ridiculous. He wore it superbly. It became him, like a brilliant jewel.

We were interrupted by the girl's return. I had expected her to come back empty-handed; but, to my astonishment, she was carrying a large white chrysanthemum. Goodness knows where, at that late hour, she had found, stolen or bought it. He accepted it as a matter of course, thanking her merely with a small gracious nod. Then, clasping my hand, he told me: 'It was a great pleasure, Isherwood. We shall meet again soon. I have something I wish to discuss with you – you will be able to help me, I think. Good-bye.'

Holding the flower like a sceptre, attended by the dark-haired girl, he turned and entered the Café.

I must confess that, after this, I began to avoid him. During the weeks which followed I heard several complaints from my friends of the tasks he had contrived to set them – one was ordered to produce letters of introduction, another to use his influence with an important uncle, a third had to translate an entire blank-verse play. He found uses for everybody, even the humblest. And no one had ventured to refuse. I knew, only too well, that I should not have the moral courage to refuse him myself – and I was extremely busy just then. So I kept away from parties at which I knew he would be present. When, two or three times, he rang me up, he was always told that I was out.

But there was no escaping him for long. One afternoon he caught me, drinking coffee with a publisher, amidst the biscuit-coloured columns and immemorially ancient leather sofas of a Pall Mall club. He sat down at once, un-invited, at our table, and mildly scandalized the waiter by asking for a cream bun: 'My task here is almost finished,' he told us. 'Next week I shall sail for the United States.'

In his hand was an oddly-shaped brown paper parcel. He unwrapped it slowly, with great deliberation, glancing up at our faces to enjoy the suspense he was dramatically creating: 'The man who gave me this has a little shop in the Tottenham Court Road. I have been in to see him once or twice . Today, he said to me: "I have read about your work in the newspapers. I wish you to take this as a present from me." Wasn't it a charming thought?'

The paper fell back. Before us stood a small bronze bust of Goethe. Neither the publisher nor myself found any suitable comment.

'Was it not charming?' he insisted delightedly. 'This poor shopkeeper – he wished to give me some token of his appreciation for what I had done. And, mind you, he was not a foreigner, like myself. He was an Englishman. Just an ordinary Englishman.'

His mood changed. He became thoughtful, preoccu-pied. He turned the bust slowly, with his long, delicately moulded fingers:

'Goethe ...' he mused, 'if he had lived today – would he have been on our side? Would he have been reliable?' He looked up at us suddenly, shook his head: 'I am afraid not.'

After a suitable pause, the publisher asked him if he would have some more coffee.

'No thank you. No.' He rose at once to his feet, cram-ming the bust and its paper into his pocket. 'I am late already.' He bowed hastily, and strode down the corridor. At the corner, he stopped – stationing himself in the shadows of the Library entrance, like an assassin. From this position he called to us, with mock-conspiratorial gaiety: 'I am waiting for the Archbishop!'

I thought I could slip away quietly, but I was wrong. Just as I had reached the foot of the staircase he called after me: 'Isherwood! One moment!' I started guiltily at the sound of my name.

'Isherwood, you must do me a great kindness. Next Tuesday I embark on the *Normandie*. While I am on board, I wish to receive a cablegram, signed by six famous writers, appealing to President Roosevelt to use his influence to help me on my mission. ... There must be at least six names – all world-famous. You understand?'

Yes, I understood. As I left the Club, I sighed deeply.

It was in New York that we met again – for the fourth and last time. Six months had passed. The Spanish Civil war was over. The dictators, in the hour of their triumph, were uttering new threats. On a beautiful cold spring afternoon I crossed Central Park to the hotel at which he was staying.

He opened the door to me himself. To my surprise, I found him quite alone:

'You must please excuse all this untidiness,' he told me. 'If I had known that you were coming I would have made some preparations.'

Even as we sat down, I was struck by the change in his appearance, and in his manner. He looked older, yellower, thinner. The black eyes were sombre, and almost gentle. And his pleasure at my visit was quite touching:

'How are you, my friend? What have you been doing? Please tell me some news of England.'

I told him everything I could think of. I did all the talking. He listened attentively, smoking one cigarette after another. I noticed that his hands trembled a little, as he lit them. At length, I asked:

'But what about your work?'

The eyes did not brighten, as I had expected. Instead, he shrugged his shoulders slightly:

'It is accomplished. The funds have been raised. We were successful.'

'I'm very glad.'

'There were difficulties, of course. . . . When I landed in New York I had hoped to make great publicity for the scheme, to give interviews to the Press. . . . But I was unlucky. Not one single journalist came to my cabin. Not one. And do you know why? They were all crowding around a foreign film actress, and a dwarf!'

'A dwarf?'

'Yes. This dwarf, it seems, was particularly important, because of his extremely small size. He was more interesting to the reporters than all the thousands of my unhappy countrymen.'

His disdainful smile, as he said this, had something of its old magnificence. But only for an instant. His face darkened again, into moody silence.

'And what are you doing now?' I asked him.

Once more, he shrugged his shoulders.

'I am here. As you see.'

'Shall you stay long?'

'Who knows?' he sighed. 'At the present, my plans are very uncertain.' Glancing round the hotel bedroom, so large and luxurious and unfriendly, and at his three scarred, shabby suitcases standing in the corner, I realized, with a slight shock, that he, who had successfully demanded so many thousands of dollars, was probably short of money. Perhaps he could not even pay his bill. He seemed to know what I was thinking, for he smiled, sadly and gently, as he walked across to the window.

'You know,' he told me, 'I long very greatly to return to Europe.'

'You don't like it here?'

'I hate it.' He said this quietly, quite without passion, stating a simple fact.

'Look,' he pointed. 'Over there is the Zoological Garden. You have seen the sea-lions?'

'Yes. I've seen them.'

'When I am lying in bed at night, I can hear them. And sometimes it seems to me that they are angry, that they are crying aloud to demand the destruction of this city.'

I laughed. We both looked out, at the white shafts of the skyscrapers, splendid in the pale sunshine, along the edge of the park.

I told him: 'A friend of mine calls them The Fallen Angels.'

'The Fallen Angels? Good. Very good. ...' I could watch his mind playing with the idea. 'One might write something ...' he began. Then he checked himself, paused; said, with sudden decision: 'Isherwood, you must write about this town. You must write a great drama, or a novel.'

It was a command – one of his many commands. But I could not accept it meekly: 'Why don't you', I suggested, 'write that novel yourself?'

He shook his head – and the finality of this refusal was the last memory of him which I was to carry away with me. 'No, Isherwood. No. I shall never write about this country. I have come here too late.'

Virginia Woolf

VIRGINIA WOOLF is dead – and thousands of people, far outside the immediate circle of her friends and colleagues, will be sorry, will feel the loss of a great and original talent to our literature. For she was famous, surprisingly famous when one considers that she was what is called 'a writer's writer'. Her genius was intensely feminine and personal – private, almost. To read one of her books was (if you liked it) to receive a letter from her, addressed specially to you. But this, perhaps, was just the secret of her appeal.

As everybody knows, Mrs Woolf was a prominent member of what journalists used to call 'The Bloomsbury Group' – which included Lytton Strachey, Vanessa Bell, Duncan Grant, E. M. Forster, Arthur Waley, Desmond MacCarthy and Maynard Keynes. Actually, the 'Group' was not a group at all, in the self-conscious sense, but a kind of clan; one of those 'natural' families which form themselves without the assistance of parents, uncles and aunts, simply because a few sensitive and imaginative people become aware of belonging to each other, and wish to be frequently in each other's company. It follows, of course, that these brothers and sisters under the skin find it convenient to settle in the same neighbourhood – Bloomsbury, in this case. It is a district just behind and beyond the British Museum. Its three large squares, Gordon, Bedford and Tavistock, have something of the dignity and atmosphere of Cambridge college courts.

Open *To the Lighthouse*, *The Common Reader*, or *The Waves*, read a couple of pages with appreciation, and you have become already a distant relative of the Bloomsbury Family. You can enter the inner sanctum, the Woolf drawing-room, and nobody will rise to greet you – for you are one of the party. 'Oh, come in,' says Virginia, with that gracious informality which is so inimitably aristocratic, 'you know everybody, don't you? We were just talking about Charles Tansley ... poor Charles – such a prig ... Imagine what he said the other day ...' And so, scarcely aware, we float into our story.

The Bloomsbury Family held together by consanguinity of talent. That you could express yourself artistically, through the medium of writing, or painting, or music, was taken for granted. This was the real business of life: it would have been indecent, almost, to refer to it. Artistic integrity was the family religion; and in its best days it could proudly boast that it did not harbour a single prostitute, pot-boiler or hack. Nevertheless one must live. Some of the brothers and sisters had very odd hobbies. Keynes, for example, whose brilliant descriptive pen could touch in an unforgettable and merciless portrait of Clemenceau on the margin, as it were, of an economic report to the Versailles treaty-makers – Keynes actually descended into that sordid jungle, the City, and emerged a wealthy man! And Virginia – the exquisite, cloistered Virginia – became a publisher. True, the thing happened by gradual stages. It began as a sort of William Morris handicraft – with Leonard and Virginia working their own press, and Virginia's delicate fingers, one supposes, getting black with printer's ink. But all this was ancient history, and the hand-press was stowed away in the cellar under dust-sheets before the day in the early thirties when I first walked timidly up the steps of the house in Tavistock Square.

It is usually easy to describe strangers. Yet, although I didn't meet Virginia more than half a dozen times, I find it nearly impossible to write anything about her which will carry the breath of life. Which century did she belong to? Which generation? You could not tell: she simply defied analysis. At the time of our first meeting, she was, I now realize, an elderly lady, yet she seemed, in some mysterious way, to be very much older and very much younger than her age. I could never decide whether she reminded me of my grandmother as a young Victorian girl, or my great-grandmother – if she had taken some rejuvenating drug and lived a hundred and twenty years, to become the brilliant leader of an intensely modern Georgian *salon*.

One remembers, first of all, those wonderful, forlorn eyes; the slim, erect, high-shouldered figure, strangely tense, as if always on the alert for some distant sound; the hair folded back from the eggshell fragility of the temples; the small, beautifully-cut face, like a Tennysonian cameo – Mariana, or The Lady of Shalott. Yes, that is the impression one would like to convey – an unhappy, high-born lady in a ballad, a fairy-story princess under a spell, slightly remote from the rest of us, a profile seen against the dying light, hands dropped helplessly in the lap, a shocking, momentary glimpse of intense grief.

What rubbish! We are at the tea table. Virginia is sparkling with gaiety, delicate malice and gossip – the gossip which is the style of her books and which made her the best hostess in London; listening to her, we missed appointments, forgot love affairs, stayed on and on into the small hours, when we had to be hinted, gently, but firmly, out of the house. This time, the guest of honour is a famous novelist, whose substantial income proves that Art, after all, can really pay. He is modest enough – but Virginia, with sadistic curiosity, which is like the teasing of an elder sister, drags it all out of him: how much time New York publishers gave, how much the movie people, and what the King said, and the Crown Prince of Sweden – she has no mercy. And then, when it is all over, 'You know, Jeremy,' she tells him, smiling almost tenderly, 'you remind me of a very beautiful prize-winning cow. ...' 'A cow, Virginia . . . ?' The novelist gulps but grins bravely at me; determined to show he can take it. 'Yes ... a very, very fine cow. You go out into the world, and win all sorts of prizes, but gradually your coat gets covered with burrs, and so you have to come back again into your field. And in the middle of the field is a rough old stone post, and you rub yourself against it to get the burrs off. Don't you think, Leonard ...' she looks across at her husband, 'that that's our real mission in life? We're Jeremy's old stone scratching-post.'

What else is there to say about her? Critics will place her among the four greatest English women writers. Friends will remember her beauty, her uniqueness, her charm. I am very proud to have known her. Was she the bewitched princess, or the wicked little girl at the tea party – or both, or neither? I can't tell. In any case she was, as the Spaniards say, 'very rare', and this world was no place for her. I am happy to think that she is free of it, before everything she loved has been quite smashed. If I wanted an epitaph for her, taken from her own writings, I should choose this:

'It was done; it was finished. Yes, she thought, laying down her brush in extreme fatigue, I have had my vision.'

Klaus Mann

IT is very easy to picture him as he was. I see him entering a crowded room, eagerly, with a vague, pleased air. He looks around him curiously, without haste, taking in the furniture and the faces. Recognizing some of them, his pleasure becomes focused and personal. He advances, greets his friends simply and warmly, and is introduced to strangers, accepting them courteously at their surface-value. He seems quite without vanity or self-consciousness. Neither frigid nor gushing, he has a certain quiet reserve, a touch of old-world politeness which holds him back from our empty modern familiarity. I cannot imagine him saying 'Very happy to know you' – yet perhaps he really *is* happy – much happier, certainly, than most of the people who say it. For it comes naturally to him to like human beings. He approaches them with sympathy and lively interest.

Soon he is talking rapidly, fluently. He moves his head quickly, tilting it from side to side like a bird, and frowning nervously whenever he cannot exactly express himself. Birdlike, he seems to be balancing upon the truth, as if upon a slender, unsteady twig. He is so anxious to say *precisely* what he means. He takes all conversation earnestly, no matter if the topic is light or serious, but always with ease and flexibility. He never lectures you. He listens, answers, discusses. His great charm lay in this openness, this eager, unaffected approach. His quiet, intimate laughter enlivened even the gloomiest subjects. For Klaus never had to pretend to be serious, to pull a long face, like a hypocrite in church. He *was* serious. He

minded deeply, he cared passionately, about the tragedies
and the great issues of his time – and he took it for
granted that *you* cared, too. I do not think I ever heard
him utter an insincere remark. Insincerity is a form of
laziness, and he was one of the least lazy people I have
known.

I suppose that, to outsiders, his life may have seemed
comparatively enviable. From his earliest days, he had inhabited the circles of the brilliant and the famous. He
had experienced pleasure and success at an age when one
is best able to enjoy them. He had travelled widely and
continuously – so much so that the huge upheaval of the
Emigration seemed, as far as he was concerned, to be no
more than an extension of his normal way of living. He
was always on the move, in and out of hotel bedrooms,
just having arrived, just about to leave, beset by telephone
calls, full of appointments. And he was always busy. The
whole continuity of his existence was in his work. How I
envied him that! I remember once asking him – it was in
Copenhagen, I think – what he was writing. He laughed,
made a little grimace. 'Oh – a pre-war novel.' This was
in 1934. The joke was so typical of him, of his sane pessimism, and of his courage. Klaus's courage was of the most
valuable kind – the kind which is shown in confronting
the circumstances of everyday life. It is, by its very nature,
unspectacular, anti-heroic. It does not demand great
crises of action and danger, though it can face them,
too. It shines most brightly in the midst of weariness,
boredom, ill-health and loneliness. It refuses to
despair.

During the last sixteen years of his life, Klaus produced
a really impressive body of work – novels, non-fiction
books and innumerable articles – under circumstances
which would have reduced most writers to impotent
silence; he played an active part in the propaganda war
against the Nazis; he learnt to write and speak a new language almost perfectly; he served in the American Army.
All this he did without complaint, without boasting, with

charm and humour. Indeed, he made his whole incredible achievement seem natural and easy. It was not.

His character had a dark underside of melancholy, seldom shown to others. He felt, with an extraordinary intensity, the sadness and cruelty of life, the coldness of the insensitive, the triviality of pseudo-optimists, the pain and nuisance of growing older. He respected, but could not bring himself to share in, the consolations of religious belief. The consolations of blind political hatred – such as they are – were also denied him: he fought injustice unwaveringly, but without hysteria. He must often have been bitterly lonely, despite his many friends and the affection of his large, closely-knit family. A wanderer himself, he was temperamentally drawn to other wanderers, the confused, the lost, the astray. I believe that he helped many of them, but they could give him little in return. He found no permanent companion on his journey.

Now he is gone. And I – like others, perhaps – feel guilty. I know now that I took him too much for granted, because he was so self-reliant, so strong. We are all of us ready with our sympathy and support for the charming failures, the amiable misfits, the cowards and the weak. I forgot, as most of us forget, that the brave need reassurance, too. It is not enough simply to love them; they need the expression of our love.

His death is our great loss – the loss of a dear friend and fellow-worker, and of a fine artist whose powers were still growing. And yet I cannot think of it as a mere disaster, altogether meaningless and tragic. Klaus had fought and worked so hard, achieved so much, inspired so many people by his example. In forty years he had suffered and experienced enough for a long lifetime. No wonder if he grew utterly weary. He had certainly earned the right to take his rest.

PLACES

Escales (I'm afraid I must have been responsible for this repulsively modish title) is a magazine article concocted from bits of the diary which Auden and I took turns at keeping during our Chinese journey. It is thus a collaboration and was published under both our signatures in *Harper's Bazaar*, in October 1938.

The narrative section of *Journey to a War* begins with our departure from Hong Kong for Canton, on 28 February 1938. But we had started keeping our diary more than a month earlier, when we sailed from Marseille on the French liner *Aramis*.

While we were on board, we worked together on our play, *On the Frontier*. Auden wrote several of the poems which are included in *Journey to a War*. (In this article there are echoes of his poem, *The Voyage*, and of his sonnet on the Sphinx.) We also drank with our fellow-passengers and later noted down specimens of their table-talk in our diary. For example:

'I'm not a planter, I'm a parasite – and, like all ticks, I've grown fat.'

'Rubber's nothing but a bloody weed. You fellows waste your time manicuring the trees.'

'Here's a snap of Tiny Tim – best chap east of Suez. This is Doc Wilson. Best tennis player west of Penang.'

'The English won't leave India as long as there's a virgin or a rupee left.'

'When I was home on leave this time, I decided to make a whole new set of friends, and I did. Next time I go back I shall make another new lot. You can't pick up old friendships.'

'These bloody directors come out here on tours of inspection. . . . There's three things that are no good to anyone – a man's breasts, a priest's balls, and a vote of thanks from the London office to the staff in the East.'

In the article, we don't mention our drive up to Kandy, during the stopover at Colombo. Our chauffeur was more than usually reckless, and his car had practically no brakes. On the way back, tearing through a tropical rainstorm, we hit a boy and knocked him down in the middle of a crowded village street. He was not seriously hurt. A Ceylonese police officer interviewed us. He referred to the villagers as 'natives' and seemed in every respect a truly sinister imitation English sahib; which muddled our feelings of racial guilt. The officer tried to get us to say that the accident had been the fault of the boy who was hit. We denied this, but he paid no attention. While we were talking to him, Auden's camera was stolen out of the car. Months later the officer mailed it to Auden's home address in England. We wondered uneasily just what he had done to 'the natives' in order to get it back.

In Cairo we had bought a batch of sex-postcards. I don't exactly know why. The pictures were yellow, dim, out of focus and altogether unstimulating. Shortly before we reached Hong Kong we began to be afraid that the customs officers would find them. We threw one of them out of the porthole, but this seemed too simple. So Auden suggested that we should scatter them from the stern of the ship; they would look pretty, he said, floating away over the water like butterflies.

Unfortunately there was a following breeze. One of the postcards blew back towards us. Craning over the rail, we saw that it had landed, face upward, on the deck below. I hurried downstairs to recover it and found myself confronted by a dozen sailors, sitting round a table, eating supper. The postcard lay only a yard or two from where they sat. I allowed them enough time to finish their meal and then returned. The postcard was gone.

I wrote this description of my first return visit from the States to England while I was there still, in 1947. Ten years later, John Lehmann wanted a contribution to his *Coming to London* series, so I rewrote it for him. Only after the book had been published did I realize that it was planned as a collection of reminiscences of one's first encounter with the London literary world. I was quite out of step with the other contributors.

The reunion with my old friends at Lehmann's house, to which I refer, was actually one of the most moving experiences of my life. I could convey the inwardness of it much better in a novel. You enter the room and there they all are. There is a moment of dreamlike unreality. Then constraint and uneasy politeness. Then the tremendous, poignant shock of recognition. Here am I, here is X. For eight years I have been living as a ghost in his memory, and he as a ghost in mine. Now, suddenly, we have to accept each other as live people, separate people who have been alive and changing, all this long while. Can we ever catch up with each other again?

In this article I feel I have conveyed only the uneasy politeness. I have cut out its last three paragraphs; they sound like a formal thank-you letter.

I should add that I have been back to England six times since then, and that my uneasiness has altogether disappeared.

Los Angeles was written for Cyril Connolly to put in his double number of *Horizon*, called *Art on the American Horizon*, October 1947. Connolly had revisited America the previous year and had written, of California, 'those who have loved the Mediterranean will not be reconciled here'.

California is always getting bad notices, from Easterners no less than from non-Americans. When their criticisms seem to be justified, those of us who love her better than the Mediterranean are torn between agreement and resentment. We are willing to admit that, in some respects, the place is not only awful but getting worse. But woe unto any outsider who dares to say so!

Both of my articles are already out of date, for Los Angeles is changing very fast. The city is being suffocated by its population. The old sleepy valley of farmlands is already a suburban wilderness, the wild hills are domesticated. The glamorous dilapidation which I describe in *The Shore* (insipidly titled *California Story* by the editors of *Harper's Bazaar* when they published it in 1952) is being tidied up, year by year. They have torn down the holy places; the mansion of Marion Davies, the St Mark's where Bernhardt once stayed, the hotel where Tennessee Williams wrote *The Glass Menagerie*. The broadwalk is respectable now. The amusement pier has been rebuilt. And they plan to construct a causeway to carry traffic clear out across the Bay. If they do, Santa Monica Canyon, my dear home, will become a yacht harbour, its water full of oil and sodden newspapers, its waves broken.

Escales

THIS ship is like a hospital. Miles from land, home, love, sanity, we lie limp in our deck chairs, gazing out dully across a sea which is as boring and hopeless as an incurable spinal disease. The nurses are very attentive. All the meals are at unnatural invalid hours.

Beneath our conversation, our eating, our thoughts, the engines throb, deep down, like a fever. This voyage is our illness. As the long days pass, we grow peevish, apathetic, sullen; we no longer expect, or even wish, to recover. Only at moments, when a dolphin leaps or the big real birds from sunken Africa veer round our squat white funnels, we sigh and wince, our bodies gripped by the exquisitely painful pangs of hope. Maybe, after all, we are going to get well; we are going to arrive. ... But the relapse is immediate and violent. We shuffle off to the bar for our evening medicine: brandy and ginger ale.

We wake to the immediate sense of a changed vibration: the ship is beating through shallow, sandy water. Port Said glitters up over the horizon into the oblique sunshine. The water-front houses, from the distance, are like a denture of brilliant teeth, waiting to devour the traveller. But the teeth, on closer inspection, are not so brilliant after all: their backs are revoltingly dirty, many are decaying, several are false. Long before we have berthed, the deck is swarming with carpet-sellers, fountain-pen merchants, touts for dancing halls and hotels. Conjurers produce chickens from empty cups. A pickpocket steals a pair of spectacles. Everybody gesticulates and screams.

We hire a car and drive to Cairo. The Delta country is as flat as Holland. Strings of Arabs, gaudily robed, with shambling camels, wander along the edges of the waterways, looking as incongruous as extras who have lost their way to the location of a Biblical film. In the middle distance are herons, bulrushes, flat-topped hovels roofed with straw and mud – and, in glimpses beyond, the desert, a slow-heaving, silvery grey ocean, obscurely reflecting the sky.

CAIRO: that immense and sinister Woolworth's, where everything is for sale – love, lottery tickets, clothes hangers, honour, justice, indecent postcards, bootlaces, disease – as much and as cheap as you like, till the buyer goes mad with boredom and guilt. And behind it, at the end of a tram-ride, the three Pyramids, looking ugly and quite new, like the tip-heaps of a prosperous quarry. For a long time we could not find the Sphinx at all. Stumbling over the litter of recent excavations, we came upon it suddenly, smaller than its photographs, in a pit. There it lies, in the utter silence of its mortal injuries; the flat cruel face of a scarred and blinded baboon, face of a circus monstrosity, no longer a statue but a living, changing creature of stone. A camera, if cameras had been invented, could have shown how that face has changed through the centuries, growing old and blind and terrible in the blaze of the sun, under the lash of the wind and the desert sand. Once, no doubt, it was beautiful. Long ago, it could see.

Now it lies there mutilated and sightless, its paws clumsily bandaged with bricks, its mane like an old actor's wig, asking no riddle, turning its back upon America – injured baboon with a lion's cruel mouth, in the middle of invaded Egypt.

DJIBOUTI: Brown emery-paper mountains heaped with thunder clouds in the background of the gulf, and a flat foreshore where a few buildings stand, very distinct and defiant in the glare, as though Life had established itself here, step by step, cell by cell, in face of superhuman difficulties, and might not be able to hold the position. A wireless station, a group of salt stacks like conical white tents, three petroleum tanks, some Arab dhows stranded in the cracked tidal mud – and always the wheeling sea hawks, which seem to the traveller to be screaming unintelligible, nostalgic news of home.

This is an outpost, a self-contained world where you could spend your life, and marry and take to drink and drugs and die – *une vie.* 'People really live here,' was our first amazed thought; and here were the people, approaching us in launches steered by tall stork-like Negroes in scarlet and orange turbans, with the tricolor trailing exhausted at the stern. All the characters of Somerset Maugham translated into French – the shrivelled but still elegant woman of thirty-five who is the mistress of an eighteen-year-old boy in spotless ducks ... and her husband, a hateful, red-faced, furry-eared brute in canvas shorts, who knows about it all, and drinks Pernod and doesn't care. Last, terrible in white and gold, comes General X. Like every French officer of high rank, he has the air of being invisibly crippled: one arm is tucked woodenly into his breast. He gives a curt, stiff salute – his face absolutely expressionless, his eyes and little moustache quite dead – and climbs the staircase to the first-class smoking room, almost unnoticed, like a plague.

The natives of Djibouti are really black, with a soft nocturnal blackness; their legs and forearms, emerging from snowy white robes, are like fragments of another element, pieces of midnight – your eyes seem to penetrate the outer surface, to gaze into their very depths. They walk superbly – approaching you from a distance across the dusty fields like the proud but courteous envoys of a great kingdom, attended by an obsequious camel or a herd of evil-eyed white goats.

In a hut near the camel market, our guide told us, it was possible to see the Belly Dance. Would we care to go there? We agreed, of course; for this, surely, would be the real thing, rank and hot from the bowels of Africa, and not to be compared with the miserable wriggling and posturing we had seen already in Brussels, Paris and Berlin. Our guide opened the door in a high wicker fence and led us into what looked like a small chicken run. He clapped his hands, and a dozen girls came running across the street, laughing and stumbling, in their huge flowered skirts. We must choose three, the guide said. They stood giggling in a row: the ones who had not been chosen ran off immediately, very gay, not seeming in the least offended.

Then the bargaining began. *Trois cent? Deux cent cinquante?* No, we said; ridiculous! We moved towards the door. The Negresses flung themselves against it, laughing riotously. *Cinquante*, we said. *Non, soixante! Non, non, cinquante! Soixante! Cinquante! Soixante! Non! Oui! Non!* But, already, they were scrambling out of their clothes. Stark naked, with their nozzle breasts which look as if they were made to unscrew, their drum bellies and absurd little legs, they suddenly appeared much younger, mere children. Facing each other, they started to clap hands, like children playing pat-a-cake, stamping the earth with their heels and chanting in high gay wailing voices. But hardly had they executed a dozen steps before one of them shouted: *Soixante!* and they all laughed, as if at a dirty, forbidden joke. The clapping and stamping continued: *Soixante!* More clapping and laughter. *Soixante! Cinquante!* we cried. *Non, soixante!*

It was plain that none of them had the faintest notion how to do the Belly Dance, or, indeed, any kind of dance whatsoever. Getting tired of the shouting and stamping, they decided to try the effect of a little romance. They tried to persuade us to sit down on a couple of upturned buckets – with the air of sirens who invite you to relax upon a voluptuous divan littered with rose petals; we were so weak with laughing that we could no longer even speak. *Soixante?* they pleaded once more, but already they were losing interest – for bargaining, like dancing and love, was only another children's game. Quite suddenly, the game was over; they dived into their clothes, took our fifty-franc note, giggled and let us out.

COLOMBO: The shabby white buildings of an abandoned international exhibition. On the breakwater an immense neon sign: 'Ceylon for Good Tea.' Groves of weary palm trees, like damp mops. The air is warm and stale.

The centre of the town is drab and clean and English, with macadams, red pillar boxes, traffic signals, gasoline stations and punctual buses. And the Singhalese officials, wearing their clipped moustaches and correct tropical drill suits, are marvellously disguised as British empire-builders. But the suburbs are gay and crowded – the superb, brittle torsos of slim, laughing natives jostle aimlessly down ramshackle lanes of shops crammed with all the gaudy, eye-catching trash of the East. Beyond the town, the countryside – despite the banana groves, the rubber plantations, the turquoise or scarlet flash of outrageous blossoms – reminded us strangely of the Thames Valley. It is as if, in the night of some freak summer, Kew Gardens had broken loose, pouring its grosser vegetation over the southern counties, strangling England's trees and grasses, scaring her shy weak flowers into terrified obscurity. Here and there, exotic shrubs on the lawns of old manor houses or country rectories have joined the insurrection, established local revolutionary committees.

Next morning, human beings look out of their foliage-darkened windows to find that their race dominance is over: the dictatorship of the plants is secure from Yarmouth to Torquay. Yes, in this country blood is inferior to chlorophyl, and all men, white or brown, are slaves, working their lives away in the dank stench of an all-powerful vegetable kingdom.

One of our fellow passengers is a beautiful Parisian girl, travelling out to rejoin her husband, a planter in French Indo-China. This morning, as we reached the mouth of the river, and the pilot came on board with the mail, she had news that he was lying in a hospital, seriously injured in a motor smash, two days ago. We know that this is a lie: he is already dead. The news has spread all over the second class.

We are all watching her, covertly, as the ship enters Saigon harbour. She must guess the truth already, from our glances and whispers; even her best friends avoid her, like an infectious disease. She paces the deck in an agony of impatience, her eyes brilliant with tears. Now and again she takes the binoculars from a passenger's hand, without a word of thanks or apology, and focuses them on the shore.

It is through her eyes that we take our first impression of the town. The huge brown kites do not care, they circle ceaselessly over the wide muddy river, swooping sometimes as if to snatch the round straw hats from the heads of coolies in the sampans. The crew of a British tramp steamer are chipping paint with brutally indifferent hammers. The crowd on the quay, waving and laughing, in their light clothes, shout gleefully to friends on board: 'How's mother?' 'Well.' 'How's father?' 'Splendid.' 'How's the family?' 'Oh, we're all fine.' They are mocking her, with their youth and health and joy. And the stolid façade of the waterfront – the big white hotel, the feathery trees, the warehouses, the French advertisements: how she will loathe them from this day onward! Perhaps the single word 'Job' will epitomize the whole sunlit scene – will afflict her with agony and nausea for the rest of her life.

Hong Kong harbour, in a chilly, drizzling fog. This might be Scotland, or the coast of Norway. Junks with patched, dragon-wing sails drift past, ancient and forlorn as wrecks fished from the bottom of the sea. A Japanese liner rests on her side in a rocky creek, beached by last autumn's record typhoon. The island towers up out of the mist, with Hong Kong at its foot – cruisers lie like watchdogs guarding the monumental banks, Queen Victoria's statue fixes China in a rigid stare; here, surely, is the ugliest city ever built upon the earth.

On the wharf two bored coolies are holding a banner: 'Welcome to the Islington Corinthians.' The members of the Hong Kong football team are waiting to receive their opponents. But where will they disembark? First the gangway is placed here, then there, then a hundred yards farther down; the banner follows it patiently, sagging in the middle. The football captain runs up and fusses and scolds; it is straightened, just in time. The team utters a dutiful cheer.

On this island, boiled shirts and banks, a cenotaph, soda fountains, American movies and English tea; over there, beyond the streaky ochre mountains, somewhere, a war. Not recovered, not even convalescent, we are routed out of our hospital into the uncomfortable, familiar world. After all, incredibly, we have arrived.

Coming to London

I DON'T remember exactly how or when I first came to London; it was probably while I was still a baby, on a visit to my grandmother. She had a flat at the lower end of Buckingham Street in the Adelphi, overlooking the old watergate, and for many years this seemed to me to be the very hub of the city. On entering, you breathed in the fine dust of potpourri and the musk of my grandmother's furs: the odour was like an incense offered before the divinity of Sarah Bernhardt, whom she adored and constantly spoke of, and it came to evoke for me the whole magic of the theatre, past and present. At the same time, the watercolours and etchings on her sitting-room walls – of Venice, Granada, Avignon and the Panama Canal – quickened my earliest longings to travel and made me see London as a gateway to the world. Reclining in a deck-chair on the roof of this flat, during the first Great War, my grandmother liked to watch the daylight raids through her lorgnette. No doubt she described the enemy as 'odious creatures'; it was her favourite phrase of condemnation – and she was later to apply it, in the singular, to George Moore, as she tore from a copy of *The Brook Kerith* the pages she considered blasphemous. She kept the rest of the book, however, because she greatly admired his descriptions of the Holy Land. She was the grandest *grande dame* I have ever known.

As a young man I lived in London myself, and left it and came back to it often. But, of all these returns, I think that only one will remain with me vividly for the rest of my life. It is my return from the United States at the beginning of 1947. I had been away from England for eight years, almost to the day.

On 21 January, around noon, our plane took off from New York. It was nearly dark when we reached Newfoundland and circled over the snow-woods and the frozen lakes to Gander, a tiny sparkle of lights in the wilderness. Transatlantic air travel was somewhat more of an adventure in those days, and less elegantly conducted. The big bare white waiting-hall, with its table of simple refreshments, seemed very much a frontier-post; here were the last cup of coffee and the last bun in the Western Hemisphere.

I did not sleep at all that night. Not because I was unduly nervous; it was rather a kind of awe that kept me awake. If you are old enough, as I am, to remember Blériot – not to mention Lindbergh – it seems incredible to find yourself actually flying the Atlantic. I sat at my little window with its doll's house curtains, vibrating with the changing rhythms of the aircraft and peering out for glimpses of the stars. Fragments of ice, dislodged from the wings, kept rattling against the pane. The cabin was dark, except for a few pin-rays of light from overhead reading lamps. Although all the seats around me were occupied, I felt curiously alone – for the journey I was making was back through time rather than forward through space, and it concerned no one on board except myself.

And then – in palest saffron, in pink, in scarlet, in stabbing gold – the sunrise. It gleamed dully on our wet metal and on the cloudfield below us, which was blue-grey like dirty snow. We were flying over an arctic aerial landscape; weirdly solid, with terraces, erosions, valleys and great rounded rugged hills. The roar of our engines, which had been so loud through the night, now sank, or seemed to sink, to a soft hushing sigh. We were gradually coming lower. The plane skimmed the cloud-drifts like a motor boat, and you had a sudden terrific sense of speed and impact, as though it would surely be dashed to pieces. We raced over them, through them, with the thick vapour whirling back in shreds from our propellers, massing, towering above us, bursting upon us in furious silent breakers. Then, through a wide rift, we saw Ireland – a country of bogs and stony fields, green and mournful in the showery morning, crossed by the winding estuary of the Shannon.

A few miles up the Shannon is Limerick, where I had lived for three years, as a little boy, because my father was stationed there. In those days, it now seems to me, I accepted our unwelcomeness as a matter of course; it did not seem particularly shocking to me that children of my own age should spit and shout 'dirty Protestant!' as I walked down the street, or that my father's regiment should occasionally be sniped at from rooftops on its march to church.

And now the green and orange flag of independence fluttered over the airport hangars, and an announcement in Gaelic was coming through the loudspeakers as we entered the dining-room. But if the political situation had changed, the local atmosphere had not. I encountered, with happy recognition, the faded grandeur of velvet curtains and the breakfast of under-cooked, disembowelled sausage and strong but tepid tea. In a brogue as rich as a 'cello, my waiter described the terrible accident of a few weeks back – pointing, as he did so, to the fuselage of the wrecked plane which could still be seen sticking out of a bog beside the airfield. 'The minute I set eyes on them coming down – Mother of God, I said to myself, they're all lost entirely!' His charming, sympathetic eyes were moist and sparkling with enjoyment of his story.

And now, for the first time in my life, I began to feel American – or, at any rate, more American than European. Standing at the bar with a fellow passenger, a businessman from New Jersey, I watched the other travellers and suddenly found myself seeing them through his eyes. There was a group of tweedy fox-hunting ladies who did not look as if they were going anywhere in particular; they might well have stopped in here for a drink after a meet. There was a party of Italian emigrants who had been waiting twenty-four hours to take off for the States; when their plane was announced, they embraced each other and cheered. And there was Sir Somebody Someone, who appeared to be running the British Empire single-handed. He had crossed the Atlantic with us, and was now in an audible state of impatience because we were delayed by the weather and London's failure to 'open'. 'They're waiting for me in Whitehall,' he kept repeating. 'All I can say is, I intend to be in India on Monday.' I was afraid he might have sufficient authority to order our departure, regardless of the risk. But it seemed that he had not.

When we finally started it must have been near two o'clock in the afternoon. We climbed steeply into the clouds and saw no more land until the coast of the Bristol Channel. This was my first opportunity to compare bird's eye views of England and the States. What a contrast between the vast rectangular sections of the Middle West and the jigsaw pattern of this countryside! Even from the air, one gets a sense of the complexity of the past – of the Domesday Book. And of smallness. How small and vulnerable it all looks – wide open to the bitter east wind of history! The churches and the little towns, where three or four straggling roads converge as if expressly to lead a bomber to its target. The all-too-evident factories and landing strips. An eighteenth-century country house with a portico, standing out tiny but sharply distinct against a wood in which clearings have been cut to form the initials G. V. R. We flew quite low, beneath the overcast; and it was cosy, like a room in the winter light of tea-time. London appeared, a long smudge of brown haze, far ahead. The plane landed at Bovingdon Airport.

Here was the scenery of the war – but already it was falling into disuse. Weeds were growing from cracks in the concrete runways; the Army signposts and the camouflage on the hangars were weather-beaten and faded. Some Germans were strolling around with spades on their shoulders – no longer with the air of prisoners but of accepted inhabitants. And here were the representatives of officialdom; an elderly gentleman and a young lady doctor of birdlike cheerfulness, waiting to examine us and our belongings in a draughty hut with an iron stove. The lady doctor was sorry I had no certificate of vaccination, but remarked consolingly: 'Oh well, never mind – you've got a jolly good sunburn!' I told her that I had been swimming in the Pacific three days before. I could scarcely believe it myself.

Throughout the years I had spent in Hollywood, I had never tired of protesting against the American film presentation of English life. What caricature! What gross exaggeration! But now – and increasingly during the weeks that followed – I began to reverse my judgement. *Is* it possible to exaggerate the Englishness of England? Even the bus which took us from the airport into London seemed grotesquely 'in character'; one almost suspected that it had been expressly designed to amaze foreign visitors. By nature a single-decker, it had had a kind of greenhouse grafted insecurely on to its back. Riding in this was much more alarming than flying. We whizzed down narrow lanes with barely room enough to pass a pram, scraping with our sides the notorious English hedgerows; then slowed with a jerk to circle a roundabout – an Alice-in-Wonderland death trap guaranteed to wreck any driver doing more than five miles an hour. And then we would pass through an English village complete with a village church in a country churchyard; so absurdly authentic that it might have been lifted bodily off a movie-lot at M.G.M. ... And as for the accents that I now began to hear around me – I could scarcely trust my ears. Surely they were playing it *very* broad? Half of the population appeared to be talking like Richard Haydn as a Cockney bank clerk, the other half like Basil Rathbone as Sherlock Holmes.

I saw little of London that night, for I went straight to John Lehmann's house; and there a welcome awaited me that I shall never forget. Looking around me at the faces of my old friends, I discovered a happy paradox – namely that, while England seemed fascinatingly strange, my friends and our friendship seemed to be essentially what they had always been, despite the long separation. That was what was to make my visit so wonderful and memorable.

During my re-exploration of London, I got two strong impressions; of shabbiness and of goodwill. The Londoners themselves were shabby – many of them staring lovingly at my new overcoat – and their faces were still wartime faces, lined and tired. But they did not seem depressed or sullen. This may sound like a stupidly sweeping statement by a casual visitor; but I have seen a thoroughly depressed nation – the German in 1932. The English were not in the least like that. For instance, the girls at the ration board, which surely must have been the most exasperating of jobs, were gratuitously pleasant. 'It seems so silly,' one of them remarked to me, 'to have to call Americans *aliens*.' And this was not just a chance encounter with a solitary xenophile, for I heard another girl being extremely sympathetic to a native lady with an obviously unreasonable grievance. On another occasion, when I was on a train, a young couple sat next to me who were about to emigrate to Australia; their baggage, already labelled for the voyage, proclaimed this fact. The other passengers in my compartment congratulated the couple on their decision and questioned them eagerly about their plans – all this without the slightest hint of bitterness or criticism. Of course, this goodwill was somewhat of the grin-and-bear-it variety which is produced by national emergencies; but it had certainly made London a much friendlier place for a stranger to visit. The only negative aspect of it was, perhaps, that the English had become a little too docile in their attitude towards official regulations. 'We're a nation of queue-formers,' someone said. I experienced the truth of this for myself, one afternoon, when I went to a cinema, found that the film I wanted to see had five minutes left to run, and decided to wait outside till it was over. When next I turned my head I saw that a line of half a dozen people had grown behind me.

London's shabbiness was another matter; it did not seem to me to have a cheerful side. The actual bomb damage gave you a series of sudden shocks – as when, one evening, I spent some time ringing the doorbell of a house, until I happened to look up through the fanlight and saw that the place was an empty shell, smashed wide open to the stars. Yet the shabbiness was more powerfully and continually depressing. Plaster was peeling from even the most formidable squares and crescents; hardly a building was freshly painted. In the Reform Club, the wallpaper was hanging down in tatters. The walls of the National Gallery showed big unfaded rectangles, where pictures had been removed and not yet rehung. Many once stylish restaurants were now reduced to drabness and even squalor. The shortage of materials made all but the most urgent repairs illegal. I heard some weird tales of builders who were smuggled into private homes in their Sunday suits as 'guests' and who did not emerge until their 'visit' – with much record-playing to drown the noise of hammering – was over. London's shabbiness was so sad, I thought, because it was unwilling – quite unlike the cheerful down-at-heel air of some minor Latin American capital. London remembered the past and was ashamed of its present appearance. Several Londoners I talked to at that time believed it would never recover. 'This is a dying city,' one of them told me.

Few of my English readers will need to be reminded that this was the winter of the coal shortage and the great blizzards. The snow started about a week after my arrival, and it soon assumed the aspect of an invading enemy. Soldiers turned out to fight it with flame-throwers. The newspapers spoke of it in quasi-military language: 'Scotland Isolated', 'England Cut in Half'. Even portions of London were captured; there was a night when no taxi-driver would take you north of Regent's Park. With coal strictly rationed, gas reduced to a blue ghost and electricity often cut off altogether, everybody in England was shivering. I remember how the actors played to nearly empty houses, heroically stripped down to their indoor clothes, while we their audience huddled together in a tight clump, muffled to the chins in overcoats, sweaters and scarves. I remember a chic lunch party composed of the intellectual *beau monde*, at which an animated discussion of existentialism was interrupted by one of the guests exclaiming piteously: 'Oh, I'm so *cold*!' Two or three of my friends said to me then: 'Believe us, this is worse than the war!' By which I understood them to mean that the situation could not, by any stretch of the imagination, be viewed as a challenge to self-sacrifice or an inspiration to patriotism; it was merely hell.

Los Angeles

IN order to get the worst possible first impression of Los Angeles one should arrive there by bus, preferably in summer and on a Saturday night. That is what I did, eight years ago, having crossed the country via Washington, New Orleans, El Pasa, Albuquerque and Flagstaff, Arizona. As we passed over the state-line at Needles (one of the hottest places, outside Arabia, in the world) a patriotic lady traveller started to sing 'California, here I come!' In America you can do this kind of thing unself-consciously on a long-distance bus: a good deal of the covered wagon atmosphere still exists. Nevertheless, the effect was macabre. For ahead of us stretched the untidy yellow desert, quivering in its furnace-glare, with, here and there, among the rocks at the roadside, the rusty skeleton of an abandoned automobile, modern counterpart of the pioneer's dead mule. We drove forward into the Unpromising Land.

Beyond the desert, the monster market-garden begins: thousands of acres of citrus-groves, vineyards, and flat fields planted with tomatoes and onions. The giant billboards reappear. The Coca Cola advertisement: 'Thirst ends here.' The girl telling her friend: 'He's tall, dark ... and owns a Ford V-8.' The little towns seem almost entirely built of advertisements. Take these away, you feel, and there would be scarcely anything left: only drugstores, filling-stations and unpainted shacks. And fruit: Himalayas of fruit. To the European immigrant, this rude abundance is nearly as depressing as the desolation of the wilderness. The imagination turns sulky. The eye refuses to look and the ear to listen.

Downtown Los Angeles is at present one of the most squalid places in the United States. Many of the buildings along Main Street are comparatively old but they have not aged gracefully. They are shabby and senile, like nasty old men. The stifling sidewalks are crowded with sailors and Mexicans, but there is none of the glamour of a port and none of the charm of a Mexican city. In twenty-five years this section will probably have been torn down and rebuilt; for Los Angeles is determined to become at all costs a metropolis. Today, it is still an uncoordinated expanse of townlets and suburbs, spreading wide and white over the sloping plain between the mountains and the Pacific Ocean. The Angeleno becomes accustomed to driving great distances in his car between his work, his entertainment and his home: eighty miles a day would not be very unusual. Most people have a car or the use of one. It is an essential, not a luxury, for the bus services are insufficient and there is no subway. I would scarcely know how to 'show' Los Angeles to a visitor. Perhaps the best plan would be to drive quite aimlessly, this way and that, following the wide streets of little stucco houses, gorgeous with flowering trees and bushes – jacaranda, oleander, mimosa and eucalyptus – beneath a technicolour sky. The houses are ranged along communal lawns, unfenced, staring into each other's bedroom windows, without even a pretence of privacy. Such are the homes of the most inquisitive nation in the world; a nation which demands, as its unquestioned right, the minutest details of the lives of its movie stars, politicians and other public men. There is nothing furtive or unfriendly about this American curiosity, but it can sometimes be merciless.

It should not be supposed, from what I have written above, that the architecture of Los Angeles is uniform or homogeneous. On the contrary, it is strongly, and now and then insanely, individualistic. Aside from all the conventional styles – Mexican, Spanish, French Château, English Tudor, American Colonial and Japanese – you will find

some truly startling freaks: a witch's cottage with nightmare gables and eaves almost touching the ground, an
Egyptian temple decorated with hieroglyphics, a miniature medieval castle with cannon on the battlements. Perhaps the influence of the movies is responsible for them.
Few of the buildings look permanent or entirely real. It is
rather as if a gang of carpenters might be expected to
arrive with a truck and dismantle them next morning.

North of Hollywood rises a small steep range of hills. In
the midst of the city, they are only half-inhabited; many
of their canyons are still choked with yuccas, poison oak
and miscellaneous scrub. You find rattlesnakes there and
deer and coyotes. At dusk, or in the first light of dawn,
the coyotes can be mistaken for dogs as they come trotting
along the trail in single file, and it is strange and discon-
certing to see them suddenly turn and plunge into the
undergrowth with the long, easy leap of the wild animal.
Geologically speaking, the Hollywood hills will not last
long. Their decomposed granite breaks off in chunks at a
kick and crumbles in your hand. Every year the seasonal
rains wash cartloads of it down into the valley.

In fact, the landscape, like Los Angeles itself, is tran-
sitional. Impermanence haunts the city, with its mush-
room industries – the aircraft perpetually becoming obso-
lete, the oil which must one day be exhausted, the movies
which fill America's theatres for six months and are forgotten. Many of its houses – especially the grander ones –
have a curiously disturbing atmosphere, a kind of psychological dankness which smells of anxiety, overdrafts, uneasy lust, whisky, divorce and lies. 'Go away,' a wretched
little ghost whispers from the closet, 'go away before it is
too late. I was vain. I was silly. They flattered me. I failed.
You will fail, too. Don't listen to their promises. Go away.
Now, at once.' But the new occupant seldom pays any
attention to such voices. Indeed he is deaf to them, just as
the pioneers were deaf to the ghosts of the goldfields. He is
quite sure that he knows how to handle himself. He will
make his pile; and he will know when to stop. No stupid

mistakes for *him*. No extravagance, no alimony, no legal
complications. ... And then the lawyer says: 'Never mind
all that small print: it doesn't mean a thing. All you
have to do is sign here.' And he signs.

California is a tragic country – like Palestine, like every
Promised Land. Its short history is a fever-chart of migra-
tions – the land rush, the gold rush, the oil rush, the
movie rush, the Okie fruit-picking rush, the wartime rush
to the aircraft factories – followed, in each instance, by
counter-migrations of the disappointed and unsuccessful,
moving sorrowfully homeward. You will find plenty of
people in the Middle West and in the East who are very
bitter against California in general and Los Angeles in
particular. They complain that the life there is heartless,
materialistic, selfish. But emigrants to Eldorado have
really no right to grumble. Most of us come to the Far
West with somewhat cynical intentions. Privately, we
hope to get something for nothing – or, at any rate, for
very little. Well, perhaps we shall. But if we don't, we
have no one to blame but ourselves.

The movie industry – to take the most obvious example
– is still very like a goldmining camp slowly and painfully
engaged in transforming itself into a respectable, ordered
community. Inevitably, the process is violent. The anarchy of the old days, with every man for himself and
winner take the jackpot, still exercises an insidious appeal.
It is not easy for the writer who earns 3,000 dollars a
week to make common cause with his colleague who only
gets 250. The original tycoons were not monsters; they
were merely adventurers, in the best and worst sense of
the word. They had risked everything and won – often
after an epic and ruthless struggle – and they thought
themselves entitled to every cent of their winnings. Their
attitude towards their employees, from stars down to stage-
hands, was possessive and paternalistic. Knowing nothing
about art and very little about technique, they did not
hesitate to interfere in every stage of film production –
blue-pencilling scripts, dictating casting, bothering direc-

tors and criticizing camera-angles. The spectre of the Box Office haunted them night and day. This was their own money, and they were madly afraid of losing it. 'There's nothing so cowardly', a producer once told me, 'as a million dollars.' The paternalist is a sentimentalist at heart, and the sentimentalist is always potentially cruel. When the studio operatives ceased to rely upon their bosses' benevolence and organized themselves into unions, the tycoon became an injured papa, hurt and enraged by their ingratitude. If the boys did not trust him – well, that was just too bad. He knew what was good for them, and to prove it he was ready to use strike-breakers and uniformed thugs masquerading as special police. But the epoch of the tycoons is now, happily, almost over. The financier of today has learnt that it pays better to give his artists and technicians a free hand, and to concentrate his own energies on the business he really understands; the promotion and distribution of the finished product. The formation of independent units within the major studios is making possible a much greater degree of co-operation between directors, writers, actors, composers and art-directors. Without being childishly optimistic, one can foresee a time when quite a large proportion of Hollywood's films will be entertainment fit for adults, and when men and women of talent will come to the movie colony not as absurdly overpaid secretaries resigned to humouring their employers but as responsible artists free and eager to do their best. Greed is, however, only one of two disintegrating forces which threaten the immigrant's character: the other, far more terrible, is sloth. Out there, in the eternal lazy morning of the Pacific, days slip away into months, months into years; the seasons are reduced to the faintest nuance by the great central fact of the sunshine; one might pass a lifetime, it seems, between two yawns, lying bronzed and naked on the sand. The trees keep their green, the flowers perpetually bloom, beautiful girls and superb boys ride the foaming breakers. They are not always the same boys, girls, flowers and trees; but that you scarcely notice. Age and death are very discreet there; they seem as improbable as the Japanese submarines which used to lurk up and down the coast during the war and sometimes sink ships within actual sight of the land. I need not describe the de luxe, parklike cemeteries which so hospitably invite you to the final act of relaxation: Aldous Huxley has done this classically already in *After Many a Summer*. But it is worth recalling one of their advertisements, in which a charming, well-groomed elderly lady (presumably risen from the dead) assured the public: 'It's better at Forest Lawn. *I speak from experience.*'

To live sanely in Los Angeles (or, I suppose, in any other large American city) you have to cultivate the art of staying awake. You must learn to resist (firmly but not tensely) the unceasing hypnotic suggestions of the radio, the billboards, the movies and the newspapers; those demon voices which are for ever whispering in your ear what you should desire, what you should fear, what you should wear and eat and drink and enjoy, what you should think and do and be. They have planned a life for you – from the cradle to the grave and beyond – which it would be easy, fatally easy, to accept. The least wandering of the attention, the least relaxation of your awareness, and already the eyelids begin to droop, the eyes grow vacant, the body starts to move in obedience to the hypnotist's command. Wake up, wake up – before you sign that seven-year contract, buy that house you don't really want, marry that girl you secretly despise. Don't reach for the whisky, that won't help you. You've got to think, to discriminate, to exercise your own free will and judgement. And you must do this, I repeat, without tension, quite rationally and calmly. For if you give way to fury against the hypnotists, if you smash the radio and tear the newspapers to shreds, you will only rush to the other extreme and fossilize into defiant eccentricity. Hollywood's two polar types are the cynically drunken writer aggressively nursing a ten-year-old reputation and the theatrically self-conscious hermit who strides the boulevard in sandals, home-made shorts and a prophetic beard, muttering against the Age of Machines.

An afternoon drive from Los Angeles will take you up into the high mountains, where eagles circle above the forests and the cold blue lakes, or out over the Mojave Desert, with its weird vegetation and immense vistas. Not very far away are Death Valley, and Yosemite, and the Sequoia Forest with its giant trees which were growing long before the Parthenon was built; they are the oldest living things in the world. One should visit such places often, and be conscious, in the midst of the city, of their surrounding presence. For this is the real nature of California and the secret of its fascination; this untamed, undomesticated, aloof, prehistoric landscape which relentlessly reminds the traveller of his human condition and the circumstances of his tenure upon the earth. 'You are perfectly welcome,' it tells him, 'during your short visit. Everything is at your disposal. Only, I must warn you, if things go wrong, don't blame me. I accept no responsibility. I am not part of your neurosis. Don't cry to me for safety. There is no home here. There is no security in your mansions or your fortresses, your family vaults or your banks or your double beds. Understand this fact, and you will be free. Accept it, and you will be happy.'

The Shore

THE place in the United States I think of as home – and I feel very homesick for it as I write these words – is the stretch of ocean front running five or six miles south from Santa Monica Canyon to Venice, partly inside, partly outside the city limits of Los Angeles.

Why does one love places? Why do I love this one so much? I might say 'because I find it beautiful' or 'because people I love live there' or 'because I have been happier and unhappier there than in any other place I know' or simply 'because I have grown used to it'. But all of these answers are partial and unsatisfactory. It is best if I merely describe what you would see if you went there yourself.

One thing I can almost promise: that you would be hugely disappointed – unless, of course, you happened, like myself, to have a taste for romantic dilapidation. For most of this beach district is down-at-heel; it has little to do with the Los Angeles of legend, city of movie studios and tycoons, stars that shed no light and searchlights that seek for nothing, glamourized graveyards, oranges and advertisements equally large and tasteless. This is not so much a waterfront as a backyard washed by waves; for Los Angeles is still really an inland city. Its port, San Pedro, is far to the south.

Santa Monica Canyon – known always simply as 'The Canyon' to its dwellers – lies just north of the city of Santa Monica. It is a shallow flat-bottomed little valley, crowded with cottages of self-consciously rustic design, where cranky, kindly people live and tolerate each other's mild and often charming eccentricities. The Canyon is our western Greenwich Village, overrun now by various types of outsiders, but still maintaining an atmosphere of Bohemianism and unpretentious artiness. And Doc Law's Friendship Bar is still, despite competition, the acknowledged *stammlokal* of the community. Doc Law, who also owns the adjoining drugstore, is a gentleman of almost excessively distinguished appearance who wears a wide-brimmed hat and floppy artist's tie, and who used to be a close friend of Will Rogers.

As you go south from the Canyon, there are a few luxurious homes – including the big white-pillared mansion which once belonged to Miss Marion Davies – but these are soon followed by hot dog stands, rooming houses, bungalow courts mostly verging on the condition of marine slums. I suppose it is the development of the private swimming pool that has killed Santa Monica as an elegant seaside resort; the fashionable prefer to swim and sunbathe a few miles inland, beyond the reach of the coastal fog. As for the rest of the population of Los Angeles, it comes swarming down to the shore. The beaches in summer are crowded like Coney Island; but after Labor Day they are almost deserted, although the warm, wonderful fall sunshine lingers on and on, and you can go in swimming till Christmas. It is then that those who love the shore most like to walk there, ignored by the standing gulls convened in parliaments, and enjoying the classic autumnal sadness of the vast, vague, golden light.

If you are lucky enough to have a room in the merry-go-round building on the pier – the merry-go-round revolves for a few hours on Saturdays and Sundays, and you soon get so that you do not hear it – you command a view of almost the whole area I am describing. Away to the north, beyond the Canyon, the big blue hills come sheer down to the water and look as grand, in certain lights, as the Andes seen from a ship off the coast of Venezuela. In the foreground, the houses of Santa Monica stand on the top of palm-fringed cliffs which are coffee-brown and vertical as slices of cake. Out at the end of the pier, the fishing boats keep arriving, and the gulls and the strong, clumsy pelicans swoop to grab fish from the catch. Then, just south of you, there is Muscle Beach, where the barbell kings lift and jerk, and the tumblers build their human towers. Tumbling makes you lithe and graceful. Barbells make you formidable, imposing and, ultimately, grotesque. Our culture has preferred barbells.

In the distance is the Ocean Park amusement pier, with shooting booths and popcorn stands, and a whip, a water-shoot and a roller coaster. These pleasures are mostly patronized by innocent out-of-town visitors. But there are sometimes serious gang fights in the fun-house; and if you look at the comic photos at the photographers' – the kind where your head emerges from the painted figure of a mermaid or a fat lady – you will recognize some of the

most famous faces of the movie world. It is a reminder of
the days of the silent film, when Mack Sennett's bathing
beauties actually bathed here and Chaplin made a two-
reeler on the beach.

More boardwalk, after that; more rooming houses and
bungalow courts, with a wide expanse of beach which was
polluted, until recently, by the sewerage outflow and was
consequently empty even in summer. An admirable desolation, which at night becomes sinister, so that you can
easily imagine yourself as the prospective murderee in a
crime story, hurrying hopelessly along by the weak light
of far-spaced lamps and hearing the elastic steps of the
killers gaining leisurely on you from behind.

And then Venice. Venice, California. (A friend told me,
during the last war, that he only knew how acclimatized
he had become when on reading a newspaper headline
'Venice Bombed', he exclaimed involuntarily, 'Good God,
have the Japs landed?') Very often, in this country,
European place-names have been borrowed with a kind
of laziness, which is apt to irritate the non-American
stranger. But this particular case is quite different. Venice
was called Venice because it was intended to be *like*
Venice, a city complete with canals and gondolas, and
architecture to match. During the early part of the century, a tremendous real estate boom developed there and
bust with the loss of millions. Today, Venice is a quiet,
shabby little place at the edge of an oil field which ex-
tends for a mile or two along the shore. But you can
still see the hotel where Sarah Bernhardt stayed. You can
still live at an address on the Grand Canal (though a
garbage raft will float past your window instead of a
gondola); you can still admire the pure curve of a bridge
which would not disgrace Italy, except that it stands
among oil derricks, is made of wood and plaster and is
apt to fall down soon.

So there you are. There you see the object of my nostalgia. Probably you are amused. Possibly you are irritated;

you think I am not serious. I hardly know what to add by way of explanation. There are plenty of people to admire the noble ruins of antiquity, the glory that was Greece and the grandeur that was Rome. I, it seems, belong to a tiny perverse minority who prefer the ignoble ruins of the day before yesterday, and would rather wander through an abandoned army camp or the remains of a world's fair than visit Pompeii or Chan-Chan. Perhaps it is simply that, in the former instance, one's sense of impermanence is stronger. What was there, on this shore, a hundred years ago? Practically nothing. And which, of all these flimsy structures, will be standing a hundred years from now? Probably not a single one. Well, I like that thought. It is bracingly realistic. In such surroundings, it is easier to remember and accept the fact that you won't be here, either.

STORIES

IN my *Notes*, I refer to the influence of the Icelandic sagas on Auden's poetry, and also to my notion that the manners and customs of the saga-heroes resembled those of small boys at a modern preparatory school. In *Lions and Shadows*, I add that I myself 'tried the experiment of writing a school story in what was a kind of hybrid language composed of saga phraseology and schoolboy slang'. *Gems of Belgian Architecture* is that story. It was written sometime in 1927.

The setting is St Edmund's School, Hindhead, Surrey, where Auden and I first met, as pupils. With a venom which has long since been dissolved in nostalgia, I once wrote a description of its appearance as follows: 'An aggressive gabled building in the early Edwardian style, about the size of a private hotel. The brick-work is varied here and there with sham frontings of criss-cross stucco. In the foreground is a plantation of dwarf conifers, such as are almost always to be seen in the grounds of better-class lunatic asylums.'

The first part of this story takes place during the 1914–18 war. Near our school was a common on which, as the war progressed, an immense army camp grew up, occupied chiefly by Canadians. Often, on our Sunday walks, we crossed a stretch of land in which the soldiers had dug trenches for training. The masters in charge of our walks would encourage us to jump these trenches. Perhaps they wanted to bring home to us something of the physical reality of war. If so, they certainly succeeded, as far as I was concerned. Many of the trenches were seven or eight feet deep; it made me dizzy to look down into them. And though there were plenty of places where I could jump across, they seemed alarmingly wide to me, with my short legs. We also played hide and seek in them. This was fun. But, one day, I got temporarily lost and experienced some of the terror of the trench-labyrinth which Robert Graves and other war writers have described.

At first, the Canadians were pictured to us by the staff as heroes who had crossed half the world to come to our defence. Later in the war, we were told that they were not heroes at all but wild, drunken, dangerous brutes, who settled their personal quarrels with bayonets, stole from shops in the village, terrorized the local girls, and suffered from nameless diseases. Finally, the camp and its neighbourhood were put out of bounds to us.

Heroes or not, we boys valued the presence of the Canadians for a more practical reason; they all smoked. We used to stop every soldier we met, from private to colonel, and ask him for the picture-cards which were contained in his packs of cigarettes. True, you could write to the cigarette manufacturers and be sent complete sets of these cards for a shilling or two; but this was considered unsporting. There actually was a set called Gems of Belgian Architecture. I owned it myself; and I seem to remember that some of the rarer cards in it were once stolen. If so, this was probably done for revenge or spite, as in my story. Stealing for mere profit was less usual, because we all loved to brag about our possessions and there was little pleasure in owning something you dared not show to others.

One important feature of our wartime school life, not mentioned in *Gems*, was our cult of the dead. Several boys, including myself, had lost their fathers; many of us had lost a near relative. It is untrue to say that we were callous; I think we mourned in our own barely conscious way. But the concept of Grief, as practised by adults, was almost meaningless to us. We could only understand it in terms of drama, over which we gloated, and of social prestige, which commanded our sincere respect. One boy was called out of the classroom in the middle of a lesson to be told that his brother had been killed in action. Afterwards, he described his sensations on hearing the news, to a select group of friends. 'Did you blub much?' we asked him eagerly. Black crêpe armbands were worn with grave pride. The wearer had privileges; he must not be unkindly ragged. On one occasion during a friendly, laughing scuffle, a boy's armband got torn. Immediately, he burst into tears of indignation, crying, 'Look what you've done, you swine!' And we let go of him at once, equally shocked at this violation of taboo. Then there was a boy who pretended that his father was dead; he was unpopular and lonely, and I suppose he was desperate for some recognition. His lie was discovered of course, and our righteous fury knew no bounds. Next Sunday he suffered what, in our penal code, was equivalent to capital punishment. He was gorse-bushed.

The school grounds were largely a jungle of pinewoods and gorse bushes. To be thrown into the midst of one of these prickly bushes was painful, needless to say, and even dangerous; but the real misery of the punishment was that it expressed complete rejection, expulsion from our society. In my story, because of its saga overtones, the gorse-bushing of Dwight has to be an act of simple revenge; but it was usually inflicted as a punishment for the sin of sins, which we called 'Side'.

For new bugs, side could be almost any behaviour which attracted attention to you and therefore suggested that you were forgetting your utter insignificance within the social system. It was even sidey for new bugs to bully each other in a senior's presence. But when a senior himself showed side, that was something far worse. It was not mere presumption, it was the Greek *hybris*, an arrogance amounting to impiety. Towards the end of my first term a senior whom I will call Parker was found guilty of side. On pay day the other seniors dragged him out of the house. He broke free, and they chased him all over the grounds. I shall never forget Parker's face as he plunged past me, nearly knocking me over. He was a big, good-looking boy who ordinarily had nice manners, carefully brushed hair, and an air of maturity. Now he was just a hunted animal, blind with panic, and we were all his

enemies, even the smallest of us who stood there watching.
He was caught and gorse-bushed at last. He dragged himself out of the bush, making a half-hearted attempt to pick
the prickles from his skin and clothes but hardly able to
see what he was doing for tears. Then he limped off towards the house, humiliated as he probably never would
be, never could be again, in his life. No one spoke to him.
We moved aside as he passed. He was truly an outcast.

An interval of at least five years is supposed to separate
the two halves of this story. But you will probably not
become aware of it until you have read on for a couple
of paragraphs, or even more. In those days I loved to
mystify my reader. Indeed, it is quite possible that you
may end up baffled; unable to guess just what it is that
has been happening. So I had better explain that the plot
revolves around Sladen. Sladen yielded to the threats of
Dog Major's spy and swapped number nine of Gems after
he had promised it to Dwight. Later, ashamed of his
cowardice, he stole the entire set of Gems from Griffin's
locker and hid them behind a loose brick in the wall of
the changing-room. Maybe he intended to give them to
Dwight after the theft had been forgotten, but was afraid
to do so. There are hints that Dwight was Sladen's
particular hero at the school; this would explain Sladen's
rather flirtatious behaviour towards Dwight in the final
episode and his drunken attempt to create a big theatrical
scene, a confrontation of the present with the past, by
producing the Gems in the presence of Dwight and his
ex-enemy, Griffin. Anyhow, the Gems have disappeared
from their hiding place, so the scene falls flat.

While I was up at Cambridge I ran into a boy who had
seemed a stupid, ruthless, altogether obnoxious person
when I had known him at school. Now he had turned
into a charming, amusing, highly sophisticated young
man; I could hardly recognize him. My surprise at his
transformation gave me the idea for the second half of
this story. I planned to show a group of characters who
have not only changed individually in the process of

growing up but have evolved historically, as it were, from the tenth to the twentieth century. Dwight, Griffin and the rest of them can revisit the school where their old saga-life is still being lived, by another generation; but they themselves can make no contact with it. They have become anachronisms. ... All this might have been marvellous if I had had the art to show it. I think my unsuccessful attempt to do so is just worth exhibiting here.

An Evening at the Bay is a prematurely written bit of autobiography. I later covered that period of my life in *Lions and Shadows*; Philip's visit, described here, is mentioned briefly in chapter seven. 'Philip Linsley' in *Lions and Shadows* is Hector Wintle, author of three novels: *The Final Victory, Edgar Prothero* and *The Hodsall Wizard*, all published during the thirties. 'Philip Lindsay' in *All the Conspirators* is also a partial impression of Wintle, but his doings in that novel are quite fictitious and the character is anyhow composite. Edward Upward appears here, in *Lions* and in *Conspirators* as 'Allen Chalmers'; his role in *Conspirators* is as fictitious as Wintle's. Upward has himself written about 'The Bay' in his novel, *In the Thirties.* 'The Bay' is Freshwater Bay in the Isle of Wight. It was once the home of Tennyson.

At the time when I wrote this sketch I had a superstitious faith in the power of exact reporting. Scraps of overheard slang and dialogue, especially the dialogue of strangers, were jotted down and treasured by me; I used them like spells which could bring an entire scene to life. One morning, when I had to leave the Bay and go back to London, I was tormented because I had forgotten a phrase used by 'the skivvy from The Boot' which one of the boys had described as being 'proper Pompey' (i.e. a typical Portsmouth expression) the night before. The bus was already waiting, but I could not tear myself away. With an air of having hours of time to kill, I engaged the boys in conversation. We laughed about this and that until

I finally felt able to refer to the girl – the oddness of my motive embarrassed me. At long last I asked, 'what was that she kept saying?' Luckily, one of the boys remembered. I jumped on to the bus, just as it started, mentally clutching my catch: 'It's like this . . .'

An Evening at the Bay was published in 1933 in *New Country*, an anthology edited by Michael Roberts.

The Turn Round the World and *A Day in Paradise* are both set in the Canary Islands. I spent the spring and summer of 1934 there and wrote *Mr Norris* at a pension at Orotava on Tenerife. The house, a climb up the peak, and a walking-tour on Gran Canaria are described, with altogether fictitious circumstances, in *The World in the Evening*.

The Turn Round the World appeared in *The Listener* some time in 1935. *A Day in Paradise* appeared in the April–May 1935 issue of *The Ploughshare*, which described itself as the organ of the Teachers' Anti-War Movement. This kind of conditional, politically motivated pacifism was characteristic of left wing thinking in the thirties. It was, of course, perfectly consistent with the advocacy of armed force in dealing with certain situations. I do not see anything dishonest about it; but it has nothing to do with the unconditional, non-political pacifism in which I now believe.

I had had the idea for *I am Waiting* for several years before I wrote the story. I did so during the summer of 1939, when I was so depressed by the increasing threat of war that I could not settle down to any serious work and yet dreaded the emptiness of writing nothing. *The New Yorker* published it in October 1939. They made several cuts, and also transposed its setting from England to Connecticut. I suppose they felt England's immediate future looked so dark that a comedy about it would be in bad taste. Here is the story as I originally wrote it.

The New Yorker is not a magazine in which one would

expect to find bona fide accounts of psychic phenomena; nevertheless, some of my readers took it for granted that this was one. One lady, a student of astrology, wrote me that she had drawn up my horoscope according to the birth date given in my story, and had found that the dates I had given for my three supernatural experiences were confirmed by it. Considering my aspects, they were bound to have taken place just when they did. ... I was obliged to reply and tell her the truth – that I was thirty-two years younger than my character, and a Virgo, not a Leo; and that the experiences and dates were anyhow fictitious. I felt terrible when she wrote back dejectedly that her family had always made fun of her astrology and that now she would never hear the last of this mistake. But I still think it was better that I should have told her, rather than someone else.

Another correspondent, equally serious as far as I could judge, urged me not to fear my great gift; because a gentleman in their town passed forth into the future and back again every week, without any ill effects.

Take It or Leave It also appeared in *The New Yorker*, in October 1942. I had written it earlier that year, chiefly to please my friend René Blanc-Roos. René was teaching French and Spanish and coaching the wrestling-team at Haverford College at the time when I was working at the Quaker hostel there. He argued furiously about art and sex, read me Rimbaud, made me laugh like an idiot, got me drunk, and was altogether an ideal vacation from Quakerdom for my free evenings. A warm but severe admirer of my work, he ordered me to write something, anything; he was determined that I should keep myself in condition, like his wrestlers. In gratitude for all this, I later dedicated *Prater Violet* to him. (He was, to some extent, the model for one of its characters, Lawrence Dwight.) He is dead now.

The Wishing Tree appeared in *Vedanta and the West*, in 1943.

I think *A Visit to Anselm Oakes* explains itself sufficiently, and can be read without reference to anything else,
as an adventure in hashish-taking. However, it was once
part of *Down There on a Visit*.

In *Paul*, the final episode of that novel, the narrator,
who is called Christopher Isherwood, goes to visit Paul
in Paris and finds him taking opium. Christopher tries to
be very broadminded about this. He even offers to smoke
a pipe himself, in order to understand the occult experiences which Paul hints that he is having. Paul is scornfully
amused. 'You're exactly like a tourist,' he tells Christopher, 'who thinks he can take in the whole of Rome in one
day. You know, you really *are* a tourist, to your bones. I
bet you're always sending postcards with "down here on a
visit" on them. That's the story of your life....'

In the version which contains the encounter with Anselm Oakes, Paul finally relents and says that, after all,
he may just possibly be able to help Chris 'see something'.
He proposes taking Chris to meet Anselm, who writes
books on witchcraft, and makes a living out of peddling
psychic mumbo-jumbo to suckers and giving hashish
parties at which the guests must pay an 'initiation fee'.

Paul tells Chris that he has realized he will never understand goodness until he can understand evil; so he has
been hunting around for someone who really *is* evil, so
far without complete success. Several people recommended Anselm to him; but, when Paul met Anselm, he
was disappointed. All he has got from Anselm, he says,
are 'a few hints'.

Christopher, as will be seen, is equally disappointed in
Anselm at first. Then, under the influence of the hashish,
he does get a glimpse of Evil, not only in Anselm but also
in his fellow-guests. But wherein does this Evil actually
reside? In Anselm, or in Christopher himself, or in Paul,
who, with characteristic sadism, has told Mokhtar to prepare the drug in such a way as to plunge Chris into the
horrors of 'Down There'?

Not long before the novel was published, in 1962, I

suddenly decided to take the visit to Anselm out of it. This section is almost exclusively about Chris and his experiences; it does not really belong to the story of Paul.

Gigi is Paul's dog. Augustus cannot be described so succinctly. If you want to know who he is, you must read the novel.

Gems of Belgian Architecture

WHEN Mr Roach found an ink-dart under his desk in the Upper Fourth classroom he made Dog Major write out two hundred times: Baby must not play with the nasty messy black stuff. People who did not like Dodgson, or his putrid little sneak brother either, said that Roach was a humorist. But after that the Craze began dying down. By Half Term there were no more Avros or bombers or torpedo darts or racing gliders in the Senior Gym. The Juniors still made a few.

People began going back to cigarette-cards and stamps. Dog Major started a cigarette-card firm. Sale and Griffin were in it. They made forced swaps and were very unpopular, but no one had the guts to stop them. At this time there were thousands of Canadians down at the Camp and the School used to meet them in the Village on Sunday Walk. All the Staff except Ciddy would let their forms ask for cards. The record was Griffin, who got thirty-four from one corporal, who had been saving them.

Gems of Belgian Architecture were just out. And there was a series of twenty-five going – Stars and Planets. They were fairly stale. Dog Major's firm had two sets, one for swapping. And Dwight had a set. Next to the firm, Dwight had the best collection. They might have asked him to join, but he and Griffin were deadly enemies.

It was a question of who'd be the first to get a complete set of Gems. One Sunday evening in the Library, when

Dodgson and Griffin were sorting out what they had got that afternoon on the Walk, numbers forty-seven and eleven turned up at last. Eleven was rare and forty-seven was super-rare. Dwight had had them but he wouldn't swap. There had nearly been a free fight about it. Griffin had told Dwight: 'You wait.' Dwight said: 'I'm waiting, ducky. Don't blub.'

So now Griffin came up to Dwight's locker and showed him number twenty-three and said: 'Wouldn't you like it?' Twenty-three was one of the two that Dwight hadn't got. Dwight tried to spit on it and missed. But after Prayers he swapped a perfect specimen with a Junior. People thought that this was snubs on Dog Major's firm.

This left number nine, which was the most terrifically rare card in the set. Nobody in the School had even seen it. At least, Ringrose-Voase said he had found what must have been half of it under a gorse bush on the Common. But it was the lower half. And, anyway, that was never proved. So it was between Dog Major's firm and Dwight. It was pretty obvious that by next Sunday one of them would have the set, with any luck.

Dog Major and Sale were in the Upper Fourth. They had agents in the Remove. Dog Minor was in the Upper Third and he organized agents among the Juniors. People who were not afraid of Dog Major sided with Dwight, so that he had spies in all the Walks. Dwight was in the Lower Fourth and so was Griffin. People thought that there was nearly certain to be a murder. Especially as it was only Amy taking the walk.

Griffin let it be published that any Junior caught swapping with Dwight would get lammed. Dwight said that nobody need be windy about that, because if Griffin started any lamming he'd get lammed himself; and anyway Griffin was such a flabster he couldn't knock the skin off a rice pudding. Dog Major and his firm then began to mention gorse-bushes. Dwight tried to raise a gang, but although people sided with him they hadn't the guts to join. Dwight had a fort in the biggest tree in the grounds.

People said that there would probably be an attack on it next Sunday morning, after Collect; but as Amy always let out the Lower Fourth hours before anyone else it was a question how Dog could prevent Dwight getting to the fort first and being ready to defend it. And, of course, this looked like another slaughter between Dwight and Griffin.

All Dwight said was: 'Oh, yes. You're the man who fought the monkey in the dustbin.'

On Wednesday, after Footer, one of Dwight's spies among the Juniors came and told Dwight that Sladen had just got a perfect specimen of number nine of Gems. He had been out with his people that afternoon. Sladen had promised Dwight's spy he wouldn't tell anyone else about it until he had seen Dwight.

Dwight couldn't go upstairs straight away, because the Juniors were still changing and Matron would be there. It was too risky. He told his spy to offer thirty for it and sent up his packet of swaps. Sladen said he'd think about it. He probably would. But Dog Minor heard part of the conversation. He came streaking downstairs and told his bro that Dwight had sent some message to Sladen. Dog Major guessed what about.

He sent his bro to tell Sladen that if he swapped number nine of Gems to anyone but the firm he's be remembered in the grounds on Sunday morning. Dog Major said he'd give the same price as Dwight offered. Sladen said All right. He hadn't much guts.

As soon as Dwight's spy got a chance, he came down to tell Dwight. Dwight was waiting in the Lower Fourth classroom, so as not to seem suspicious. But Sale and Griffin were on the lookout at the bottom of the stairs. They told Dwight's spy he'd better not try bringing any more messages. After a bit, Dwight got tired of waiting. He went upstairs by himself and dodged Matron and met his spy, but it was too late. He heard how the swap had been made and how Dog Minor had taken number nine of Gems downstairs and given it to his bro in the Library.

While they were talking, Ciddy came in and gave Dwight lines for being upstairs without leave.

After that, of course, Dwight had to hear a lot of Dog Major's firm's triumph. Griffin told everybody in the Library how clever Dwight thought he'd been and all the plans he'd made and how they were foiled. Dwight lost his bate and asked Griffin to come into the Gym and get hurt. Griffin said very cuttingly that he wasn't coming, out of kindness to Dwight. People thought that this was rather feeble, especially as Griffin obviously knew that Dwight wouldn't dare attack him in the Library for fear of getting into a worse row with Ciddy. Dog Major and Sale laughed and backed Griffin up, however.

On Thursday there was work as per usual. Nothing special happened in the morning. Dwight seemed very cheerful and in good spirits. He never once said anything about the Gems. He kept discussing Meccano models with Fernandes and Baines and making bad puns. Griffin asked him: 'Feeling better this morning?' He said: 'Yes thank you, ducky.' People who heard this decided that he must be planning some very cunning revenge.

On Friday at tea it began going round that Dwight was swapping off his whole collection. Dodgson and Griffin wouldn't believe the rumour, but it turned out to be absolutely official. Dwight swapped his set of Stars to Horniman for two golf balls and an old set of Wonders of the World to Fernandes for a Brownie film. Parry-Evans bought the Gems for one-and-six at the end of Term. People thought that was rather a Jewish bargain on Parry's part. Ringrose-Voase said afterwards that he'd willingly have given two bob if he'd known. Dwight didn't sweat to advertise the swaps at all. He quissed most of his duplicates in the Library when none of Dog Major's firm were there.

Dwight let it be published that he'd simply got fed up with collecting, but most people said 'Oh yes. They thought it was more likely that he'd done it just to show Dog Major's firm he didn't care about the Gems, or to spite them by trying to make the cigarette-card Craze un-fashionable. Dwight could never stand being loser at any-thing. Anyhow, he didn't succeed, if that was what he wanted, because Dog Major and Griffin and Sale went on as usual and the next Sunday afternoon they had all their agents at work and made a record.

On Monday, after lunch, Griffin said to Sale: 'There's a quarter of an hour before the changing-bell. Let's gloat over the new swaps.' So they went to Griffin's locker to get out the firm's albums. Griffin's locker was one of the marvels of the School. He had fixed up a torch inside it which switched on as you opened the door. There was also a patent man-trap which caught your fingers if you put them in the right place. That happened to be bust, how-ever. And there was a hole bored through the back into the locker opposite, which belonged to Dog Major, so that Dog and Griffin could have secret conversations with-out getting up from their chairs. The latest thing was a notice in red letters: This locker is the private property of D. H. Griffin Esquire. Trespassers will be prosecuted. People considered that this had been put up out of swank, because all the Juniors could see it on their way through the Library into the Dining Hall. The letters were filled in with luminous paint. Ciddy was expected to say that Griffin must take it down. But so far he hadn't.

Griffin took the albums out of the locker, and first he opened the swap album. Sale counted the duplicates for swapping. There were sixty-four of them. Then Griffin opened the album of whole sets, including the set of Gems. The next thing he saw was fifty blank spaces. All the Gems were gone. He said to Sale: 'Go quick and fetch Dog Major.'

So Dog came and they showed him and wondered what to do next. Sale wanted to raise the alarm. Griffin wanted to search all the Senior lockers at once. But Dog said no, better wait a bit in case some humorist is trying to be funny. So they decided to wait until the evening, and not say a word. Then, if the Gems had been hidden for a weak joke, the idiot who'd done it would probably put them back and feel rather feeble. Later on, they could probably find out and lam him.

That afternoon, on Senior Game, they couldn't help looking very suspiciously at everyone. Griffin was so busy thinking about the disappearance of the Gems that Mr Roach cursed him for funking. And of course that gave Dwight, who was on the other side, a chance of making his usual remarks, which were followed by several juicy hacks.

After tea Dog Major and Griffin looked at their album again. The Gems still weren't there. So they held another long consultation. It seemed practically certain now that this was a real robbery and not a joke, so it was a question of taking drastic steps. Griffin said he was pretty sure he could track down the criminal by his private methods. He already had suspicions, but wouldn't say more until he'd followed up one or two clues. They agreed to keep quiet for that night.

Next day the Gems still weren't there. And at lunch Griffin admitted to Dodgson that he hadn't been able to find out anything definite yet, although his suspicions were just as strong as ever. They agreed to publish the news. By changing-time it was all over the School. When Dwight heard it, he said: 'Good.' Nothing else. People talked a great deal about the robbery that afternoon, and there were various suspicions. Most people agreed who they suspected, but they were careful not to say anything publicly until it was known what Dog Major and his firm would do next.

That evening, after work, Dog Major and Griffin were in the Library, and there were a good many others there too. Parry-Evans came up to Dog and offered to let his locker be searched. Some people thought this was quite the right thing for Parry to have done, because he was known to have bought the incomplete set of Gems from Dwight. But most said it was merely to suck up to Dog and that anyway searching his locker didn't prove anything when he was ready for it. Griffin and Dog did search, however.

Griffin said he was quite positive that Parry had Dwight's old set and not the firm's. Besides, he hadn't yet got a number nine, although there were now two going in the School. After this, several people offered their lockers to be searched. Nothing suspicious was found in any of them.

In the middle of the searching Dwight came into the Library. At first, Dog Major and Griffin took no notice of him, but it looked as though something would be sure to happen. Then Griffin went up to Dwight and asked him if he'd let his locker be searched like the others. He said this in a rather loud voice on purpose so that everybody should hear. They looked at each other very hard for a minute, but neither of them would be stared out. Then Dwight said: 'No.' People thought this looked bad. Then, after a bit, Griffin asked: 'Why won't you?' And Dwight said: 'If you want to know why, you can ask the cat's grandmother.' Then Dog Major chipped in and asked whether Dwight thought they wouldn't search it by force if they wanted to. And Dwight answered No, he didn't think they'd do that. And Griffin said: 'Oh?' And Dwight said: 'Exactly.' And Dog asked why not. And Dwight said: 'Because a sneaky little friend of yours has had a good sniff round there already.' He gave a very sarcastic look at Griffin while he was saying this. Griffin got red and told Dwight that he'd better be careful what he was dithering about. Dwight said: 'If I'm dithering, it's rather odd that you can understand me so easily.' Dog Major wondered whether Dwight had been spying when Griffin searched his locker, or whether it was just a guess.

After this Griffin went about openly accusing Dwight of the robbery. Most people thought things looked very bad against him, but there were no actual proofs. People were inclined to think that Dwight had taken the Gems more as a revenge than anything else. It was rumoured that he'd thrown them away in the grounds or burnt them in the incinerator.

Dwight kept quite calm about all this. He seemed to think it was funny. He called Dog Major Sexton Blake and Griffin Sherlock Holmes. Sale was My Dear Watson. Every time he saw them he asked if they'd got any new clues. Griffin watched him very suspiciously and got spies to report things he'd said. Dwight pretended to be fearfully surprised that anyone should suspect him. 'As if I wanted the greasy old cards,' he told people. Once, Griffin wanted him to swear on the Bible that he hadn't taken them. Dwight said he wouldn't. It was wicked. But, the next day, he said: 'All right, I will.' So Griffin got witnesses, and Dwight took a solemn oath in front of them in the Lower Fourth classroom that he'd never opened Griffin's locker or taken out the Gems or hidden them or destroyed them. When Dwight had done that, he held up the book he'd been swearing on and showed them it was Pendlebury's Arithmetic wrapped up inside the cover of an old bible, which Amy used for Divinity and which had come to bits. Dog Major said that was Blasphemy and he'd a jolly good mind to report it to Ciddy. Griffin said well, anyway, the oath was just as binding, because part of the Bible counted just as much as the whole Bible. Dwight said in that case he supposed it'd be enough to swear on a bit of thread pulled out of the cover. Dog Major said: 'Shut up, and don't be a blasphemous little swine.' Griffin said: 'The oath's binding, and I advise you to remember it.' Dwight said he'd write it down in his diary to make sure. But he seemed a bit funky, all the same, after what Dog Major had said about being blasphemous.

It wasn't till later that Griffin thought Dwight might have had an accomplice. 'We ought to have made him swear he doesn't know who's done the robbery,' he told Dog Major. 'That would have had him.' But Dwight refused to swear any more oaths. Griffin and Dog and Sale took this as silence gives consent. They did a lot of detective work trying to find out who the accomplice was. Dog Minor made inquiries among the Juniors and searched their lockers when they weren't there. Most people were inclined not to believe much in this new idea. And, as time went on and there were no definite proofs against

Dwight, he rose a bit in popularity and it didn't seem so positively certain that he was guilty at all. People stopped giving him the frozen mitt; and, by the end of Term, the robbery wasn't being discussed except occasionally. However, Dog Major and his firm didn't consider that they'd finished with Dwight by a long chalk.

On the Saturday before Pay Day, the last Sunday in the Term, Dog and Griffin and Sale made up their minds that tomorrow they'd pay Dwight enough to satisfy him and slightly extra. Griffin was really the leader in this, but Sale and Dodgson were quite ready to back him up, whatever happened.

Sunday morning was cold and drizzling. Very few people went out into the grounds. Most of the Seniors stayed in the Library. Dwight was there, reading. After a few minutes, Dog Minor came in and told Dwight he was wanted down at the miniature range. Dwight seemed a bit suspicious. He asked: 'Who wants me?' Dog Minor said: 'Mr Roach.' Dwight had seen Fernandes and Ringrose-Voase going down there that morning to practise. Mr Roach often took shooting and sent for people he thought were slacking. Dwight hadn't been to the range lately. So he decided it must be all right. He started off at once.

Dog Major and Sale and Griffin were ambushed at a narrow part of the path, well away from the house. They came out and surrounded Dwight as he passed. Griffin was carrying a piece of rope. Dwight said: 'Well, what do you want?' Griffin said: 'It's Pay Day.' Dwight said: 'Oh, that's a pity, isn't it?' Griffin said: 'Yes, a great pity.'

Dwight asked what they were going to do, and Dog Major told him: 'You'll see, soon enough.' Then Dwight gave a yell and pointed straight up into the air over their heads. He went streaking off down the path towards the range, but Sale, who was a good sprinter, headed him to the left. Then he made for the wild part of the grounds. They kept close behind him. Sale and Griffin tried to get between him and the fort, but he dodged. Sale got to the foot of the tree just as Dwight started to climb. He caught hold of Dwight's feet. Dwight kicked him in the wind. Sale sat down on the ground. He wasn't much winded. He said: 'You wait, you cad.' Griffin came up next, but Dwight had got on to the lowest bough. He broke off a piece of branch for a spear. Then Dog Major came up. Dwight dared them to attack him. 'Three to one,' he shouted out. 'I've seen better things than you in cheese.'

Griffin started to climb, and so did Dog Major; but Dwight kept them off with the branch. He hit at them as hard as he could. They had to look out for their eyes. Then Dwight, who'd been jumping about, suddenly lost his balance. He fell out of the tree. It wasn't very far to fall. When Dwight hit the ground he just rolled over and lay still. His eyes were shut. Dog Major said: 'I believe he's broken his neck.' Dwight waited until they were bending over him. Then he jumped up and gave Griffin a terrific beat in the face and made off towards the house at top speed. They thought they'd lost him for a minute, but Sale, who'd recovered, did a record sprint and got him headed off. First he turned to the right and then to the left. Then he rushed straight at Dodgson. Dog half collared him. He got away, but the others drove him back. Then he was caught. Griffin tied his feet and hands up with the rope while Dog and Sale held him. He struggled the whole time. Once, he got his teeth round Sale's ear. They had to bend his fingers till they cracked before he'd let go. Then they carried him to a great juicy gorse-bush. Griffin and Dog swung him. Sale counted: One. Two. Three. Off. Dwight landed right in the thickest part of the bush. At first, he didn't move, but when he did they saw he wasn't just shamming hurt. Dog called out: 'Hard luck. We had to do it, you know.' Sale said: 'Hard luck,' too. Dwight began getting out of the gorse. The rope had come untied. His cheek had got blood on it and his hands were cut. He was half blubbing and half laughing. He went straight for Griffin. Griffin saw that Dwight had lost his bate hopelessly and that he didn't know what he was doing. All three of them were in a funk. Then Griffin turned round and began to run. Dwight went after him like a mad dog. The others followed. Griffin made for the range, because that was the nearest place of safety. He only just got there. As luck would have it, Mr Roach had gone. Voase and Fernandes were cleaning their rifles. Griffin rushed into the shed yelling: 'Look out, Dwight's gone mad.' A rifle Mr Roach had been using was lying on the table by the door. He'd gone away in a hurry and told them to give it a pull-through before they went. What's more, he'd left it loaded. He was very careless over things like that. Dwight came tearing into the shed after Griffin, and before any of them could say knife he'd picked up the rifle and fired it at Griffin's head. Griffin said later that he'd felt the bullet go through his hair. And, from where they found the mark on the wall, he couldn't have been far wrong.

After this Dwight sat down on the floor. He said he thought he was probably going to be sick. But he wasn't. When they saw he wasn't dangerous, they made him come with them to Matron. Fernandes explained that Dwight had had a fall, which was true. Matron took his temperature, and it was three points up. She gave him white mixture and put him to bed. In the morning he was quite all right again.

When Dwight came down, Dog Major and his firm asked him to make peace. So they made peace and it was fairly well kept. There was no more talk about the Gems. Dog Major and Griffin gave up their detective work. The mystery remained unsolved.

It was the last day of Term. Everyone was very busy packing or quissing the things they didn't want to take home. Now and then a bell rang and Ciddy put up a notice on the board to say that journey-money would be given out in five minutes or that it was time to fetch clothes from the Linen-Room or that all Juniors *not* travelling by the London train are to see me in the study. And there was a punt-about going on outside. A good many Old Boys had come down for the Match – Plumtree, who had been Captain of the Eleven last year and was now at Charterhouse, and Legge and Hardwick from Tonbridge and Ross from Malvern and several who'd left their Public Schools and were in business or up at the Varsity. People recognized Horniman, the Cambridge right-half, from pictures in the papers. He and Mr Roach were to be captains and pick up sides.

Two of the Old Boys caused great amusement by having a race over the wall-bars in the Senior Gym. One of them got stuck. 'No, Philip,' he said, 'that was distinctly unfair. I shall take off my coat.' So they had the race again, but the same thing happened. And then they made the people race who were watching and put penny bets on the winners. The general opinion was that the senior Old Boys were sportsmen, but that the junior ones, like Plumtree and Hardwick, had got a swank on.

After this, the two Old Boys who had been racing said that they were going out to look at the new carpentering shed and the pavvy. A good many people followed to listen to their remarks. Philip made them all laugh. He imitated Ciddy saying: 'Dwight, I didn't know you were that particular kind of fool.' He told them about a Mr Rice who used to be on the staff and was called Amy, and how he was ragged so much that he had to leave. Ciddy had come into the Lower Fourth classroom one morning and found people actually jumping about on the desks. When he asked what on earth was happening, Amy said with a feeble sort of grin: 'You see, Headmaster, now and then I just give them three minutes' break. It helps them to concentrate better, I think.'

While Dwight was saying, in a very loud voice, what he thought Mr Roach used to keep in the back room of the old pavvy, regardless of Matron, who had come out to get a breath of fresh air watching the punt-about, they saw a taxi coming up the drive. It was another Old Boy arriving. He was leaning out of the window. Dwight said: 'Christ, Leonard, it's Griff.' Leonard said: 'My God, so it is.' Dwight let out a terrific yell and began running towards the taxi, waving his arms. Leonard and everyone else followed. Griff was now waving too. Dwight jumped on to the running board and pulled open the door. The driver thought it was best to stop. Dwight was saying: 'What the hell do you think you're doing here, you old bastard?' Leonard said: 'Well, Griffin, this is a piece of incredibly good work.' Griffin got out of the taxi. 'Hullo, you awful man,' he said to Dwight. 'Hullo, Fernandes; the last time I saw you, you were –' 'Hush,' said Fernandes, 'you mustn't corrupt the Young.' After this, they all went into the house.

'Did you let them know you were coming? We're about twenty in a bed as it is. You'll probably have to sleep with Matron.'

'Or with Nasty Nellie. Which would you prefer?'

'Oh, he'd rather have Nellie, I'm sure.'

'Or we might fix him up with that new music mistress. Did you get her name?'

'I didn't, unfortunately.'

'That's a pity.'

'Unnecessary, surely?'

'As a matter of fact, I'm only down for the day. Going back to Town on the midnight train.'

'Oh, you gay dog.'

'You'll be here for the doings this evening, though?'

'You bet.'

'Ciddy wants us all to do a turn. I'm going to sing. Leonard's playing the piano.'

'God, are you really? Who else is here?'

'Bill Horniman.'

'Good.'

'Rupert Sale.'

'Bad.'

'Godfrey Sladen.'

'Sladen? Were we here with him? I know the name.'

'Yes, you remember.'

'What's he like now?'

'Still at Harrow. Bit of a rat.'

'On the contrary, Philip. He's an extremely charming child.'

'Oh, well. Griff can judge for himself at lunch.'

'Any more?'

'Nobody we know. Four little ticks who've been at Public Schools a term. Come back to tell their friends what it feels like to be bummed.'

'Yes, I did that too. I came down with Dog.'

'How's Dog getting on now?'

'Oh, stenching of money, as usual. He's got a flat in Knightsbridge. Every time you meet him he's driving a new make of car.'

'Is it true he's living with a lady who keeps a hat-shop?'

'I hadn't heard it. Quite probably.'

'I'd heard she was an Art Photographer.'

'She's need some Art if she photographed Dog.'

'How's his brother?'

'I've only seen him once. He was playing golf with Pa at Ranelagh in complete Yankee sporting togs. He's very, very nasty.'

'Tell you who I met the other day. Hawkins.'

'Not Michael Hawkins? Philip, you never told me.'

'He used to be rather a sound man.'

'Oh, Michael's a dear man. He really is.'

'What about that marvellous job he was getting in the City?'

'I don't know. He didn't mention it. He's sailing for India next month. Going into the Mounted Police.'

'Wonder if he'll run across Parry-Evans.'

'I should think he's bound to. And Leslie Stagge.'

'Oh, yes. Poor old Leslie.'

'Did he go out there, too?'

'I believe so. Someone told me.'

'Was he the man who went to a co-educational school and got bunked?'

'Yes. A bit of a humorist.'

'Do you know, the other day a friend of mine said he'd point out to me the most boring man in Cambridge; and who do you think it was?'

'Teddy Baines?'

'No. Stephen Dykes.'

'Teddy would be a close finisher.'

'He really is an intolerable creature.'

'He thinks he's going to become President of the Union.'

'Nobody else does, I trust.'

'What's become of Ringrose-Voase?'

'I haven't the faintest. He's one of those people one never hears of.'

'Like Bagshaw.'

'Oh, I can tell you why you never heard of Bagshaw. He's dead.'

'Really, when was that?'

'About a year after he left. I'm surprised you didn't see it in the Terminal Letter.'

'He went to one of those sinister Scotch academies on the edge of the Arctic Circle and they killed him.'

'He was a wreckish sort of dud, anyway.'

'Whenever I heard his voice I used to try to kick him.'

'Tomlinson was worse.'

'Where's he?'

'Abroad, somewhere.'

'Does anyone know what's happened to Alan Fraser?'

'He's gone into a bank.'

'And Waters? Tell me, where's our Waters?'

'He's in a bank, too.'

After the Match, Ross and Plumtree walked back together from the pavilion to the house.

'If you want my opinion,' said Plumtree, 'that's one of the most putrid games I've ever played in.'

'Same here,' said Ross.

'Our attack was absolutely useless.'

'So was theirs.'

'I know. . . . Honestly, could you see anything in Horniman's play? I thought he was pretty rotten, myself. He kept sending me the most utterly impossible passes. He never seemed to look what he was doing.'

'He wasn't sweating himself.'

'In that case, I don't see why he need have condescended to play.'

'The others were all as slack as hell, too.'

'I know.'

'I suppose they thought that was the smart thing.'

'And isn't the School side ghastly this year?'

'Awful.'

'I mean, there's simply nobody who's got the vaguest notion how to play Football.'

'I can't imagine how they managed to win a single match.'

Walking ahead of them, Plumtree suddenly noticed Horniman, in conversation with Legge. Legge was looking up at Horniman and giggling admiringly.

'My God, Ross, do you see that? If that isn't the bloody limit. . . . Do you know, I'll bet you anything you like Legge deliberately worked it so that everybody shall see him talking to a Blue. It's just the sort of idiotic prep-schoolish thing he'd do. He probably went straight up to Horniman and simply tacked himself on.'

'Why shouldn't he, poor boy, if it amuses him?'

Ross glanced at Plumtree with an inquiring smile. And Plumtree began to blush. He blushed until his hair looked almost white.

'It's in the most filthily bad taste, that's all.'

Between tea and supper Ciddy got hold of Horniman and asked if he'd lend a hand at putting up the stage in the Library. Horniman cursed and said: Oh yes, he'd love to. Sale insisted on helping too.

'I must say,' he remarked, when Ciddy was out of the

room for a moment, 'I do think the others might have offered to do something; or, at any rate, shown a little interest.'

'They'd only be in the way,' said Horniman. 'Besides, I can't blame them; I'd have dodged this job myself if I'd had the chance.'

'Still, it looked bad. I shouldn't wonder if Ciddy isn't quite hurt about it.'

Sale had gone into the Drawing-Room a few minutes before to fetch the curtains, and had been irritated to see Fernandes at the piano trying over some songs with Sladen, while Griffin and Dwight lolled in opposite chairs before the fire, reading magazines. They were behaving, quite frankly, as though the room belonged to them. Plumtree and his companions, feeling ill at ease there, had already gone out to rag in the Senior Gym.

'I do bar that man Dwight,' said Sale abruptly.

'Why, what's wrong with him?'

'He seems to think he can put his feet on the mantel-piece wherever he goes.'

'Oh, Philip's all right,' Horniman answered vaguely, 'once you get to know him.'

He was rather bored by Sale and only kept up the con-versation to distract his mind from the bluntness of the screwdriver he was trying to use. Sale draped back the curtains with a careful frown:

'I like Griffin, although –'

'Yes, Griff's a decent sort, isn't he?'

Sale, walking several paces from the stage to see the effect, added:

'Although it entirely beats me how he and Dwight can possibly stick Fernandes. That really is the very worst type of dago.'

Horniman said nothing. He looked worried, as though by an unpleasant smell. Sale, frowning austerely at the curtains, began to whistle some bars from a fugue. He admired Bach.

Just before supper, Dwight said that he must have a drink. Griffin was quite ready. Fernandes didn't want one. He and Sladen were still at the piano.

'You've torn it with Leonard's little friend,' said Griffin, when they were outside. 'He was itching to come too.'

'Let him itch and scratch. He's nasty. I do wish Leonard wouldn't collect things like that about the place. There's usually some around when you go to his digs.'

At the end of the lane beyond the School gate they could see the lighted windows of the Cock Pheasant.

'To think,' said Griffin, 'of the number of times we used to pass that pub; and this is the first we go inside.'

'Better sometime than nowhen,' said Dwight.

Fernandes and Sladen had stopped playing and singing as soon as their audience had left the room.

'You know, Godfrey, you ought to go on the Stage.'

'Oh, rot, Leonard. . . . You don't think so really.'

'Yes, I do.'

'But I can't act.'

'You'd soon learn. It's Personality that matters.'

'But I haven't got any Personality.'

'You're fishing for compliments, Godfrey.'

'No, honestly, I'm not.'

'You must know that you're an incredibly attractive creature.'

'Oh, rot, Leonard . . .'

Then the bell rang for supper. The Dining-Hall was hung with streamers and holly. The School filed in and the Staff and Old Boys followed. Fernandes was annoyed to find that he'd been put at Ciddy's table, with Horniman and Sale. Plumtree, Ross, Legge and Hardwicke sat by Mr Roach. The others were with Matron.

Griffin and Dwight came in late, after grace had been said. They were rather short of breath, and their cheeks were very pink. They explained, apologizing, that they'd been out for a stroll. It was such a glorious night, with all the stars shining.

'Just to get your appetites up?'

'Yes, that's right, Matron. Just to get our appetites up.'

Dwight's voice was loud and confident with pleasure. As he sat down next to Sladen, who was on Matron's right, his wide, pleased smile circled the table. Everyone who encountered it began unconsciously smiling. Griffin was opposite.

'Awfully nice to see this old hall again, isn't it, Griff?'

'You're glad to be back?' Matron beamed.

'Glad to be back? I should just think we are ...'

'Let me give you some lemonade, Matron,' interrupted Griffin, scowling and grinning at Dwight. The jug of lemonade was passed round.

'What have you been doing really, Philip?' Sladen asked, in a flattering, confidential whisper.

'What every young boy should know, ducky,' answered Dwight, very loudly. Luckily, Griffin had started discussing the Match with Matron. His voice trembled with enthusiasm:

'And then, why, you wouldn't believe ...'

The boys at Matron's table were all watching Dwight, realizing instinctively that he would soon do something to amuse them. He began a mock balancing trick with his knife and fork, making his hand tremble violently, so that they kept crashing on to the table or the floor. Everyone laughed. Griffin frowned delightedly, signalling. Matron gave him a quick glance and suddenly began talking to Sladen about Harrow.

Dwight was answering Griffin's signals. Griffin sank visibly in his seat. He was stretching his legs forward under the table. Dwight also stooped down. He talked the whole time. Sladen saying 'Yes, Matron,' 'Oh, no,' 'Well, you see, it's arranged like this,' was confused by a distinctly audible recitation of There was a young lady of Kent and A certain old man of Tibet. Also, Dwight kept asking for more lemonade. One of the boys volunteered to fetch another jugful.

'You see,' Dwight explained, 'the beauty of this stuff is that it can't hurt a fly. Unless the fly got drowned in it,

of course.' The table was in an uproar. Griffin, now that
he was not being talked to by Matron, leant forward,
laughing louder than anybody. Occasionally, he and
Dwight made the same stooping and stretching movements in their seats. Once Dwight exclaimed: 'Oh, bitch
the thing,' and Griffin dived right under the table, but
only for an instant. Matron went on talking to Sladen,
very intently.

Then Ciddy got up to make his speech. Dwight's stage
whisper: 'Now then, boys, quiet for the Head Beak,' was
the last sound heard. Ciddy began the old, old story: 'I
think most of us may congratulate ourselves on a fairly
successful term.' Sladen, glancing down, surprised Dwight
in the act of adding to his half-drunk glass of lemonade
from a small flat bottle. He did this very cleverly, guarding the bottle with his wrist and sleeve, so that it would
be quite invisible to anyone but Sladen himself. He met
Sladen's eyes with a derisive grin. 'Like some?' he asked.
Sladen looked round guiltily. Everyone was watching
Ciddy. He blushed and nodded, moving his glass towards
Dwight. This was his first taste of gin. He smiled reck-
lessly as he drank it off and just avoided making a face at
the smell. 'Sailors don't care,' he whispered. But Dwight
did not seem particularly impressed. He merely shook
his head and said, in his ordinary voice: 'Naughty,
naughty.'

Ciddy wound up. Applause. Horniman, answering for
the Old Boys: '... want to thank the Headmaster and
Miss Forrester for all their kindness to us (applause) ...
and, of course, Matron (applause) ... and last, but certainly not least (laughter) ... and hope very much that,
next Christmas, all being well (applause) ... Mr Roach
told me just before the game this afternoon that (laughter) ... won't keep you any longer, but would just like to
say (applause) ... hope that (laughter) ... all hope
(applause) ...' The Break-Up Supper was over.

While the actors were getting dressed there was a sing-
song in the Library. First, Mr Roach's old success, 'The

Choir Boy', repeated every term, was called for. Then Horniman, after a lot of protestations, sang 'Linden Lea'. He had a nice voice. Sale congratulated him. 'I suppose it'll be my turn next,' he laughed. 'Bit of an ordeal, this, isn't it?'

But now the boys set up a tremendous yelling for Dwight. 'We want Dwight. We want Dwight,' they shouted and stamped. 'Dwight seems to have become very popular all of a sudden,' Sale remarked. And Dwight hesitated, fidgeting in his chair and smiling vaguely. 'Better not, old boy,' Griffin whispered. 'Shall I give them The Ram of Derbyshire?' asked Dwight, as though in a dream. 'No, no. Better not. We'll do our singing later on,' said Griffin uneasily. Dwight rose to his feet.

There was terrific applause as he came down the room. Fernandes, who had accompanied Horniman, rose to follow, then apparently changed his mind and sat down again. There was a sudden, complete silence. The news had spread all over the School that Dwight had been wonderful at supper and would be sure to be wonderful now. Dwight stood facing his audience, still faintly smiling. He kept his head bent forward like a deaf man. Then he began to sing: 'Drink to me only,' at the top of his voice, and without the least expression. At the end of the fourth line he stopped short, said, quite distinctly, 'that's enough', and went back to his place.

Everybody was completely taken by surprise; but the applause was louder than ever. Plumtree and Ross were delighted. Ciddy himself clapped. Griffin, thumping Dwight on the shoulder, kept saying: 'By God, you've pulled it off. By God, old boy, you've done it at last.'

After a little, when the excitement had died down, Fernandes bent towards Sladen and whispered: 'Now, Godfrey.' They had arranged before supper that Sladen should sing something pretty lively from one of the revues on in Town. It would give the place a bit of a shake-up. But Sladen scowled and said, in a quite unfamiliar, aggressive voice: 'I'm not going to do anything, so you needn't think I am.' His face was flushed. Fernandes shrugged his shoulders and grinned at Dwight, who remarked unexpectedly: 'You're a very rude little boy.' Sladen sniggered.

Word came that the actors were ready. There was a re-arrangement of chairs. Dwight and Griffin took places right at the back of the room, against the door. Sladen kept beside them. The other Old Boys and the Staff were in the next rows, in front. Sale worked the curtains. Scenes from the Merchant of Venice began.

'Take me out of this, quick,' Dwight whispered suddenly.

'Right you are, I've had enough,' said Griffin.

Rising, they slipped through the door and were gone in a moment. Sladen had followed them.

'Let me come with you, Philip.'

'No. Go away.'

'Please let me come. I've got lots of money, if you're going to the Cock Pheasant.'

'What do you know about the Cock Pheasant, my boy? They don't allow schoolboys there.'

'I'm nearly eighteen.'

'I don't care if you're one billion trillion. Get Leonard to take you. We're busy.'

'Oh, let him come, Philip. He'll blub if we don't.'

'All right, come along then.'

'Thanks awfully,' said Sladen, whose eyes had really been full of tears.

Dwight's peevishness vanished when they got out of doors. 'Hurrah', he yelled, running as he had run that morning, his arms stretched out. He began climbing a tree. They pulled him down.

It was some time before Fernandes noticed their absence. When he had done so, he gave them five minutes to return. After this, he followed. He visited Dwight's bedroom and the bathroom. His third guess was correct.

The bar of the Cock Pheasant was crowded. Evidently, they had already created something of a sensation.

Through tobacco-smoke Dwight's face first appeared, radiant with joy. He took Fernandes aside and whispered in his ear.

'You see, the truth is, Leonard – you mustn't tell these people – but we're most terribly, terribly drunk.'

Griffin, with his eyes tight shut, evidently encouraged by the applause of the onlookers, was playing some form of Up Jenkins against the potboy. Sladen leant on the counter, very pale.

'Well, Godfrey,' began Fernandes.

'Go away, bastard,' said Sladen. Some navvies laughed.

'And now, Leonard,' Dwight was skipping about like a sheepdog, 'you must get just nice and happy like us; and then we'll go and burn the dear old School to the earth.'

'We'll burn every bleeding, blazing building in this village to the bloody ground,' agreed Griffin, enthusiastically, over his shoulder.

'Well, come back and do it now,' said Fernandes. 'They're all waiting for you.'

'Waiting for us? Do you hear that, Griff? They're waiting for us.'

'But why are they waiting for us?'

'I'll tell you if you come outside,' said Fernandes coaxingly.

'I've got something to tell you, too, Philip,' said Sladen, suddenly joining in the conversation. He spoke in a low but excited voice. Nobody but Fernandes heard him.

'Just this one little glass,' Dwight was pleading. 'It's only beef-tea.'

'I'll drink it if you'll come.'

'You will? My God, Griff, isn't Leonard a sportsman? Every inch of him ... What would you like? A sherry? Or some port? Or have a Horse's Neck?'

'Anything. Only be quick. Or everybody'll wonder where we are.'

Dwight stopped, suspiciously; half-way to the counter.

'Why are you in such a hurry, Leonard?' he asked smiling.

'Because Ciddy will notice what a long time you've been gone.'

'It isn't a plot, is it?'

'No, of course not. Why should it be a plot?'

'I was rather afraid it might be a little plot of yours, Leonard.'

'But why?' Fernandes was half-laughing, half-furious with impatience.

'A little plot to get us away from this nice house before closing time. Because we're not going, are we, Griff?'

'I should just think not, Philip.'

'That's all right then. And now you'll stop and have a nice little drink, won't you, Leonard? I'm sure it'll be good for your cough.'

'But I haven't got a cough.'

'You will have when you've drunk this, though. Won't he, Griff?'

'By God, he will. By. God. He. Will.'

At last it was closing time. They shuffled down the lane, Fernandes in the middle. He was wondering how to get them quietly into the house. Griffin and Dwight sang. Fernandes asked:

'How are you feeling, Godfrey?'

'I'm all right,' said Sladen, greenish white, 'only I want to show Philip something.'

'Well, little man,' said Dwight, 'what do you want to show me? Where is it?'

'Over there,' Sladen pointed towards the outbuildings of the Senior Changing-Room. The moon was well up.

'Can't we see it tomorrow?' asked Fernandes. 'They're probably hunting for us.'

'No, I want to see it now,' said Dwight. 'Is it a present?'

'They belong to you by rights,' Sladen answered.

Having led them to a corner of the building, he knelt down on the ground against the wall. The others stood beside him. Fernandes, being sober, felt the intense cold.

He kept stamping his feet and looking about; praying that Ciddy wouldn't appear.

'For God's sake be quick,' he said.

'Just one moment, Leonard. Only just one moment.'

Sladen was clumsily removing a loose brick from the wall.

'In there,' he said faintly.

'What are?'

Dwight put his hand into the opening.

'Completely full of nothing.'

'It's a long time ago,' said Sladen. 'Someone's found the place out since.'

'But what did you put in there, Godfrey?'

'Our young friend's slightly overcome,' said Dwight.

Sladen had begun being sick. Dwight and Fernandes supported him.

'Whoa, up. That's a good boy. Fetch 'em up.'

'Out she comes. Let 'em have it.'

'And the next please. Right up. Café and Roof Garden.'

'Better now, Godfrey?'

'Let's get him indoors.'

'It'll be quicker to carry him.'

'Sure you can manage, Philip?'

'You bet. Bury the Great Duke with an Empire's lamentation.'

Sladen was now quite limp. His staggering bearers moved towards the front-door. Again, they began to sing. The lights of a stationary car showed by the porch.

'That's my faithful taxi,' said Griffin calmly. 'I ordered it, and there it waits.'

'Good God, is it?' Fernandes left them to manage Sladen as best they could and raced towards the house, expecting to encounter Ciddy on the doorstep. But there was only the maid talking to the driver. She had been in to find Griffin and they had told her he was somewhere about; sure to appear in a minute. They had not been waiting long. The play was still on. Fernandes got rid of her before the group approached. He found Griffin's hat and coat on a chair just inside the hall and had them ready for him.

'Well, old boy, it's been a delightful evening. Most delightful.'

'Do hurry up,' said Fernandes. 'You'll miss your train.'

'It's frightfully hard to tear oneself away. . . . I mean – to tear away oneself; if you understand me.'

'I understand you, old boy.'

'Thanks. I knew you would.'

'Well, goodbye, Philip.'

'Not good-bye, Griff. Au revoir. I'm coming with you. Here, Leonard,' Dwight swung Sladen forward, 'here's your little chum. A thousand thanks for the loan of him.' He jumped into the taxi after Griffin.

'But Philip, what about all your things? What'll everybody think?'

'Never mind. Never mind. Best of luck, old boy.'

'Where to, sir,' asked the driver. 'Clanford Junction?'

'No, the Arc du Triomphe.'

Dwight waved back from the window. Fernandes shouted something, but the driver had already touched his cap and nodded. The tail-light vanished up the lane. Sladen, lolling forward in Fernandes' arms, was again being sick.

An Evening at the Bay

'GOOD evening, Mrs Grainger,' said Allen. 'Can we have two large stouts, please? This is a friend of ours. What would you like to drink, Philip?'

Philip asked for a gin and ginger. A small gin. Mrs Grainger, touching her waved fringe with the tips of her fingers, asked if he was staying long.

'A fortnight? That's nice. You'll get a lot of good from the air here. It's done your friends good. They're looking a lot better than they did.'

'They are that,' said Mr Peck, the coastguard, to a man called Bruiser, who worked in the quarry.

'They've come into their own again,' Bruiser agreed.

'You're from London, I expect?'

Philip said yes. He was rather embarrassed.

'I was in London last September,' the waiter from the Hotel, an amateur humorist, rolled his eyes: 'Oh, my word!'

Mr Peck nodded with serious interest.

'What I mean to say – in London you can always get real enjoyment for your money. What I mean, if you've got five shillings to spend you can get five shillings' worth of real enjoyment.'

'That's right.'

The waiter winked at me. Allen took Philip through into the Lounge Bar, where there were armchairs and little tables. It had been fitted up that summer, for the use of visitors from the Hotel. A few came at first, but there was no way in except through the Public Bar and this discouraged the fastidious.

I waited for the drinks. I wanted to tell Mrs Grainger to double Philip's gin.

'We've got to feed him up.'

'This is the centre of the dress circle,' Allen was saying.

Philip sat down in the corner by the window. He could see the whole of the Bay. The ruins of the little esplanade, undermined and broken up by the sea five years ago. The large stucco house with boat-shaped verandas in the hollow of the swampy meadow. The gorse-bushes and the sandy lane stretching away to the left. The boarding-houses and lodgings with notices: Teas. Non-Residents Catered For. Marine View. Ocean Villa. Beach View, where we were staying. Bathing-dresses hung from windows blazing in the sunset. The opposite cliff was lit bright orange. The roofs of the new bungalows gleamed. The monument caught the light at the top of the swollen Down. On the right, the rocks of the bar were slowly drowning in a stagnant tide.

'Maud's watching,' I told Philip. 'She must have seen us come in here.'

'There's not much those two don't see, between them,' said Allen.

He pointed. There was a face above the half-curtains in the upper bow-window of the stucco house.

'Where's the other one?' Philip asked.

'Christine? She'll be out in a minute now. This is just to watch we don't get away.'

Philip was obviously thrilled.

Through the half-open door into the Public Bar we heard Mrs Grainger's voice rather confidentially telling Mr Peck about her nephew and how he was in the Flying Corps, and liked coming home on leave from Egypt.

Two girls came strolling round the corner from the left into our view. They sat down on a seat at the top of the shingle-bank and looked at the sea. The waiter probably waved to them from the window of the Public Bar. They turned their heads away with a curious deaf movement, like pigeons. The waiter smirked in comic falsetto.

'They all want me. I don't know if it's my hair or what it is. Oh, dear!'

'Of course,' said Mrs Grainger, 'it was so different from what Egypt. ... Of course, he was so fond of the bread and butter and that. ... It was so different from Egypt. ...'

'Here she comes,' said Allen.

Philip watched the fair-haired girl step with a conscious skip from the veranda of the house.

'She's got her new blouse on tonight. That's a good sign.'

Christine paused, looked back over her shoulder, sauntered towards the gate, paused, moved on. She did not even glance up at Maud.

'She's seen you,' said Allen.

Philip took a sip of his gin and ginger. He leant against the sill of the window, watching.

'So has Maud,' I said. 'I expect they tossed up for you.'

Christine had passed out by the gate into the road. She

was pulling grass out of the hedge. A piercing whistle sounded from the left. It was one of the errand-boys lounging against the wall by the sweetshop. Christine took no notice. She turned casually and began walking up the road towards the Down. The two girls on the seat were sitting as though they felt a draught at the back of their necks. There was another loud whistle.

'Did you see,' Mrs Grainger was saying, 'where that young fellow was drowned at Southsea? Sad when you're on a holiday.'

Jock had arrived in the Public Bar.

'Evening, Jock. Still fed up?'

'Still f-fed up?' Jock must have put on his Woolworth monocle. 'Bai goom?'

Loud laughter.

'When I was young,' said Mrs Grainger, 'the days never went slowly enough, I'm sure.'

Christine was climbing the path, skipping every few yards and throwing back her head. Already the light had gone off the cliff. The girls on the seat looked chilly.

'Are them two parties friends of yours?' Bruiser asked Jock.

'They so-soon will b-be.'

Philip was sipping his drink, watching Christine's figure get smaller up the cliff. Maud was still at the window of the house. My eye caught Allen's.

'Be a man,' said Allen to Philip.

Jock had lounged out to speak to the girls on the seat. He was being watched from the window of the Public Bar. There were loud guffaws. The waiter's titter. One of the errand-boys, invisible, made a noise like a sea-gull. Two elderly visitors from the Hotel walked past, briskly, to take their evening look at the sea.

'She's waiting for you,' said Allen.

Christine was walking out along the cliff, moving more slowly. She stopped, looking down into the Bay. Philip blushed and grinned.

'Be a little man,' I said coaxingly.

The visitors came slowly back. They seemed bored and depressed. Philip took a big sip, finishing his drink.

'You'll have another of those,' said Allen.

'No, thanks very much.'

Allen rose, picked up Philip's glass and went through with it into the Public Bar. He met Jock bringing in his two girls. Jock was rather drunk. He winked at me, showing the girls to a table in the corner of the Lounge Bar. The girl Jock liked sat down neatly, crossing her legs, patting her skirt straight, and pointing the toe of her shoe. One could see how she must appeal to Jock. She was a City typist. The Bumpkin's Dream. As exciting as an undressable doll. She didn't sprawl or giggle. She glanced at her friend and smiled. The friend, of course, was a dud. She looked dejected. She felt uncomfortable in here, knowing that she was a tack-on and tomorrow evening would not be invited. Mrs Grainger switched on the electric light in both bars. Jock's girl powdered her nose. She asked for a port and lemon. Her friend would have the same.

'Two ports and lemons and a p-pint of draught. And will you give me a t-timber-yard on a s-small scale?'

'Why, whatever do you mean?' Jock's girl asked.

'This here.' Jock held out the box of matches. 'This here's a t-timber-yard, isn't it?'

'Oh, the idea!' She laughed lightly, genteelly, being careful not to show her teeth. They must be bad. And a moment later, with a violent snort, the friend laughed too. One convulsive snort, and she was silent, blushing crimson. Jock's girl pretended to be very much astonished.

'Why, Elsie, whatever *is* the matter?'

The figure of a young man had appeared on the edge of the cliff, quite close to where Christine was standing. He lit a cigarette. The errand-boys at the corner were watching. There was a long mournful howl which echoed round the rocks.

'Who's that?' asked Philip. Allen and I exchanged glances.

'Frank Chalk. From the Garage,' said Allen. 'We near-ly tripped over him, two evenings ago, up on the Down. He doesn't wait for Nanny to introduce him to the girls.'

'I'm afraid,' I said, 'that you're about to become a mem-ber of the Antlers Club.'

'It doesn't worry me.' Philip began to sip his second drink.

The bald man from the station banked down the corner on his tuned-up Norton, chugged forward to the edge of the breakwater, glanced at the sea, paddled the bike round and was off again up the road within the half-minute.

Jock was entertaining his girls. They were down for a fortnight from Ealing.

'Oh, I like this place. I think it's ever so nice.'

'You do?' Jock winked at Allen. 'I reckon I'm about fed up with it.'

'I suppose it must be quiet in the winter.'

'Quiet?' Jock brought out his monocle. 'B-bai goom!'

Christine had turned away from Frank. She was coming down the path from the cliff.

'She's not having any,' Allen whispered to Philip. 'You see? She's waiting for you.'

'Oh, rot,' said Philip, gulping his drink.

'Be a man.'

Jock's girl was asking: 'You have business down here, I suppose?'

'I have b-business whenever this p-place is open.'

'Why, whatever do you do here?'

'I d-drown my s-sorrows.'

Christine was half-way down the path. It was too dark now to see whether Maud was still at the window. Frank had disappeared. There were screams from the corner, where the errand-boys stood. They were teasing the skivvy from The Boot.

'Now look here,' said Allen. 'All you have to do is to walk along the road. And as you pass her say good even-ing. And she says good evening. And you say: It's a lovely evening. I was just going for a ramble. Would you care to come?'

'Oh yes,' said Philip, 'you know the Etiquette Book backwards. You'd better come with us and tell me what to do.'

'I will, if you like.'

'Oh, the idea,' Jock's girl was saying. 'Whatever do you want to do that for?' Her voice was raised a little, for our benefit.

'Because I'm f-fed up.'

'You poor thing!'

'P-poor *w-what* did you say?'

'I'm very sorry.'

'I s-should just think you ought to be s-sorry.'

'Suppose she doesn't answer?' Philip asked.

'Ask her if she's ever been pushed off a cliff. Say you've often heard it's a most extraordinary sensation, and that, of course, if there's any damage done, one can always pay.'

With a loud scream, the skivvy from The Boat appeared round the corner, chasing one of the boys. She boxed his ears. He dodged, mocking. The others stood round and jeered.

'Give it 'ere, Ted. Be a sport. Look it's like this. I've got to be in by ten. I'll come tomorrow night.'

'I'm surprised at you. Reely I am.'

Christine had reached the road. And there was Frank again on the cliff.

'Don't you have any tea-dances down here in the winter?' Jock's girl opened her eyes very wide, squinting at Allen. 'You don't? Fancy. It wouldn't suit me, I'm afraid. I'm ever so fond of dancing.'

'I bet you sixpence she doesn't answer,' said Philip.

'Done. Now run along and lose it.'

'Bet both of us sixpence, won't you?' I said.

'If you like.'

'Where's Ethel tonight?' they were asking the skivvy.

'Well, it's like this. She's in 'er skin somewhere.'

'It's like this. It's like this,' the boy mimicked. 'That's proper Pompey, that is.'

Philip drained down his second glass. He stood up.

'I'll be back in five minutes for the money.'

'Give her our love. Oh, and I say, do find out whether she really believed what I told her the other night about Christopher being German. And ask her whether she's forgiven me for the present I gave her. She'll know what you mean.'

'We'll leave the permanganate in your room.'

'Optimists.'

'Don't wake us.'

Philip went out through the Public Bar. Allen moved his chair so that we could both watch. Christine had got down nearly to her own gate. She kept her eyes on the ground. But gradually she walked more and more slowly, paused, turned. Philip, lighting a cigarette, began to stroll after her, down the road. With a little gesture of townish swank he flipped the ash from the cigarette, shooting his cuff.

Allen grinned. 'At last.'

We hugged our knees with glee.

The errand-boys had stopped ragging the skivvy. They were watching. I thought I could see Maud's face pressed against the window. Frank was like a sentinel on the cliff, looking down at them. Christine was getting kittenish again. She made little dashes up the path, brandishing a handful of grass. Philip didn't hurry. He admired everything – the bathing-huts, the houses, the sea. Sauntering past the stucco house, he gave it a good look up and down, from Maud's window to the veranda, like a tourist regretfully deciding that he hasn't got time for a peep inside Westminster Abbey.

'Do you know,' said Allen with admiration, 'I shouldn't wonder if he really has done this kind of thing before?'

'Yes. I didn't believe a word he told us this morning, though.'

'Neither did I.'

The errand boys uttered a miaow. It was getting very dark. We peered out at the cliff. The plump, cocky little figure of Philip moved leisurely up the path after the white skirt, which drove forward in short rushes and kept stopping, like a paper bag being blown up the slope and getting stuck and being blown on again. But Philip didn't give up. They were drawing nearer to each other. Frank turned away, disgusted.

'He's rather a little marvel.'

'Perhaps she'll let him. You never know.'

'Catch her. He'll get a bit of geography, with luck. She's only a teaser.'

'You know,' said Allen, 'I should be quite annoyed if she let him. I don't mind anything else. But after the fuss she made on Thursday.'

And now they were actually walking abreast. Two yards apart. A yard. Side by side. They never stopped. Their little figures grew smaller and smaller, keeping right on over the dark smooth belly of the Down, towards the monument sticking up into the sky. The darkness swallowed them. The errand-boys, moving up the road with the skivvy, sounded one last, mournfully derisive whistle.

'Let's go.'

We passed out through the Public Bar, nodding good night.

'Your friend's enjoying his visit,' said Mrs Grainger, smiling.

'Boys will be boys.'

We strolled out to the wall of the breakwater. The spark of a cigarette moved down the road. It was Frank. Allen dropped a pebble into the tide.

'The two pimps.'

The sea was like a black pond and stank of weed. From beyond the headland, the beam of the lighthouse moved gropingly clockwise.

'Yes, I must say,' said Allen, 'I really shall be damned annoyed if she lets him.'

The last bus came down the road from the village, empty, brightly lit, late. The young driver bounded from his seat, nearly too late for a drink. Walking stealthily into the Public Bar, he kicked Bruiser hard from behind. Shouts.

The weed stank of cold bad fish. The lighthouse searched the empty Bay.

'The appalling tragedy of the heterosexual,' said Allen. 'They've burnt us out of our homes. Now we've got nothing left but the Beach Girls. We're the Great Doomed Tribe.'

'Be naturalized Bulgarian.'

Allen yawned 'It's probably only the sea which makes me talk like this. One should never, never look at the sea.'

As we passed the window of the Lounge Bar, Jock was leaving with the girls. We heard Jock's girl say: 'And now I suppose you'll go home and drink till you look like it.'

'That's certainly an idea,' said Allen.

I hurried into the Bar. They were just closing.

'We nearly forgot something, Mrs Grainger. Four large bottles of Draught, please, and two packets of Iona Fingers and two packets of Potato Crisps.'

The Turn Round the World

WE saw him the moment we came on board the little steamer in La Palma harbour. From beneath an enormous battered topee his thin, unshaven goat-face looked out with wistful, bleary eyes. He wore a very old, stained khaki uniform which might once have belonged to an officer in the British Army. His puttees were ragged. His feet, in leather sandals, were bare. His luggage, a most unmilitary-looking large cardboard suitcase, stood beside him on the deck.

He was so odd, so lost, that he might have arrived from almost anywhere remote: equatorial Africa, a film studio, the moon. But nobody except ourselves appeared to be taking the least notice of him. Yes, there was one other passenger who seemed faintly interested and amused; a dapper, sunburnt young man in a light grey flannel suit who lounged against the rail next to us, smoking a cigarette. We exchanged glances. The young man nodded in the direction of the topee, tapped his forehead, winked at me, and grinned.

And now the odd traveller in the topee had spotted us too. His face lighted up, as if with relief – we might have been friends he had momentarily lost sight of in the crowd. A would-be ingratiating smile parted his damp protruding lips. He made towards us: his manner at once hearty and wheedling.

'Hullo, Johnny,' he greeted us. 'You two English boys, eh? Jolly good. Yes, sir. You bet.'

'*Es tut mir leid, mein Herr, ich spreche nur Deutsch.*'

I hardly expected this to work. It didn't. Quite ignoring my answer and my manner, he continued.

'Jolly good. You take my card, eh? You give me what you like.'

I gave him one peseta. And, certainly, the card was worth the money. It had pictures on both sides. On one side was our friend himself, in white uniform and knee-boots, complete with pack, water-bottle, two revolvers, hunting-knife, compass and field-glasses. He was trying, heroically, to stand upright beneath the weight of his equipment, but the rifle which he held in his left hand was obviously being used as a prop. His eyes had the patient burdened stare of a mule. Beneath this portrait was printed: *Capitan Explorador Español Juan Martianez se desea una buena voluntad por esta tarjeta.* The inscription went on to say that the Explorer-Captain had already visited North, South, and Central America. He had travelled twenty-four thousand kilometres on foot. His journey had occupied eighteen years.

'Fancy,' said Heinz, awed. 'He's been walking all my life!'

On the other side of the card was a picture called 'Indian Women from the Andes Mountains'. The two plump little creatures were doing their best to look dainty in stiff, ugly native costumes. They were probably professional models from a studio in Madrid.

When we had finished examining the card, I looked up to say something polite, but the Explorer-Captain Martianez had already returned to stand guard over his cardboard suitcase.

'Silly old fool – dressing himself up like that. He's a regular scarecrow, isn't he?'

This was from the young man in the smart flannel suit. To my surprise he spoke fluent German. The bitter contempt in his tone made me, illogically, rather indignant: why hadn't *he* bought a card, too?

'I don't see why you should sneer at him,' I said. 'He's got to live, poor devil, like everyone else.'

The young man didn't seem offended at this retort. Indeed, he smiled with considerable charm, showing white, even teeth: my warmth appeared to amuse him. His brown skin was so clear, his eyes were so bright, and his figure was so slight and lithe that he looked almost a boy. Yet he couldn't really be very young, for I now noticed several streaks of grey in his thick, bushy black hair.

'Oh yes,' he agreed, amused. 'We've all got to live.'

'You're not German, are you?' I asked.

'No. I'm Hungarian. Look here.' As though I were an official, he had whipped out his passport and was turning over the stamped pages for my inspection: 'Austria, Germany, Belgium, Holland, Denmark. . . . Here you are – twelve countries, so far.'

'Very interesting.' Not wishing to seem too inquisitive, I paused to offer him a cigarette. But his eyes and his thoughts had returned to the bizarre figure of the Explorer-Captain.

'Such an idiot,' he muttered. 'The way he came straight up to you – before we'd even started. Couldn't let you alone for five minutes. He always does it like that.'

'Do you know him, then?' I was very much surprised. The two hadn't exchanged so much as a nod.

'Know him? I should just think I do!' The Hungarian flicked his cigarette ash carelessly over the rail. 'I've known him for years.'

We reached Hierro at three o'clock in the afternoon. It is the smallest of all the islands – a last, tiny volcanic crumb of Europe, cloud-bound and desolate, at the verge of the tropics. There is no harbour. Jumping wildly into a rowing-boat which skidded on a nasty switchbacking swell, we were washed ashore at the foot of a precipice, near some huts. Crammed into a rickety motor-bus, we roared up an alarming corkscrew mule-track to Valverde, the capital village, which lies fifteen hundred feet high, in a perpetual Scotch mist. Coming up out of the brilliant sunshine, in wet clothes, we were shivering, seasick, and wretchedly hungry. The Explorer-Captain also seemed deeply depressed. The Hungarian had disappeared.

He turned up, however, just as we were finishing our meal. By this time life looked brighter. The food was unexpectedly good, the Fonda was fairly clean, and we had been given a bedroom which did not, for a wonder, open on to an inner courtyard with latrines and hens. The Explorer-Captain had created some diversion by bargaining with the landlord for special terms. He promised, rather pathetically, to eat very little and never to ask for a second helping. The Hungarian had, presumably, had his meal somewhere else in the village. He was sleek and smiling, in the highest spirits.

'Well, that's that,' he told us. 'My business is settled, I've seen all I want to see. Nothing doing here.'

I laughed: 'You seem to make up your mind very quickly.'

'Oh, it doesn't take me long. I've just been having supper with the Mayor.' (He brought this out quite casually.) 'He advised me not to waste my time here. I'm going on tonight.'

He explained to us that the steamer would leave for Gomera at nine o'clock. If we missed it we should have to stay on the island for four days, until the next boat arrived. The landlord, not unnaturally, had omitted to mention this. However, we both agreed that we couldn't face a night of seasickness so soon. We would stay here. Perhaps the weather would clear up.

'All right,' said the Hungarian. 'Then I'll see you later.' He indicated the Explorer-Captain, who was to be seen from the window trying to press his cards on some unwilling villagers in the drizzle below: 'I suppose he's staying on here, too?'

'Yes, I think so.'

'Good,' said the Hungarian, with what seemed unnecessary brutality. 'I knew he would – the fool.'

Then he shook hands and left us.

We got through our four days somehow or other. On the first, we climbed to the central plateau of the island, high above the clouds. It is hot here and very dry. Three cinder-hills rise from the desert of sand and pumice-stone. One of the cinder-hills must, we knew, be the highest peak on Hierro – but which? They all looked much the same size. At last we decided to climb each of them in turn. It took us most of the day. The rest of the time in Valverde we were in a state of convalescence: I tried to understand three-year-old Cuban newspapers. Heinz played billiards with the village notables. The rain seldom stopped for longer than a quarter of an hour.

We often talked about the Explorer-Captain, who was away on a walking tour of the south end of the island, and about the Hungarian. We speculated a good deal as to the Hungarian's profession. I thought he must be some kind of commercial traveller. Heinz was sure he was a spy.

Commercial travellers, he insisted, don't wear such light flannel suits.

San Sebastian, on Gomera, is a pleasant change: a shallow, open valley, with the little town on the edge of the beach. Columbus stayed here once: there are palm-trees and camels and flowers. We found, to our astonishment, that the landlord of the Fonda was expecting us.

'Oh yes, your friend told me you were arriving. He has engaged a room. You will find him waiting for you.'

He showed us into a room with two beds. In one of the beds lay the Hungarian, in his shirt. He seemed very much at his ease and greeted us like old friends.

'I wasn't sure what time the steamer would get in, so I engaged this room for you last night.' He smiled charmingly and added, as if to forestall any possible objection: 'Of course, if you had come, I should have slept on the floor.'

'I hope you're not feeling ill?' I asked, with some sarcasm.

'Oh dear, no!' He laughed at the mere idea. 'I'm only waiting here until they've pressed my suit. It's all I have, you see.'

I frowned. I wasn't pleased. Both of us were dirty and sleepy after a night on deck. I had been looking forward to a wash and bed at once. The Hungarian must have guessed this, for he jumped out of bed in his underclothes and said kindly: 'You get in. You look tired.'

'There's no hurry,' I answered crossly, unwilling, in my stupid British way, either to lie in his sheets or to tell him I wanted the bedclothes changed. The Hungarian smiled and sat down on a chair. He began scratching his muscular brown calves.

'Was Martianez on the boat with you?' he asked.

'Yes.'

'You didn't tell him you were coming here?'

'No. I didn't see him after we landed, at all.'

The Hungarian chuckled.

'The old donkey. I gave him the slip on Hierro, all right. I bet he didn't get a *centimo*, there. As for this island, he's welcome to it. I've collected all there is to get. When he goes round they'll only set the dogs on him.'

I suppose we were both staring at him blankly, for he added: 'Why, I've never shown you *my* card, have I?'

Hurrying to a suitcase in the corner of the room, he produced two cards – one in German, which he gave to Heinz; one in English, for me. My card read as follows:

THE TURN ROUND THE WORLD

I am an Hungarian estudiant, walking round the world with the object to know all countries, nations and people, with habits, etc. Later, when all is accomplished, I shall publicate my memorial. I have pleasure to beg a welcome and encouragement for this efforts.

And there was a picture of the Hungarian, in his immaculate flannel suit, with stick and gloves, leaning against an ornamental column in a photographer's studio.

'What do you think of it?' he asked us, with pride. 'Better than that old-fashioned rubbish Martianez carts around? And I've got them printed in all languages. A waiter in Marseilles who's a friend of mine translated them for me. He speaks seven languages perfectly.'

Later in the day, the Hungarian gave us some valuable hints on how to succeed in his profession:

'You must always be smartly dressed,' he told us, 'especially if the village is very poor. No peasant gives much to a shabbily dressed man. They think he's a swindler – that's quite natural. Why, you yourself: who do you pay to see at the cinema – Greta Garbo or some down-and-out actress nobody has heard of? You don't think to yourself: Garbo's rolling in money and this girl hasn't got enough for a meal? Of course you don't. . . . Another thing: always start at the top. When I arrive anywhere I go straight to the Mayor. Then the others see me coming out of his house and they think: that's an important person. A lot of the country people are so ignorant they believe I'm a tax-collector. . . . When I see the Mayor, I don't ask for money straight away, like that camel Martianez; I ask for a letter of introduction to the authorities of the next village. Then I talk to him for an hour or two about my travels. I make jokes, I entertain him. Then, at the end, I ask straight out for a *duro*. If he won't give it, I say: "They gave me two at the last place." And if he still refuses, I say: "This village seems to be full of Arabs." That always makes them wild. . . . It's very seldom I fail. But you have to keep yourself smart and you have to be able to talk to them.'

That evening we saw him off on the steamer to Tenerife. The Explorer-Captain had left San Sebastian already, for the interior of the island.

'I think I've got about five days' start on him,' said the Hungarian. 'I work faster than he does. And then, with luck, he mayn't be able to get a boat for another day or two. ... But he always manages to catch up on me somehow, the old swine. I met him first in Granada, three years ago, and I've never been able to shake him off since. He follows me about, because he knows I always find the best places. He simply lives on my brains – the beastly old parasite.'

Just as the Hungarian was going on board, our landlord came running along the quay to demand an extra two pesetas for pressing the flannel suit. I couldn't quite understand what he said, but the Hungarian translated it to me without the least embarrassment. I paid up as pleasantly as I could.

He had been on Tenerife before, he told us: but there were still a number of small villages he hadn't visited, at the west end of the island, under the mountain. 'It would be a pity to miss them,' he added casually. At parting, I rather shamefacedly pressed ten pesetas into his hand. I wanted to surprise him, but he was not surprised. He accepted them pleasantly, simply; as his due, his absolute right – an instalment of the very moderate tax he levied upon Society. We waved to our fellow-parasite on the departing steamer and he waved gaily back. We never saw him again.

A Day in Paradise

OUR first glimpse of the island is always a disappointment. After the brochures, the travel-posters, the adjectives in the guide-book, we may be excused for expecting the incredible: a flower-berg towering solitary from the tropical ocean, thirteen thousand feet high, crowned with snow. Instead of which, crowding to the rail in our blazers, our summer frocks, with our cameras ready for the first historic snap, we find ourselves entering a large, dirty, modern harbour: cranes, oil-tanks, shabby houses and, in the background, a low range of barren volcanic hills. The central peak itself is hidden by dingy clouds. Not a palm-tree, not a flower is to be seen.

Our faces fall, but we say nothing; we reserve judgement. After all, we have paid our money, we have cruised for eight days, we are not going to admit, even to ourselves, that we have been swindled. This is a great moment for us. We have saved up for it, talked about it, dreamed of it, through these long hours in the classroom, behind the counter, over the kitchen sink. We must be patient. This can't be all we came to see. Look, already the launch with the Customs officials is speeding towards us from the jetty. In half an hour we shall all be on land.

And, even as we set foot on the mole steps, we are reassured. Look! Look! There's a real Negro, selling postcards. There's a camel, carrying a load of bananas. What funny carriages, with striped green hoods. All the drivers are yelling at us, waving their arms. Soon we are rattling through the streets, wishing we could turn our heads all ways at once, so as to miss nothing. Here, in the public park, are palm-trees like feather mops, like the most exquisite ferns. And there, in the opulent gardens of villas, roses grow in banks, blossom spills over from veranda and trellis. Notice the fountains, notice the boot-blacks before the café, the officer playing with his string of coloured beads; notice the cathedral. Notice how the peasant women balance huge baskets of oranges on their heads. It gives them natural grace and an erect carriage even in old age, the guide-book says. No doubt that's why they do it. Goodness, whatever is that? Daubed on a whitewashed wall, the sign of the hammer and sickle. Are there communists here, too? What a joke! How funny, how silly, how charming everything is!

The interior of the island, to quote the guide-book again, is as fertile as a garden. Every inch is under cultivation. The whole mountain-side is parcelled out into little plots. Beside each plot stands a tiny shed; you could hardly describe it as a house at all. Yet often, as our motor-coach rolls past, a family of a dozen or more will emerge from one of these sheds to watch us. If we had more time we might pause to wonder how all these people can possibly contrive to exist. As it is, we merely wave our hand-kerchiefs. Besides, haven't we read somewhere that peasants in warm countries require scarcely anything to eat? The climate doesn't seem to have had that effect on us, however. We are very glad indeed when a stop is made at the Mountain Hotel for lunch.

Back in the port, we find that we have just time for a stroll on our own account before returning on board. Naturally, we turn our steps, this time, in the opposite direction; towards a part of the town which the guides didn't show us. Soon we have left the main street. We find ourselves in a district of narrow lanes running uphill and down. The houses here are so ruinous that we wonder if they hadn't been damaged by an earthquake, yet people are living in them, as in the tumbledown sheds on the mountain-side. Children with great dark eyes are playing in the dirt. All of them are half naked and most of them have open sores on their arms and legs. The sores are disgusting if you look at them too closely; flies are crawling over them. And the stench from the little shuttered ruins of houses is most distressing. But the guidebook, that invaluable psychological prompter, rescues us from an uneasy moment. 'The life of the port', we read, 'is extremely typical and picturesque.' So we take a snapshot of the most typical of the children (he appears to be mentally deficient), pat him, rather gingerly, on the head and give him some money. Immediately, twenty or thirty others are after us, shrieking: 'Penny! Penny!' They become rather a nuisance and have to be shooed off.

Our ramble is terminated by a high wall with barbed wire along the top. This wall, it appears, cuts off the town from the peninsula at the north of the island. One can't go beyond it. On the wall are huge letters in whitewash and several times we read the inscription: *No Mas Guerra!* Out comes our dictionary: No More War! Well now, that really is the crowning absurdity of this ridiculous, romantic island! As if anybody here had reason to bother about War! Consulting the guide-book, we learn, from a footnote, that the buildings on the walled-off peninsula are military barracks and forts.

By the time we have got back to the jetty it is quite dark. We notice, as we take our places in the launch, that numbers of men and boys are settling down to sleep under sacks, with a bundle of straw for a pillow, on the stone. 'You know,' says a girl in our party, 'I envy them. It must be fun to live like that, without any worries or responsibilities.' Many of us agree with her.

That night, after supper, we say good-bye to the island. Nothing is visible, now, but a string of flickering lights, stretching far along the shore. Southend and Brighton are equally beautiful at night from the sea; but then one knows, unfortunately, that they are only Southend and

Brighton. Here we are in the Tropics. Here is Romance. Some of us, almost certainly, will get engaged to be married.

And now we're home again, at the school, behind the counter, in the kitchen; back to the old grind, but with something to dream of, something to talk and boast about for the rest of our lives. Colleagues and friends ask what the island was like. To be quite frank, we find we've forgotten a good deal, a great deal, nearly everything. We remember only the liner, the deck-quoits, the ices, the dancing on board. But we still have our photographs. And there's always the guide-books to prompt us: 'Oh, it's a paradise!' And if, just for a moment, passing through the slums of our native town, we are reminded of that filthy lane down by the port; if we remember, for an instant, our first dismayed impression of the island before the guide-book began to reassure us, of a sinister, squalid place where human beings are living as no animals should be allowed to live; if, seeing a poster in the street, we think of *No Mas Guerra!* scrawled on the whitewash and wonder whether, perhaps, there is some truth in it; whether the struggle against hunger and war isn't more immediate, more universal than we dream: then quickly the image of the island, as the travel-bureau and the guide-book present it, will slide, like a brightly-coloured magic-lantern picture, between us and our real memories, and we shall repeat, as hundreds of others have repeated: 'Yes, indeed . . . it's a paradise on earth.'

I am Waiting

THE incidents which I am about to describe are true; but that does not matter. I can offer you no proof – at least not for the next five years. By that time you will probably have forgotten that you ever read this story. So please believe it or disbelieve it, just as you wish.

I will call myself Wilfred Smith. I choose that name because it describes me rather well; much better than my own. 'Wilfred' suggests (don't you agree?) a certain softness of character, a lack of driving-power, coupled with intellectual refinement. It is uncreative, harmless and weak. 'Smith' is self-effacing, anonymous. All those adjectives suit me.

Today, 25 July 1939, is my birthday. At the age of sixty-seven, I am what you, or anybody else, would call a failure. I have no career, no outstanding achievements behind me. I have established no reputation for wit, intelligence or specialized knowledge. I have never married, and I cannot truthfully say that I have ever been loved – though half a dozen people are, perhaps, mildly fond of me. I cannot even claim to be a paragon of quiet, unappreciated virtue. I am just a fairly selfish, fairly amiable, elderly bachelor – happy with my pipe and book after a good dinner; happiest of all when lying half asleep in bed.

I live in a pleasant house, on the outskirts of a provincial town in the West of England. The house belongs to my younger brother, a successful and energetic solicitor. Mabel, my brother's wife, is very kind to me, on the whole – as long as I am careful to be tidy and not unnecessarily visible. There are three sons, all grown up and all married; they frequently visit us with their wives. All these people call me Uncle Wilfred, or Wilfred, or Wilf. They are well-disposed towards me, I think. Why shouldn't they be? I am no sponger: I pay for my board and lodging from a small inherited income. I do not try to be a nuisance though I know I am sometimes rather a bore.

Once upon a time I used to dream that I might become a tolerably gifted writer. I produced some poems and several short stories, but none of them were ever published, and I was cured of that fancy long ago. Today, I am entirely without hobbies and pastimes. I have never learnt golf – partly, perhaps, because my brother is an excellent player. I cannot remember the rules of even the simplest card-game. A child of seven years old could beat me at draughts.

Like many other idle, middle-aged people in this country today, I spend far too much time reading the newspapers and listening to the radio. In consequence, I have become, during the past ten years, a chronic worrier. I worry endlessly about the future, about the dictators, about wars and rumours of wars. Goodness knows, the times we live in are serious enough. The latest political happenings have made even the most optimistic spirits turn grave. But my kind of worrying is different from theirs; it is altogether less practical, more neurotic. It is, I sadly recognize, an incurable mental disease. Even if all reasonable grounds for alarm were to be magically removed overnight, I am sure that I couldn't recover. I should continue to worry throughout the millennium.

With reference to the story which follows, I need only add that I have never, at any time, had reason to believe that I possessed psychic powers. I have never been particularly interested in spiritualism, astrology, or the occult. And I know no more of the works of Professor Einstein than does the ordinary semi-educated man in the street.

On Friday, 6 January, of this year – I can be exact, for this was the day after the anniversary of my brother's marriage – I was sitting in the drawing-room of our house, alone. The others had all driven into the town to go to the cinema; so I could enjoy the luxury of drawing my arm-chair into the very middle of the hearth-rug, facing and monopolizing the fire. Anybody who has to share a room with a number of other people will know how delightful this occasional and somewhat furtive pleasure can be.

From this position I could see only what was directly in front of me: the fender, the fire-irons, the flaming coals in the grate, the mantelpiece, and the picture which hung above it – a coloured reproduction of Titian's *Nymph and Shepherdess*. The time was about twenty minutes to

nine in the evening. I remember this because I kept
glancing at the clock on the mantelpiece, in order to be
ready to turn on the radio and listen to the news bulletin.

This clock is a wedding-present given to my brother by
the members of his firm. It is made of china, and vaguely
supposed to be valuable. A boy and a girl, in peasant cos-
tume, are supporting the clock itself, contained in a basket
of purple and green fruits. It would probably have
joined several of the other wedding-presents in the lumber-room, years ago, for my brother says it is hideous; but
my sister-in-law likes it; she finds it 'amusing' – and so it
remains.

I may have dozed off, as I so often do. At any rate, I had
closed my eyes. When I reopened them it was with a violent start, as though somebody had called my name. Perhaps the others had returned, unexpectedly early. Some
such thought passed through my mind, but I didn't turn
my head. I don't know why. All my drowsy attention was
focused upon the clock. And what I immediately noticed
was that the left hand was missing from the china figure
of the peasant boy.

It is very difficult for me to describe my precise sensations at that moment. It is difficult because, in order to do
so, I have to think back to a time when this discovery had
no particular significance. I saw only that the hand had
been broken off, wondered how long it had been broken,
and was surprised that I had never noticed it before.
Mabel would be cross, I thought; and this led me to a fear
that I might somehow have done the damage myself,
while I was asleep. I rubbed my eyes, and sat up suddenly
in my chair. I blinked several times. How absurd! I must
have been dreaming. For now, as I examined the clock,
fully awake, I saw that I had made a mistake. The
clock wasn't damaged after all: the china hand was still
intact.

One morning, about a week later, when I was walking
in the garden, Mabel came out of the house with an ex-

pression of extreme annoyance on her face. 'Wilfred,' she said, 'I'm afraid I shall have to sack Annie, after all.' Annie was our new maid; and she wasn't being a success.

'Why?' I asked. 'What's she done now?'

'Can you imagine!' Mabel exclaimed. 'That girl is really worse than an elephant. She's managed to break the drawing-room clock. She was dusting it, she says. She must have used a sledge-hammer.'

But already I was pushing past her, towards the french windows which open into the drawing-room. I hardly knew why I was so excited. Entering the room, I saw what I had dimly expected to see: the china boy's left hand was broken off at the wrist.

One's memory is more cunning than the most adroit minister of propaganda. It can impose the most absolute censorship of inconvenient facts, only to reproduce them, weeks or months later, when the occasion suits its purpose. Half an hour after Mabel had shown me the damaged clock I had forgotten all about my dream. That evening I sat alone in front of the fire and regarded the mutilated boy without a flicker of recognition. Next day the hand was mended, almost without a trace; there was nothing left to remind anybody of the accident. And yet, when the time came to remember, I remembered everything, down to the smallest details, as you can judge for yourself.

The second occurrence took place at eleven twenty-five a.m. on Monday, 20 February. I was in my bedroom, standing near a bookcase which occupies the corner behind my bed. Mabel, as far as I know, was in the kitchen, with the cook. The maid was cleaning the bathroom. My brother was at his office. None of my nephews were staying at the house.

It was a grey morning. Although, from where I stood, I could not see out of the window, I knew by the pattering noise on the glass that it had begun to rain. I had just decided to look up some passages from *The Ring and the Book*. I am very fond of reading Browning.

As I reached out my hand for the volume, I experienced an extraordinary sensation, which I can only compare to that of acute rheumatic pain. Yet I cannot say that it was actually painful. It swept over me, leaving my body tingling and trembling, and the sweat breaking out on my forehead. Violent as the attack was, it didn't alter my position. I stood there as if frozen, with my hand outstretched. What followed cannot have taken more than a minute. Perhaps it occupied only a few seconds.

At first I was aware only of a change of *mood*, very difficult to describe. I felt lighter, happier – as though some oppression had been lifted from my mind. *Lighter*, yes, that was the exact word; for my room was actually full of light, of bright sunshine. The sun was casting shadows on the wall above the bookcase. I could feel its warmth on my hands and the back of my neck.

As I stood, I began not only to feel and see, but to hear also. Sounds were coming up through the window from the garden below. I heard laughter, voices, and the noise of a tennis-ball being hit backwards and forwards across the net. Then one voice, much more distinct than the others, called out: 'Come on, Joyce. Give them hell. They're beginning to crack.' It was my youngest nephew. Joyce is the name of his sister-in-law, my eldest nephew's wife.

No words of mine can describe the strangeness of those familiar words and sounds, I listened to them as a dead man might listen to the voices of the living. They were so near to me, and yet so immeasurably remote. 'Oh, tricky! Very tricky!' I heard Joyce exclaim. And Bob, my eldest nephew, retorted: 'You cow, what do you think you're playing – ping-pong?'

That was all. The next moment the contact – or whatever you like to call it – was broken. My fingers had touched the book; and there I was, back in the grey clear continuity of normal consciousness, with the rain pattering fast on the pane behind me, and the light of a February morning all around. I heard the maid come out of the bathroom and begin to descend the stairs.

I forget exactly what I did next. I think I must have paced the room several times, backwards and forwards, pausing to look down, through the window, at the wet tennis-court and the empty garden beyond. I was deeply excited and disturbed. Although I still wasn't entirely clear what had happened to me, I was aware that something *had* happened, something so dimly tremendous that it dwarfed every other experience of my whole life. This couldn't, like my earlier adventure, be comfortably dismissed as a dream. For an instant I had actually looked, with blurred eyes and confused senses, into some other plane of reality. Was it the future? Or the past? Or neither? I couldn't tell. I only knew what I had heard and seen. This I carefully wrote down, as I have described it here. When I had finished, I felt very tired. I lay down on my bed and slept soundly till lunch.

Thereafter, I was like a reader who searches for some half-remembered passage in a book. I had a kind of assignation with a certain moment in time. Could I find that moment, or would it find me? Obviously, if I had really travelled into the future, and not back into the past, I should have several months to wait. It was very difficult to be patient.

Towards the end of May, Jack, my youngest nephew, came to visit us. He was to stay a fortnight. The fine weather had started, and the tennis-court was already put in order. Whenever anybody spoke of 'Tennis', I, who have never taken any interest in the game, felt my pulses throb with suppressed excitement. But where were the other actors in the strange meaningless little drama I hoped to witness? I repeatedly asked Mabel and my brother if Bob and Joyce were expected. No, they said, not yet. Bob, who is a chartered accountant, had an auditing job in Portsmouth. He wouldn't be likely to visit us before August.

On the afternoon of Saturday, June 3, I returned by bus from shopping in our neighbouring town. It was about a quarter to three. Hearing a confused sound of voices from the garden, I decided to slip into the house by the back door, not wishing to meet the visitors, whoever they were, while I was hot, dusty and laden with parcels. Encountering nobody, I climbed the stairs to my room. I had bought several books at the local antique shop and my first thought was to unpack them. As I moved towards the bookcase I heard Jack's voice on the lawn below, calling the score: 'Fifteen all!'

A girl's voice, which I didn't recognize, cried: 'You skunk, you're cheating!'

'Oh, well played!'

'Lousy!'

'Don't try that Wimbledon stuff here!'

'Damn!'

'Come on, Joyce. Give them hell. They're beginning to crack.'

It was there, my moment. And even as, with a gasp, I recognized it, it was past – it flashed by me and was gone. Long before I recovered my wits sufficiently to hurry to the window the actors had spoken their familiar lines. The drama was over. Looking down into the garden, I saw Jack, Bob, Joyce, and a strange girl chatting and joking across the net at the end of their game. The girl was a friend of Joyce's. She had been brought over in the car from Portsmouth, I later discovered, when Bob planned this surprise visit. He had come to stay for the weekend.

So that was that – and what was I to make of it? If only the evidence had been more satisfactory! If only the voices I had heard that February morning had said something more memorable, more convincing! Jack might at least have named the winner of the Oxford and Cambridge Boat Race. Bob might have quoted some figures on the Stock Exchange. Something you could take hold of, something irrefutable. The truth was, I felt horribly, illogically disappointed. I suppose I had hoped great

things from my moment. Surely such glimpses aren't revealed to us without a purpose? Those words, banal as
they were, should have heralded some cosmic event, some
huge catastrophe or natural phenomenon. Instead of which
– nothing. The sun still shone. The birds still sang. The
heavens hadn't fallen. And here we all were, having tea.

I studied the faces of my relatives, so reassuringly familiar, and new doubts began to trouble me. Granted that
I had been able to predict, with absolute accuracy, a
certain combination of words they would utter on a particular summer afternoon; was that, after all, so remarkable? Couldn't anyone, with any talent at all for catching
tricks of speech, have done the same, for people he knew so
well? Certainly, I had had some very vivid kind of super-
sensory experience. I had imaginatively created a scene;
and this scene, perhaps by the purest coincidence, had
later been enacted in real life. It was all very odd. But
plenty of odd things happen. They prove nothing. No, if
I wanted to be certain I should have to wait.

I didn't have to wait long.

Almost exactly two weeks later, on the afternoon of
Sunday, June 18, I had gone into the lumber-room to
hunt for some old photographs. The lumber-room is at
the top of the house; it has no windows, only a skylight
let into the roof. It is crowded with bits of damaged furniture, cardboard boxes and old trunks. Mabel, who was
sitting in the drawing-room, had made me promise to put
everything back exactly as I found it. She also suggested
that I should wear one of her aprons.

Wondering where to begin my search, I decided upon a
scarred and much-labelled Gladstone bag, which looked
large enough and ancient enough to contain the entire
family archives. Blowing off some of the dust, I knelt
down beside it and undid the fastenings and straps. No
sooner had I done so than the contents began to spill out
over the floor. It was packed full, almost to bursting,
with papers, bills, copies of old magazines, theatre pro-

grammes, newspaper clippings, dance-cards, autographed menus and all kinds of other fascinating relics, many of them dating back to the end of the last century. I was delighted, and began examining all these treasures, quite forgetting what it was that I had originally set out to look for. In this way I must have passed about a quarter of an hour.

Then, as I still bent over the papers, the attack seized me.

This time the sensations were different, and incomparably more violent. My ears began to sing, my limbs stiffened, and a convulsion like an electric shock seemed to take place at the base of my spine. A spasm of giddiness caught up my senses and swept them around, as if into a vast whirlpool. Half fainting, breathless, dizzy, I had barely time to think: 'It's going to happen again!' Then I closed my eyes.

How long the fit lasted I don't know. Probably it was very brief. Gradually my arms and legs relaxed, my head cleared, I began to inhale deeply and easily. The sense of relief was exquisite. Very cautiously I opened my eyes and looked about me.

In the course of my two previous experiences I had felt dazed and confused. Now, it was just the opposite. I had the sensations of a man who wakes from a bad dream. My brain was absolutely under control – indeed, it seemed to be functioning with abnormal ease. My body felt light and active. My eyesight was remarkably clear. Only my heart beat more rapidly than usual, under the influence of an intense and ever-increasing feeling of excitement.

At first, I hardly recognized the room in which I found myself. It was the same room, but now entirely empty. The papers, the trunks and the furniture had all disappeared. The floor on which I knelt seemed to have been recently scrubbed, for it was quite clean; and the cobwebs had been dusted away from the corners. Looking up at the skylight, I saw a patch of clear sky above my head. Its brightness suggested an early summer morning.

For several minutes I didn't move. I hardly dared to –
lest I should bring an end to this adventure. Besides, I
needed a little time to accustom myself to my surroundings, and to think. I have said that my mind was clear. I
am really astonished at the rapidity with which I found
myself able to accept my predicament. Undoubtedly I had
made a genuine time-journey, either into the future or
the past. I had been picked up by the scruff of my neck,
like a kitten, and deposited somewhere. But where?
'When am I?' I asked myself – and the question made me
laugh.

I was scared, of course; but much more excited than
scared. For, come what might, I was determined to ex-
plore the place in which I found myself. Outside this
room there were other rooms; there were people; there
was a world. What kind of world? What kind of people?
I had got to find out. Rising to my feet, I performed what
was, unquestionably, the bravest action of my life. I
walked over and turned the handle of the door.

It was locked.

This was a stunning and unexpected blow to my hopes.
For some moments I stood stupidly twisting the knob in
my hand. Then I began to rattle it, to beat the panel with
my fist. Finally, I shouted aloud: 'Let me out! Let me
out!'

There was no answer; and, after a while, I stopped. It
was no good, The house must be empty.

Slowly, I returned to the middle of the room. My heart
was beating so fast, now, that it almost choked me. My
brain was racing like an engine. 'I've got to get out!' I
kept telling myself. I looked at the skylight; but it was too
high above me, and I had nothing upon which to climb.

From boyhood I have been accustomed to admire,
albeit somewhat grudgingly, the extreme lucidity of my
brother's intelligence. Now, as I stood there baffled, I
asked myself: what would he, who was never at a loss,
have done in my place? He would have applied himself,
as he always did, to the available data, no matter how

scanty. Well, that must be my method also. Wouldn't this
bare room yield up some small clue? I started to examine
it, foot by foot, with the eyes of an amateur detective.

It was then that I made my great discovery. In the
shadows of the far corner, crumpled against the skirting-
board, lay some dirty sheets of paper. Sitting down upon
the floor, I smoothed them out with trembling hands.
They were the inside pages of a magazine. I read its
name: *The Cage Bird Fancier*. And the date: July 1944.

Only an archaeologist can imagine the intensity of my
excitement at that moment. Here was my Rosetta Stone.
Here was the frail, precious link between my known
present and the immense, uncharted regions of the future.
Here was an actual tiny fragment of the future itself,
palpable to my present-day fingers. It had been manu-
factured by men who could answer, off-hand, many of
those burning questions which still perplex the wisest
mortals of 1939. Surely the printers had left some hint of
their knowledge here? Shaking with eagerness, I began to
read.

I suppose I was very silly. I suppose I ought to have
realized from the start the utter futility of my search. But
I was too perturbed to be capable of reasoning. My mind
shouted questions: 'Has there been a war? Has there
been a revolution? What is happening in Europe? In
China? In the Near East?' And the men of the future, as
if teasing my impatience, would only answer: 'It is rather
difficult to give exact dimensions for stock cages as they
often have to be built to suit the individual breeder's
accommodation. Generally speaking, however, they
should not be less than thirty-six inches long, twelve to
fifteen inches high, and twelve inches wide. . . .'

For all the information it gave me, *The Cage Bird
Fancier* might equally well have been written in Turkish
or Japanese.

Yet I read on, with the obstinacy of desperation: 'We
have a hen siskin which was very faddy about feeding her
young, and it was quite by chance that my father squeezed

a mealworm (after breaking its head off) and gave it to her when she was sitting on the nest.'

'If anyone can make chaffinches feed their young solely on a suitable soft food consisting of a really scientific formula, most of our troubles would be at an end.' ('Most of our troubles,' indeed! I cursed the single-mindedness of the monomaniac.)

'Owing to present conditions,' ('At last!' I thought. 'Now we're getting on to the track of something!') 'the June meeting of the East Cheshire Bird Society had to be postponed.' I read on avidly, only to discover that the Society was in a state of temporary suspension, because three of its most prominent members had lately died.

I read on and on, learning all manner of highly relevant and unfruitful facts – that the legs of a canary will sometimes denote its approximate age, that narrow perches are best for birds which have slip claw, that baldness is not unusual among greenfinches. These tiresome details are imprinted upon my memory for ever. But nowhere, nowhere could I find a trace of any wider implication. And even as my eyes hurried along the last lines of the print, I knew, in the deepest marrow of my bones, that I had outstayed my welcome. 'Come along, now,' something seemed to mutter in my ear. 'It's time. You must be getting back.'

'No, no!' I protested. 'Wait! Give me one more moment!' But the singing noise was growing louder inside my head, my sight was dimming fast. Painfully, I spelt out the concluding sentences: 'Time, unfortunately, prevented my visiting any more High Wycombe fanciers, but I hope to pay them a return visit at some future date. In the meanwhile, I should just like to add....'

Everything went black. Clenching the paper in my two fists like a fraying life-line, I pitched forward into oblivion.

When I recovered consciousness I found myself in bed, in my own room, with Mabel hovering anxiously around me. It was she who had discovered me, when she came upstairs to call me down to tea, lying senseless on the lumber-room floor. 'Was there anything in my hand?' I asked her; and she replied: 'Yes. You found them all right. Don't you remember?' 'Found them?' I echoed, stupidly. 'Why yes. The photographs. One of them is rather crumpled, but I'll iron it out. ... And now you're not to talk any more. The Doctor will be here any moment.'

The Doctor, when he arrived, could find nothing much the matter. He advised a thorough rest; a little trip to the sea later on. Both he and Mabel were curious to know the exact circumstances under which my fainting-fit took place. I answered their questions as vaguely as possible. I had decided, of course, to tell them nothing. I have no wish to end my days in a mental home.

And now, here I am, waiting for whatever may come next. Sometimes I feel frightened; but, in general, I manage to regard the whole business quite philosophically. I am well aware that the next adventure – if there ever is another – may be my last. The conditions of time-travel may prove too violent for my elderly frame. Perhaps I shan't survive the journey. But I wouldn't refuse to make it, on that account, even if I could. What other experience can be comparable to this? What else have I to live for now? So let the moment call for me when it will – at whatever time, in whatever place. I shall be ready.

Take It or Leave It

I HAVE an idea for a story. Maybe it's good. Maybe it's terrible. I only know that it isn't my kind of idea. So I am passing it on to you.

All writers get ideas which don't really belong to them, especially while they are shaving, or maybe fixing their hair, if they are girls. (You notice, I'm even beginning to talk with a different accent? It's not my voice any longer. That's the influence of this story, which isn't mine.) Well, as I was about to say, such ideas are like wrong telephone numbers. You can simply answer, 'Sorry – no, this isn't the Navy Yard' and hang up. Or, just for the hell of it, you can pretend to be someone else, play around for a while, and take the consequences. Literature is cluttered up with the consequences of authors' playing around with a wrong number: *A Tale of Two Cities*, for instance, or *Dr Jekyll and Mr Hyde* or *The Picture of Dorian Gray*.

The government says we should save everything. So let's save this idea. Maybe one of your boys could handle it. Give it to the brightest boy you've got, because this story has to be very bright indeed, dressed in the latest slang and the latest fashion, right up to the minute. Take it off the ice, let it stand a while, a couple of months, even, and perhaps – don't say I didn't warn you – perhaps it will start to stink.

The characters? I can't waste time inventing names for them. Her I see as dark, with the kind of black, dissatisfied eyes which seem to adhere slightly to faces and mirrors, and to pull away from them with an elastic tension and a sudden snap. (You'd better consult your fashion editor about the shade of her lipstick and how she should be dressed.) He's chunky, a bit older than she is, used to wrestle and play football at college, has a cauliflower ear, very shrewd grey eyes, untidy, short grey hair sticking up in a tuft behind, and a mailbox mouth. He looks good-natured, and so he is – with other men. They have been married about ten years.

They live in a big apartment overlooking the East River, on, let's say, Fifty-fifth Street. Be careful how you furnish it; readers expect that sort of thing to be authentic. Look, I'll give you a couple of hints: a white corduroy cushion shaped like a human hand, a lunar bone-scape (school of Yves Tanguy), a set of sham Chinese chairs supposed to have come from the Royal Pavilion at Brighton. (Important note: The painting is his choice, not hers. This gives the first hint of something tricky, feline, and incalculable in his character.)

Before the war he was a marketing consultant, something of that sort. He's an expert on statistics, price curves, consumer psychology. He reads books on economics as though they were crime stories, skimming through the thickest of them in a few hours as he puffs at his short, heavy pipe. When he reads he wears black-rimmed glasses, which look, one can't quite say why, like a sort of ironical disguise. He turns the page with a thick finger, one eyebrow goes up, a pencil is fished out of a vest pocket, a note is scribbled in the margin. As usual, he has detected the particular type of fallacy in this particular author's reasoning. Watching him from behind her novel (Romains' latest dose of goodwill), she frowns.

Ever since their marriage began to go wrong (at first, almost without their noticing it) her life has gradually speeded itself up until now, as she leaves a room or a house, her lips begin to move automatically, murmuring apologies for being late at the next appointment. She works on all the newest committees, wraps bundles for the latest united nations, speaks at the inauguration of victory clubs, has dates with British naval officers on leave, fills her dining-room with military experts, Chinese poets, South American diplomats, and any Russians she can lay hands on. In fact, she's running around in circles, always with her eye on him, always hoping he'll react and play up to her and finally let himself in for what she wants more than anything else in the world – a long, long, long talk. But he, the old wrestler, is much too smart. He acts as if this state of affairs could go on eternally for all he cares. 'Do we have to bring *that* up again?' He yawns, and slips off to Washington or to bed. It drives her nearly frantic.

Of course, she discusses the situation, not vulgarly but very objectively, very analytically, with her friends. Oh yes, she is determined to be absolutely fair. She blames herself. She gives him the benefit of every doubt. She questions her motives; she defends his. Then she rests her case gracefully, leaving the world to bring in the verdict – he's guilty on all five hundred counts. She doesn't protest at this. She just shakes her head and smiles gently and sighs. It is understood that she is tired out, and, oh, tremendously brave.

Does he discuss her? No one knows.

Just as my story (I mean your story) opens, she has begun to keep a diary. The scene where she buys it will be your bright boy's first problem, and I don't envy him the job, because that ole man stream of consciousness who jest keeps rollin' along is getting to be fiction's number one bore. Maybe Bright Boy will be able to bridge it or build a dam; that's not my worry. I merely have to inform him that his heroine is walking down Fifth Avenue and happens to look into the window of a small, very expensive store, and there it is, not a diary of the ordinary kind but a most beautiful manuscript book, bound in tooled leather, like a volume of somebody's collected works. The minute she sets eyes on it she knows she has to buy it, and take it home and write in it.

Write what? Everything. The entire story of her marriage. The special pleading she used on her sympathetic friends fooled everybody but herself. And now that she is facing her merciless private tribunal she must be utterly frank. Somewhere, in the deepest coils of her conscience, she knows darn well that she has done her share in the double-crossing. She knows she's been cold and cattish and disloyal and selfish and vain. And, oh, what a relief it will be to be able to admit this at last, however grudgingly! As she takes up her pen to start, she remembers those other diaries she used to keep, years and years before, in school, and suddenly the reader, who has been hating her guts, glimpses the little girl behind the tired, sharp mouth and the crow's feet and the too youthful makeup, and his eyes fill with sympathetic tears. (This passage must be marvellously written or we're sunk. Bright Boy had better be good.)

One afternoon, a few days later she comes home from the hairdresser, hears a sound in his bedroom, goes in and finds him there, just returned from a trip. (Since he began working for the government his movements have become more and more erratic. He turns up at all kinds of unexpected moments. This gets terribly on her nerves.) He's dumped his bag on the bed and is on his way out again, in a clean shirt and a different suit. He mumbles something about having to meet a fellow at the club, see you later, and is gone. She crosses to the bed, opens the bag, and begins to unpack it – from sheer force of habit, perhaps, or simply because she's thinking about him, wondering what sort of girl he has in Washington. A stenographer, probably. She sees him, essentially, as a man's man.

Hello, what's this? A fat notebook, bound with elastic. But the elastic has sagged and slipped off, and several visiting cards and folded scraps of paper with scribbled addresses have fallen out of it. She collects them, automatically opens the book to slide them back between the leaves, as automatically begins to read.

Well – I imagine Bright Boy has got the point already: the writing in the notebook is all about *her*. Of course, the style is entirely different, terse, factual, sarcastic. She's amazed to find how closely he's been following her daily life: how he quotes, ironically, the silliest parts of her public speeches; how he knows exactly when she's had lunch with Jimmy or supper with John. She's amazed, and furious with him for his cutting little comments, and indignant at being spied on, but, above all, terribly intrigued to discover that he cares enough to notice such things and put them down when all the time she'd imagined him a cross between an ostrich, a cow, and an elephant.

When next she sits down to her diary, something – caution or shame or both – prevents her from writing about her latest discovery, but she can't keep alluding to it indirectly. His picture of her as outlined in his notebook is too unfair for anything; she simply *has* to correct it. 'He doesn't understand me one bit,' she protests. 'He thinks I'm just a ...' Pages of explanation follow. She's back on her favourite job; pleading the case of her number one client. The vow of frankness is forgotten.

Needless to say, she lives and breathes for another peek at his notebook. A week passes. He leaves home again. Returns. By this time she's wild with impatience. Teddy and Una have been asking for him every single day, she tells him. He must go around and see them before supper, at once, this minute. She practically pushes him out of the apartment. Before the door closes she's in his room, rummaging in the writing desk.

Here it is. She gives a faint gasp of satisfaction: another long entry. She reads it through without breathing, without relaxing a muscle, and then again through, to the end. No, it isn't possible. He wouldn't. He couldn't. She runs into her bedroom, whips open the drawer where she keeps her diary, takes it in her hand, turns the pages, sniffs them, looks for traces of tobacco ash. Nothing. And yet. . . . She hurries back to the notebook, rereads. No, there can be absolutely no doubt. He has taken every one of her points and answered them clearly and concisely. In fact, he does everything but actually quote her verbatim. And he makes out a pretty good case for himself; she has to hand it to him – he's a better lawyer than she is. But to think he had the nerve! Why, the old so-and-so. ... She looks in the mirror and discovers that she's started to grin.

You can imagine the rest, can't you? How a new kind of life begins in the apartment. They are watching each other. She knows that he knows, and he knows that she knows that he knows. It is a game, but they have to play it seriously and very carefully, because, however absurd and childish the situation may appear to us, it is deadly impor-

tant to them; perhaps their last chance of happiness together is at stake. One wrong, premature move by either
partner and the thread of contact will be broken. It could
hardly be repaired.

Slowly, slowly, they advance towards one another.
Gradually, she drops her accusations, makes certain admis-
sions and concessions. He does likewise. The diary grows
warmer. The notebook responds. There is a great deal of
face-saving to be done on both sides. They help each
other with this: 'I am sure she never really intended ...'
'If it hadn't been for his work, I know he would have
seen ...'

But the rules are still strictly adhered to. Never any
direct reference to what is going on. The diary and the
notebook lie in their respective places, each, apparently,
unspied on, undisturbed. He and she avoid being alone
together more than ever now, for both are embarrassed,
and neither is sure of being able to handle an emergency
climax. Nevertheless, at the rare dinner parties which they
both attend, their eyes meet from time to time, asking the
question 'Can't we drop this? Can't we risk it, now? Can't
we trust each other?' and always the answer, sadly
acquiesced in, is 'No – not yet.'

And how does it all end?

Well, one day she can stand it no longer. She opens the
diary and writes to him, openly, directly, swallowing the
last of her pride, a love letter. 'Darling: Everything was
my fault, right from the beginning. Can't we start all
over?' She writes on and on, feeling, not thinking, utterly
reckless. Then, as she loses impetus, she puts the book
hastily back into the drawer without rereading it – for
fear she would tear out the pages and burn them – and
runs out of the apartment, gloriously late for another
committee.

All day long she is thinking of him, picturing his face
as he reads, imagining their next meeting. How will he
react? How will he handle it? Will he be waiting for her
when she gets home? Will he take her in his arms? Will

he blush and stammer, the cute way he did when they got engaged? Or, best of all, will he say nothing at all at first, just put her into a taxi and drive to one of the little places where they used to go after their honeymoon and dine with her, watching the lights on the water and being wonderful and gentle and understanding? Perhaps, if he could get leave, they might even fly down to Florida for a couple of days. Like a wartime wedding, almost....

She gets back to the apartment around five, the earliest she can manage. It is a little shock of disappointment to find that he isn't in the living-room, or in his bedroom, or the study. She had prepared herself to go straight into the big scene. But maybe he has just run out to buy – orchids? And, anyhow, she quickly reflects, I must be looking like the wrath of God after that crush at the Fighting French tea. I'll have time to bathe and slip into something a bit more suitable.

She opens the door of her room. And stops, as though she'd run slap into a brick wall. There he is, by the writing table, with her open diary in his hand.

They stare at each other. It's difficult to say which one looks the more guilty, the more idiotically surprised. Then, with an instinctive gesture which is straight out of the nursery, he tries to hide the book behind his back. This is the final, fatal mistake. The situation, which the wit of a Voltaire, the grace of a Casanova, might, up to this moment, still, conceivably, have saved, now passes beyond all human control; the conditioned reflexes swoop down and tear reason to shreds. 'How dare you!' she screams, snatching the diary from him. She tries to rip it across and fails, for the leather is tough, so she throws it at him instead, and misses. After this there is nothing to do but run away, anywhere, out of the room, out of the house. He shouts after her to come back, she's crazy, but he's mad at her, too, for he has been very badly startled; then he starts to laugh trying to steady his nerves, presently, when she doesn't return (she has gone to an aunt on Long Island), he packs his bag and moves to an hotel, where he gets drunk. He writes to her next day, and the letter is returned unopened. He is a bit surprised to find that, after all, he doesn't care much; the link has been well and truly broken. Some months later they are divorced.

But perhaps I am being too pessimistic? Maybe Bright Boy could straighten things out for them? He has my blessing. Let him try.

The Wishing Tree

O N E afternoon, when the children are tired of running around the garden and have gathered for a moment on the lawn, their uncle tells them the story of the Kalpataru Tree.

The Kalpataru, he explains, is a magic tree. If you speak to it and tell it a wish; or if you lie down under it and think, or even dream, a wish; then that wish will be granted. The children are half sceptical, half impressed. Truly – it'll give you anything you ask for? *Anything?* Yes, the uncle assures them solemnly: anything in the world. The audience grins and whistles with amazement. Then someone wants to know: what does it look like?

The uncle, pleased at the success of his story-telling, casts his eye around the garden and points, almost at random: 'That's one of them, over there.'

But this is too much of a good thing. The children are mistrustful, now. They look quickly round at their uncle's face, and see in it that all-too-familiar expression which children learn to detect in the faces of grown-ups. 'He's just fooling us!' they exclaim indignantly. And they scatter again to their play.

However, children do not forget so easily. Each single one of them, down to the youngest, has privately resolved to talk to the Kalpataru Tree at the first opportunity. They have been trained by their parents to believe in wishing. They wish when they see the new moon; or when they get the wish-bone of a chicken. They wish at Christmas, and just before their birthdays. They know, by experience, that some of these wishes come true. Maybe the tree is a magic tree, maybe it isn't – but, anyhow, what can you lose?

The tree which the uncle pointed out to his nephews and nieces is tall and beautiful, with big feathery branches like the wings of huge birds. It looks somehow queer and exotic among the sturdy familiar trees of that northern climate. There is a vague family tradition that it was planted years ago by a grandfather who had travelled in the Orient. What nobody, including the uncle, suspects is that this tree really *is* a Kalpataru Tree – one of the very few in the whole country.

The Kalpataru listens attentively to the children's wishes – its leaves can catch even the faintest whisper – and, in due time, it grants them all. Most of the wishes are very unwise – many of them end in indigestion or tears – but the wishing-tree fulfils them, just the same: it is not interested in giving good advice.

Years pass. The children are all men and women now. They have long since forgotten the Kalpataru Tree, and the wishes they told it – indeed, it is part of the tree's magic to make them forget. Only – and this is the terrible thing about the Kalpataru magic – the gifts which it gave the children were not really gifts, but only like the links of a chain – each wish was linked to another wish, and so on, and on. The older the children grow, the more they wish: it seems as if they could never wish enough. At first, the aim of their lives was to get their wishes granted: but later on, it is just the opposite – their whole effort is to find wishes which will be very hard, or even impossible, to fulfil. Of course, the Kalpataru Tree can grant any wish in the world – but they have forgotten it, and the garden where it stands. All that remains is the fever it has kindled in them by the granting of that first childish wish.

You might suppose that these unlucky children, as they

became adults, would be regarded as lunatics, with horror or pity, by their fellow human beings. But more people have, in their childhood, wished at the Kalpataru Tree than is generally supposed. The kind of madness from which the children are suffering is so common that nearly everybody has a streak of it in his or her nature – so it is regarded as perfectly right and proper. 'You want to watch those kids,' older people say of them, approvingly. 'They've got plenty of ambition. Yes, sir – they're going places.' And these elders, in their friendly desire to see this ambition rewarded, are always suggesting to the children new things to wish for. The children listen to them attentively and respectfully, believing that here must be the best guides to the right conduct of one's life.

Thanks to these helpful elders, they know exactly what are the things one must wish for in this world. They no longer have to ask themselves such childish questions as: 'Do I honestly want this?' 'Do I really desire that?' For the wisdom of past generations has for ever decided what is, and what is not, desirable, and enjoyable, and worthwhile. Just obey the rules of the world's wishing-game and you need never bother about your feelings. As long as you wish for the right things, you may be quite sure you really want them, no matter what disturbing doubts may trouble you from time to time. Above all, you must wish continually for money and power – more and more money, and more and more power – because, without these two basic wishes, the whole game of wishing becomes impossible – not only for yourself, but for others as well. By not wishing you are actually spoiling their game – and that, everybody agrees, is not merely selfish, but dangerous and criminal too.

And so the men and women who were shown the Kalpataru Tree in the garden of their childhood grow old and sick, and come near to their end. Then, perhaps, at last, very dimly, they begin to remember something about the Kalpataru, and the garden, and how all this madness of wishing began. But this remembering is very confused.

The furthest that most of them go is to say to themselves: 'Perhaps I ought to have asked it for something different.' Then they rack their poor old brains to think what that wish, which would have solved every problem and satisfied every innermost need, could possibly have been. And there are many who imagine they have found the answer when they exclaim: 'All my other wishes were mistaken. Now I wish the wish to end all wishes. I wish for death.'

But, in that garden, long ago, there was one child whose experience was different from that of all the others. For, when he had crept out of the house at night, and stood alone, looking up into the branches of the tree, the real nature of the Kalpataru was suddenly revealed to him. For him, the Kalpataru was not the pretty magic tree of his uncle's story – it did not exist to grant the stupid wishes of children – it was unspeakably terrible and grand. It was his father and his mother. Its roots held the world together, and its branches reached behind the stars. Before the beginning, it had been – and it would be, always.

Wherever that child went, as a boy, as a youth, and as a man, he never forgot the Kalpataru Tree. He carried the secret knowledge of it in his heart. He was wise in its wisdom and strong in its strength: its magic never harmed him. Nobody ever heard him say, 'I wish', or 'I want' – and, for this reason, he was not very highly thought of in the world. As for his brothers and sisters, they sometimes referred to him, rather apologetically, as 'a bit of a saint', by which they meant that he was a trifle crazy.

But the boy himself did not feel that he had to apologize or explain anything. He knew the secret of the Kalpataru, and that was all he needed to know. For, even as an old man, his heart was still the heart of that little child who stood breathless in the moonlight beneath the great tree, and thrilled with such wonder and awe and love that he utterly forgot to speak his wish.

A Visit to Anselm Oakes

ANSELM OAKES lived way out in the suburbs, some-where near Meudon. It took an immensely long taxi ride to get us there; and first we had to drop Gigi off at the Rue de Bac. 'I don't trust Anselm,' Paul told me, half seriously: 'I know he's got his eye on her. He wants to sacrifice her to a devil he likes, called Eazaz.'

At last we arrived at a block of modernistic flats, per-haps not more than fifteen years old, but already dilapi-dated. The elevator came down very slowly, making sounds as if its shaft was too narrow for it and it was scraping against the sides. I was nervous anyway at the prospect of the mysterious adventure ahead, and suggested walking upstairs. Paul told me, with a certain malicious amusement, that we couldn't. Part of the staircase above had collapsed, and would probably never get repaired again.

When we stopped at the top floor, the door opposite the elevator flew open with uncanny force and banged loudly against the wall, revealing a dark passageway, lit only by a tiny, red spark within a Moroccan hanging lamp. The effect was strangely intimidating and, no doubt, designed to be. Then, out of the darkness, a big man came striding towards us. He had bold, bright, dark eyes and the kind of sallow skin which looks as if it had been soaked in oil. The eyes were the reverse of 'hypnotic', in the usual journalistic sense; they seemed restlessly inattentive. An-selm (as this obviously was) wore a dirty white terry-cloth bathrobe. On his head was a turban, with a jewel (almost certainly red glass) set in its front. On his fingers were a number of big rings with entwined serpents and other emblems, zodiacal or cabalistic. The trousers of a con-ventional suit were visible below the bathrobe. On his feet were yellow leather pointed Moroccan slippers. The whole outfit suggested a sort of emergency compromise between everyday and ritual dress, as when a priest hurriedly puts on his stole over his street clothes to hear a dying man's confession.

Anselm bowed to us now with palms pressed together, Hindu style. Then he intoned, 'The Will is the Law, the Law is the Will; the Great Serpent has arisen to the Third Lotus and bids you enter.' (I was suddenly tempted to challenge this mumbo jumbo and possibly bewilder him by replying with an authentic quotation from the Tantra; but that would have been spoilsport as well as bad manners.)

As we entered the apartment Anselm switched on more lights within the hanging lamp, so that the walls of the passage were better illuminated and I could see they were hung with pictures. Anselm signed to Paul to come with him into a room on the left; I could tell by his manner that I wasn't supposed to follow. As I started to examine the pictures, I could hear them talking in low voices. The pictures were crudely but strikingly painted; mostly pornographic and all rather frightening. One was of a bare stubbly field, across which two men dressed like Mexican peons were walking. In the foreground, behind a clump of cactus, a ferocious-looking penis with a fanged shark's mouth and slitty pig's eyes was lurking ready to rush out and attack them. Another showed a screaming man being swallowed by an immense grinning vulva with closed eyes on either side of its opening; this was captioned 'love is blind'. In another, a young man was standing outside the window of a small house looking at what appeared to him to be an attractive nude girl. All *he* could see of her were her head, arms and naked breasts, as she leaned on the window-sill, looking out at him and beckoning him to come inside, with a seductive smile. But the side wall of the house had been removed so that you could see what was invisible to the young man – that the girl's body ended in the tail and rattles of a snake.

At the end of the passage I entered a room which was

decorated and furnished in conventional 'mystic' style. The signs of the Zodiac were painted around the walls. There was a crystal on a velvet-draped table, beside a pack of tarot cards. A cheap Buddha, which could have come from any Japanese goods store, stood on a book-case, with two joss-sticks burning in front of it. In a corner there was a filing-cabinet of the usual grey-painted metal. On its drawers were descriptive cards: *plagues, mantrams, mudras, curses, love-spells, power-words, runes, boons, talismans, miscellaneous mischiefs*. These were printed in large clear lettering and were obviously meant to catch the eye and make a suitable impression on any-one who found himself in the room. 'The man's just a common conjurer,' I said to myself, in disappointment.

At this moment Paul appeared. He drew me over to the window, which, I now noticed, opened on to a balcony.

'Have you got five thousand francs on you, Chris?' he asked, almost in a whisper.

'Why?'

'Because we need it.'

'Why do we need it?'

'Oh, please, now, Chris, be reasonable – don't argue? *You* need it. It's sort of a fee Anselm charges. An initia-tion fee ...'

'*Initiation?* Look, what goes *on* here?'

'Keep calm, will you, sweetheart. Didn't you promise your Auntie...?'

'Okay. Forget it. Here you are....'

I paid out the bills to Paul – remembering how you pay that extra fee to the guide who shows you the 'naughty' frescoes at Pompeii – and he opened a door into a room on the right; a much smaller room, which was nearly bare of furniture. Around it were black velvet mattresses placed end to end. The walls were entirely covered by hangings with intricate Arab designs on them, coloured purple, orange and green.

There were three other people in the room already; a middle-aged woman with henna'd hair, a young Jewish-

American girl with a long nose and a very sexy figure, a young Englishman with long thin legs and a certain boyish prettiness. Paul said, 'this is Chris – Prim, Boots, Dexter'. I took a mild dislike to Dexter, because of his face and clothes; he was dressed like a bohemian poet of the nineties. I had no particular feelings, at first, about either Prim, the woman, or Boots, the girl. And they obviously felt very little interest in me. I sat down on one of the mattresses. It was uncomfortably hard.

Anselm now came in, followed by an Arab youth with a big copper tray on which were various kinds of food. 'Isherwood,' said Anselm, in his deep voice, 'this is Mokhtar, my assistant – or, as some believe, my familiar.'

Mokhtar grinned. He wore Moorish clothes; bag trousers and an open sleeveless jacket which showed parts of his lithe brown body. There was a slyness about him which reminded me of the boys on Ambrose's island. He was evidently very much in control of the situation – whatever the situation was.

'I wonder if you'd prefer to start with kif or majoun?' Anselm said to me. He was polite, but somehow not quite in the right way, like a car-salesman. I analysed his accent as Irish veneered with Old School Tie. I must have looked blank at his question because he added, 'Our Mutual Friend tells me you're a stranger to the subtleties of *cannabis indica*?'

'He means hashish,' Paul told me, 'or, as we backwoods Americans call it, marijuana. Honey, you'd better put yourself in Auntie's hands. ...' He turned to Mokhtar, 'let's start him on majoun, because it's so delicious my baby'll just love it!' He slapped the boy familiarly on the buttocks. 'Mokhtar can make majoun do *anything* to you – and I've already explained to him exactly what it is *you* need, Chrissikins. ... Let's see now, you'd better not drink anything, as this is your first time. While you're eating the majoun, I'll fix you a kif cigarette.'

Paul was right about the majoun being delicious; it looked and tasted rather like Christmas pudding. I ate it with a tiny coffee spoon, while Paul slit open an ordinary American cigarette, mixed kif with the tobacco and re-rolled the mixture in a new cigarette-paper. The kif smelled like newly-cut grass in the catcher of a lawn-mower. (Even now, the memory of that smell gives me a very faint sensation of fear.) When Paul had finished doctoring several cigarettes he began drinking a Martini. I asked him if he wasn't going to take any hashish. He shook his head and smiled. 'That stuff doesn't do anything for me now,' he said, like an adult who had outgrown soda-pop.

Anselm, meanwhile, had lighted a long wooden kif-pipe, hung with charms and amulets made of gold, silver and tortoise-shell; he told me he had brought it back with him from the Sahara. Anselm puffed at the pipe, occa-sionally handing it to Prim, Boots and Dexter, who smoked it in turn while they chatted. Paul made me eat a bowl of mutton stew from the tray, and drink mint tea; these he said, would help the action of the drug. I smoked two kif cigarettes, inhaling deeply in my eagerness for the intoxication to start. All of a sudden I had lost my fear of it. In this way, I think, about an hour passed, I don't remember saying much, if anything, to Paul. As for the others, I had a definite disinclination to talk to them. Already I was withdrawing into myself.

My symptoms began with seasickness. The room rolled slowly but heavily to starboard, righted itself, rolled to port. I tried to roll with it, forcing what must have been a queasy smile. This wasn't too bad. But now I began to be conscious of the smallness of the room. It was exceed-ingly small. *And it was getting smaller.* If I stayed here, *it would soon get smaller than I was*; but that was un-thinkable. *Out* – out before it's too late! I got to my feet with perhaps exaggerated casualness. 'You all right, honey chile?' Paul asked.

'No.'

'You mean it's started, already?'

'Sure has.'

'Good.'

I strolled out into the 'mystic' room with the Buddha and the crystal. Paul didn't offer to come to my assistance and I was glad, because I was only just holding on to my self-control. Nobody seemed to take notice of my leaving. I was probably moving fairly normally, though I have an impression that I walked with a high-stepping gait, like a *haute école* horse.

I opened the window and went out on to the balcony, wanting to be as far away as possible from the smallness of the small room. But this was a hideous mistake, as I realized at once. For, out here, the windy, empty, gaping, all-swallowing blackness was too *big* to contain me – much much too big! I must get *out* – out of the outdoors – before I was sucked up into it, and lost for ever. I fled back inside, and peeped cautiously into the smaller room. It was all right now; merely small. I sank back into my place on the mattress with panting relief.

But my relief was very short-lived. And what now followed was worse. It was the beginning of the *slyness; the first of the tricks*. As I lay there with my back against the wall I became aware that there *was no wall*. Oh yes, I was still being supported, but that was irrelevant. I was sitting, as it were, on the sheer edge of Glacier Point, with my back to the three thousand foot precipice and the chasm of all Yosemite yawning one inch behind me. If I turned my head I should see that my support didn't really exist. So I didn't turn my head.

My next problem was the doorway to the room. No – that expressed their relation wrongly. One should say, *the room to the doorway*. The doorway, not the room, was the problem. I called it a doorway, not doorways, because I was still aware that this was really – whatever 'really' meant – a room with only one doorway. What I was now perceiving was an infinite potentiality of doorways, out of which one was being, you might say, 'recognized', as a speaker is 'recognized' by the chairman of a meeting. But *how* and *why* had this particular doorway been chosen? The very thought of having to make such a choice was mental torture. All of the potential doorways were now visibly present, in a tight, endlessly complex and somehow menacing relation to the chosen one. And now, in a flash, I saw what an unspeakably terrifying thing Cubism is. Picasso must have known this, and Braque and Juan Gris. Naturally, they did not talk about it. They did not want to be locked up as madmen. They were the bravest men who have ever lived.

As without, so within. The shifting, sliding planes of potentiality weren't only outside and around me. *I* was potential. *I* was shifting. *I* was no longer in focus as I. The thumbscrew had been touched, ever so slightly, and now all my edges were blurred. One more touch and I should be infinitely nothing. I shut my eyes and held my breath, lest the desperately delicate balance should be upset for ever.

And now, in the next room, Anselm had started a phonograph playing some popular records. Their words, he told us, were Hungarian; but they must have been directly translated from French cabaret songs, for they had exactly the same breathless archness and *oo-la-la*. These records were exquisitely painful to my nerves. I felt literally trapped within the limits of their strict triviality. I paced these limits like a caged animal. I looked around me in desperation for some relief, with the result that my eyes got trapped too, within the Arab designs on the wall-hangings. I couldn't get my eyes out of the design or my ears out of the music. The limits of the music and the limits of the design were parts of the same cage!

But the songs were painful to me for another reason; they were in a foreign language. Ordinarily, this would have enabled me to ignore them altogether. But, in my present state, it was impossible for me to do this; I had not only to listen to them but to try to understand them. And I could! I now found myself possessed of this useless and burdensome psychic power. As long as I listened only to the rhythm of the language – making no attempt to guess at or deduce the meaning of its individual words – I understood it totally, without any question of error. If, however, I said to myself 'that's Hungarian', then at once I ceased to understand. I kept doing this, because I didn't *want* to understand the songs. They meant nothing but their own cruel banality, from which I was straining to escape.

I strained too hard, perhaps; because now my mind began to slip its gears and race and whirr. It was actually running away with me, and I was scared as I had been once when the brakes of my car failed on the steep part of La Cienega Boulevard. Something had to be done instantly. I turned to Paul for help. He wasn't there. I'd had no awareness of his having left the room; but then, I'd had no awareness of any event outside my own area of attention. Dexter was sitting nearest to me, so I hooked my attention on to him; it was like drawing another boat to you with a boathook. And it worked! Gradually, my mind slowed down, the whirring stopped. I felt, with relief, that a new phase of the intoxication was announcing itself. And indeed this *was* the beginning – of the *great horrors!*

Dexter seemed altogether different from the young man I'd seen on coming into this room. He was utterly revealed to me now; and my mild dislike of him was changed into horror and loathing. There he sat, facing life with a pout of greed; boyishly imperious, capricious, endowed with a certain power to do harm which he exercised petulantly. At life's hotel, his complaint to the manager would be that he was bored. And, for this, someone had got to suffer – by George they had! And, at the same time, he was watching out of the corner of his eye, hoping that a real Adult, a Father-Figure, would notice him and bother to come over and take away the toys he had broken and smack his bottom. That would be his greatest thrill. So far, no one had bothered.

Nevertheless, he wasn't negligible, wasn't pitiful, wasn't merely a nuisance. He was intensely, actively bad.

Astonishingly venomous for his size, like that tiny-mouthed viper you can scarcely see in the dust. Ah, how obscene he was – sipping his cocktail and cutely puffing at his kif and telling old red-headed Prim, 'Let's face it, dear, she's nothing but a crashing bore, since she went blind. ...' The innermost accent of evil was in the sentence. I saw his jaw harden as he pronounced the words; it was the clacking wooden jaw of a ventriloquist's puppet. 'Silly old bag!' he added, with screaming cockatoo laugh, 'the other day she put her hand *right in the fire,* hunting for a ring she'd dropped!' His jaw wagged, then snapped shut on its string.

But where was the ventriloquist? I looked up. Anselm was standing in the doorway. He must have just turned off the phonograph. Now he clapped his hands. Mokhtar appeared.

The situation was becoming complex. I now had to try to attend to several people at once; and this, in my condition, was nearly impossible. Each redirection of my attention cost me a conscious effort. I did my best.

Mokhtar squatted on the floor and began to play a kind of flute. The thin wailing music that it made had an extraordinary power. Never have I heard any sound so nakedly sexual. It didn't provoke or entice; it *was* Sex. You had to recognize that, even if you didn't want it at the moment. *I* didn't want it; no doubt that was because of the way my majoun had been prepared. Boots *did* want it. She stripped off all her clothes and lay down on her belly on the mat, well within Mokhtar's reach. He merely grinned, however, and went on playing.

And now Anselm started to chant; this was evidently some of the rigmarole he used on his disciples or customers or whatever you could call them. 'Take and it shall be given unto you; rape and ye shall find. Only in the sacrament of sham is virtue to be found. Behold me! I roll in excrements. I enter in by the forbidden aperture. I feast on the uttermost vileness. I make free with the flesh that I require. ...'

As Anselm reached this point in his chanting, he stooped down over Boots, gripped her shoulder, turned her over on her back and suddenly scratched her with his old yellow claw-nails right across the belly, so hard that they left bloody marks on the skin.

Three things were peculiarly horrible about this scene. First, the whinny of excitement uttered by Prim. Prim's excitement was horrible, just because it *wasn't* plain old ordinary sadism, that much overrated horror. Prim wasn't even being fanatical. Her whinny expressed the simple glee of the average non-involved civilian: *goody-goody for our side!* That uncritically adopted team-spirit which moves nice wholesome men and women, millions of them, to accept and applaud lynchings, pogroms, concentration-camps, without bothering to understand what they are all about. Prim was for Anselm, so – *goody-goody!* Anything he chose to do was perfectly all right with her.

Boots' reaction was equally horrible in a different way. How to describe that smile with which she accepted the scratching? She was no more a masochist than Prim was a sadist. No – what I saw in the way she smiled at Anselm was sheer cynical depravity. She was one of those who let themselves be outraged because, in spite of everything, it is *less trouble* than any kind of resistance or positive response. By their consent, they become the parents of future atrocities.

But if Prim and Boots were horrible, Anselm himself was a hundred times more so. The look on his face as he clawed Boots! As I watched him, I understood that, if a Devil *did* exist, the most terrifying thing about him might be simply this: that he wasn't interested in anything, even in damnation. Anselm didn't for one instant believe in his tarot cards, spells, incantations. He didn't believe in scratching Boots. Then why had he scratched her? *For no reason whatsoever.* As he was doing it, his face had shown no cruelty, no lust; nothing but absence of attention.

And now, suddenly, Anselm, Prim, Boots, Dexter,

Mokhtar – all of them – were leaving me. Some of them might have walked out already, some might still be in the room; that made no difference. In either case, like balloons with their strings cut, they were drifting away; and at an immense speed. Or you could put it that the room was expanding immensely; the distance across it could now only be measured in light-years. Now they were all gone. I was alone.

All right then, so I was alone. Was that bad? why should I mind? What had Augustus taught me? What had I been learning through my own experience all these last yeas? Did I believe what I claimed to believe, or didn't I?

Yes. I looked for my belief, and yes – here it was available to me. My experience was true. 'This thing' was with me. I didn't have to move one inch. I was right here where everything was. And would always be. Nothing else mattered. I didn't need other people. I didn't need the room. The room could go. It *was* going, faster and faster. I could no longer see the walls. I didn't need the walls. 'This thing' was all I needed. Only ... the speed made me dizzy ... I shut my eyes. For an instant, I felt a great soaring joy, such as I had never known before. I was soaring towards the joy, and everything but the joy was receding from me. But – not so fast! No – wait – wait for me! I couldn't let myself go so fast. Make it stop! And then I was in a panic, and falling. I tumbled back into the room, opening my eyes.

The room was back to normal, and empty.

They had all gone and left me alone. I wanted them back, even if they were horrible. Anything, rather than being alone. All, all alone. My misery became poignant. I was a little kitten, locked out in the winter snow. A poor helpless tiny thing. I was ready to beg them not to desert me. I didn't care what they thought. I was shameless. I was desperate. ...

'Paul! Paul! *Where are you?*'

'Right here, honey,' said Paul, appearing at once in the doorway.

'Where have you *been*?'

'Just stretching my legs. I stepped into the other room a minute.'

'*A minute!* You've been gone *for ever*!'

Paul gave me one of his searching, medical looks. It was as if I'd unconsciously revealed something to him. He came over and sat down beside me on the mattress.

'Look at your watch,' he said.

He seemed somehow abnormally real, and even more *visible* than usual; more boldly printed, in stronger colours, on the field of my vision. (No doubt this was because I had dimmed the identity of the others by transforming them into symbolic figures, while Paul had remained simply Paul to me, throughout the evening.)

'Why? Why should I look at my watch?'

'Look at your watch.'

I looked at my watch.

'What time is it?' Paul asked

'A quarter past two. Why?'

'No – tell me *exactly*.'

'Two seventeen. ... Why do you want to know?'

Paul didn't answer. I felt the horrors coming on again, very big. This was different from the being alone; worse. It was the bottom of everything. The ice-cold awful opposite of joy. I sat with the back of my head against the wall.

'Paul – what is this place?'

'Don't you know, honey chile?'

We were talking in a quiet, conversational, almost dreamy manner.

'I mean – where *are* we?'

'I know where *I* am. I don't know where you are.'

'Could we be in two different places?'

'Why not?'

'Paul – I'm *scared*!'

'There's nothing to be scared of, baby. Nothing in this world. Let's us two just talk this over quietly, shall we? Only you've *got* to keep calm. Nothing bad'll happen to you as long as you keep calm. So will you promise me to?'

'All right. I promise.'

'That's my boy! And now you tell me, *just for the sake of argument*, why you couldn't be some place else, right here at this moment?'

'But that's impossible! I mean – we're in a flat in a house on a street. It's part of a city, in France. It's marked on the maps. It has a name. ... It can't be two places at once, *can it*? And what about all the people who live in this city? The ordinary people. They'd know about it too. They'd notice something was wrong ...'

'Not necessarily.'

'Why not?'

'You *really* want me to explain that to you?'

'Of course I do!'

'This is just for the sake of argument, mind. *I'm* not saying where you are or where you aren't. Only *you* can say that.'

'All right – just for the sake of argument ...'

'Take a hold on yourself, now. You may not like this.'

'What won't I like?'

'You want me to go ahead?'

'Sure!'

'Okay, then. ... What time was it when you looked at your watch? No – don't look again! Just tell me.'

'Let's see – two seventeen. ... But what's that got to do with ...?'

'*Now* look at your watch.'

I looked at my watch. There was no difficulty about reading it. My mind and my eyesight seemed perfectly clear. I stared and stared. I couldn't at first believe what I saw. But there was no question whatsoever. It was two-seventeen. *Even the minute-hand hadn't moved.*

'Oh Jesus Christ,' I heard myself saying, quite quietly.

'You see what I mean?' said Paul pleasantly, as though he had scored a point in a purely theoretical discussion. 'You *could* be some place else, right here and now. None of the ordinary people, as you call them, would notice anything. They couldn't possibly. It takes time to notice something – even if it's only an instant. But suppose you're in a place where being there doesn't take any time at all?'

I felt the sweat cold on my forehead. I was starting to shake all over. The times I'd thought I'd been *really* scared – when the plane nearly crashed in Mexico over the mountains, when I waited in the surgeon's office to show him my little tumour – why, they were nothing now, mere trifles, huge fun . . .

'Augustus knows the score all right,' Paul was saying. 'The only mistake he makes is trying to tell other people. You can't. Everyone has to find out for himself. If you talk about it, it's nothing at all – just another lousy word. . . .'

'What word?'

'Eternity.'

It was then that I completely lost my head. I got up and went plunging into the next room, where I knocked over the table with the crystal. There was the passage leading to the door of the flat. Architecturally, it was maybe thirty feet long; psychologically it was at least a mile. But I had to get to that door. I had to find a way out of the Arab design on the wall-hangings; for the design had suddenly *become* the flat itself, and I was trapped in it. I began running down the passage. I ran and ran and ran. I gasped for air. My lungs burned. I had a stabbing pain in my side.

Through an open doorway I caught a glimpse of Mokhtar, Dexter, Boots and Prim. All of them were naked, and, under ordinary circumstances, I should have said that Prim was being raped. That is to say, she was fighting and yelling, and Boots and Dexter were holding her down and Mokhtar was behaving erotically. But the word 'rape' had no meaning now, because a rape is an act, and an act has a beginning and an end, and exists in time. There was no time in this place. And there was no place, either.

Then – quite suddenly – I was at the door. Anselm

appeared briefly. He was wearing a heavy gold-embroidered bishop's cope over his bathrobe. 'The Great Serpent forbids ...' he began. But already I had got the door open and burst out of the Arab design, and was frantically pushing the button of the elevator.

Nothing happened. Nothing happened. Nothing happened. My voice had come back now, so I screamed and screamed. Paul came quietly out of the flat and opened the elevator door for me, showing that it had been up on the top floor and waiting, all along. He wanted to ride down with me, but I wouldn't let him. I hit at him to stop him from getting into the elevator. Even in the midst of my hysteria I was aware that he understood how I was feeling and didn't really resent this.

When I got out of the building I ran along the street until I came to lights and a bistro which was open. Here, I summoned up the courage to look at my watch. Time had started up again – but in bottom gear, it seemed. For my escape had taken less than five minutes.

The worst was over now. But when I got back to my hotel room and into bed I found I was afraid to switch the lamp off.

MORE ABOUT PENGUINS

Penguinews, which appears every month, contains details of all the new books issued by Penguins as they are published. From time to time it is supplemented by *Penguins in Print* – a complete list of all our available titles. (There are well over three thousand of these.)

A specimen copy of *Penguinews* will be sent to you free on request, and you can become a subscriber for the price of the postage – 4s. for a year's issues (including the complete lists). Just write to Dept EP, Penguin Books Ltd, Harmondsworth, Middlesex, enclosing a cheque or postal order, and your name will be added to the mailing list.

Some other Penguins by Christopher Isherwood are described overleaf.

Note: *Penguinews* and *Penguins in Print* are not available in the U.S.A. or Canada

Also by Christopher Isherwood

MR NORRIS CHANGES TRAINS

This book was originally conceived as part of a longer novel, another section of which was made into the successful play and film, *I am a Camera*, and the musical, *Cabaret*.

'From the first word to the last, this book is alert, intelligent, original and amusing. It is successful as a picture of pre-Hitler Germany, in a more general way as a study of society moving towards dissolution, as an imaginative treatment of sex problems, and just as a highly amusing story' – *London Mercury*

'Here is a true original: a flabby rogue without, as one would say, a single redeeming quality, who is nevertheless one of the most delightful persons one has met in fiction' – *Daily Telegraph*

'An impertinent, amusing, shameless story' – *Observer*

GOODBYE TO BERLIN

Goodbye to Berlin continues and completes Christopher Isherwood's picture of that vanished city, in scenes that range from the tenements and night-bars of the slums to the fantastic villas of the very rich; the extraordinary, the tragic, and the ridiculous are blended on almost every page. These impressions of Berlin in the days immediately before the institution of the Hitler régime are vignettes of history as well as writing of the first order.

Also available

PRATER VIOLET

THE WORLD IN THE EVENING

A SINGLE MAN

Not for sale in the U.S.A.